D1645226

The Regional Books Series

GENERAL EDITOR: BRIAN VESEY–FITZGERALD, F.L.S.

THE VALE OF BERKELEY

THE REGIONAL BOOKS SERIES

Edited by BRIAN VESEY-FITZGERALD, F.L.S.

THE Regional Books *deal in the fullest manner with certain highly individual and remarkable areas of Britain. In every instance the Region itself is a clear-cut entity, with a marked individuality of its own.*

The following volumes have been published or are in preparation.

Other titles will be announced later.

PLEASE WRITE TO THE PUBLISHERS
FOR FULL DESCRIPTIVE PROSPECTUS

THE VALE OF BERKELEY

LEWIS WILSHIRE

ROBERT HALE LIMITED
63 Old Brompton Road, London S.W.7

BY THE SAME AUTHOR

Novels
SPRING ROAD
NEWS FROM THE HAMLET
SUMMER OF ENCHANTMENT

Editor of
WEST COUNTRY SHORT STORIES

First published 1954

MADE AND PRINTED IN GREAT BRITAIN BY
WILLIAM CLOWES AND SONS, LIMITED
LONDON AND BECCLES

CONTENTS

ILLUSTRATIONS

ILLUSTRATIONS

Present-day difficulties do not permit of a comprehensive map of the area being included in the book. For more detailed information readers are referred to the respective Ordnance Survey sheets.

ACKNOWLEDGMENTS

The illustrations numbered 2, 4, 16, 17, 18, 19 and 22 were supplied by Eagle Photos, of Cheltenham; Nos. 3, 5, 7, 10, 11, 15 and 23 by Reece Winstone, of Bristol; No. 8 by "The Dursley Gazette"; No. 12 by "The Bristol Evening Post"; No. 25 by "The Gloucester Journal". The remaining eight illustrations were reproduced from photographs supplied by the author.

BY WAY OF INTRODUCTION

THE chief advantage of introducing your own work is that you can, at the outset, try to anticipate or even disarm criticism by apologising for your shortcomings. For the subject of this book, however, I shall make no apologies. So far as I know, this is the first book to deal exclusively with the Vale, and that in itself is justification enough. Admittedly it is not as famous a region as Cotswolds, Exmoor, Mendips, Lakes or Fells; but that is because its scenery is of a quieter, more intimate, kind; not so dramatic or obvious; not so easily comprehended. Certainly its situation is a splendid one, lying as it does between Cotswold and Forest of Dean, alongside the magnificent estuary of Severn, and possessing ancient camps and castles, an internationally famous wildfowl conservation centre, lovely villages, rivers and rhines, characters of unusual richness and eccentricity even for the West Country and even today, a great reputation (fast dying in the face of mass-production and centralised control) for noble cheeses and fine cider, and some of the best pasturage in England. No, I am not going to make any apologies for the *subject* of this book, which is a superb one; only for its *treatment* by the author. It is only fair to the reader to acknowledge my limitations, and to indicate some of the deficiencies he will encounter in reading this book.

For instance, it will be found that my interest in statistics and my knowledge of period architecture are not all that they might be, and I have no doubt that some readers will be contemptuous of my overriding interest in the human stuff, the personalities, the —if you like—common gossip of the Vale, which at times crowds out the factual detail. They will discover that I am very credulous, and that—possibly because I am by profession a novelist—I can *never* resist a good story.

One thing is certain. Your pleasure in reading this book is unlikely to equal mine in writing it. Or rather, my pleasure in collecting the materials for it; because writing is really a heart-breaking, nerve-racking, wrist-wearying old job, in which blood and toil, tears and sweat, curses and ink are mixed in about equal proportions.

My researches took me into mansions and into cottages: threw me into all sorts of company: sometimes left me stranded, at nightfall, on strange roads: several times involved me in Severn mud of a peculiarly adhesive and affectionate kind: caught me in thunderstorms—I remember one, in particular, which found me hatless and coatless in Michaelwood, where I'd managed to lose myself, and which I weathered by using an Ordnance Survey Map as a primitive tent. It saved me from a wetting, but the map was and is a pitiful sight! They also took me into libraries, both public and private. For although I think one's own observations are sharpest and best, they would be of little value if they took no account of historical background. I freely and unashamedly confess that I often trespassed, and, though frequently caught in the act, was only once admonished. That was by a very eminent gentleman, who caught me skulking on his precincts just as he was pointing out the beauties of his estate to an American visitor. He was, understandably, irate, and requested me to vacate the neighbourhood as early as possible. As I had walked some considerable distance that day, and collected an appreciable quantity of mud, got wet through and dried out in the sun, was dusty and bedraggled and had no kind of excuse for being where I was, I *may* have appeared to him somewhat disreputable. At any rate, he pointed the finger of scorn and told me to go—and I went!

Many have expressed curiosity about, or put forward their own opinions concerning, the boundaries of the Vale. There are no exact boundaries, for the Vale defies exact definition. I have been assured, by people who have lived in the Vale all their lives and ought to know better, that they've never *heard* of any Vale of Berkeley. And inclusion in it has been claimed by people farther north, south, east and west than I am willing to concede. Naturally, then, I put forward my definition with some hesitancy; the more so because, during the actual writing of this book, I have shifted most of the original boundaries to suit my own convenience, or because I genuinely felt that my first view was mistaken. Broadly speaking, the Vale of Berkeley lies between Cotswold and Severn, below Gloucester and above Bristol. Its north and south boundaries, as finally established, are Stonebench and Severn

Beach, with an arbitrary eastern boundary embracing Almondsbury, Tytherington, Cromhall, Tortworth, Damery, Coaley, Frocester, King's Stanley and Moreton Valence.

I am unable to produce historical authority for this. It is in no way related to the Berkeley Hundred, and I can only refer dissatisfied readers to the Ordnance Survey Map and to Marshall's *Rural Economy of Gloucestershire* (1789), in which he describes the Vale as follows:

> "The outlines of this charming plot of country form the segment of a circle nearer than any other regular figure. The Severn an irregular chord; the hills to south and east a curve, which the Painswick and Matson hills continue to the northern angle. . . . The extent, from Aust Cliff to the foot of Matson hill, is 25 miles. The medium width of the district has been estimated at four miles. . . . Including the skirts of the hills, it may contain 80 square miles, or about 50,000 acres."

Apart from an adjustment of a few miles north and south, that is essentially the Vale as it appears herein.

Were I to list all the people who have helped me in the writing of this book, hundreds of names would follow, and shortage of space makes that impracticable. But it would be more than churlish if I did not, at any rate, mention those without whose help and advice I could never have completed the book. They are: Dr T. A. Ryder, Vicar of Cam, geologist and historian; Mr R. J. C. Atkinson, M.A., F.S.A., of the Department of Prehistoric Archæology, Edinburgh; Miss Olive Lloyd Baker, of Hardwicke Court; Mr Brian Vesey-FitzGerald, F.L.S.; Mrs Elizabeth S. Rickards, of Almondsbury; Mr and Mrs Richard Leakey, of Tytherington; Mr B. Stafford Morse, M.A., Hon. Secretary of the Society of Thornbury Folk; Mr W. M. Blair, director of the Tortworth Estates Co.; Mr Peter Scott and the staff of the Severn Wildfowl Trust; Mr Alfred Keys, J.P., of Eastington; Mr Gordon E. Payne, O.B.E., F.R.G.S., F.R.Econ.S., author of *A Survey of Gloucestershire*; the Women's Institutes of Almondsbury, Alveston and Frampton-on-Severn; Mr Percy Bennett of Blakeney; Dr Olive Griffiths, of the Gloucestershire Community Council; my friend "George"; and the editors of *The Field, Country Life, West Country*

Magazine, Gloucestershire Countryside, Gloucester Citizen, Bristol Evening Post, Bristol Evening World, and the *Gloucestershire Gazette* series, who published certain parts of this book in serial or article form.

Readers who are impatient to get through the suburbs of explanation to the countryside itself may, if they wish, turn straight to Chapter III and explore it with me afoot, if they will solemnly promise to return to the opening chapters later.

LEWIS WILSHIRE

CHAPTER I

THE COUNTRY LIKE A MAP

An easy land of quiet, friendly corners,
Cradled by Cotswold, bounded by Severn,
Shaped into beauty by the hand of time.

CLIMB the Nibley or Hawkesbury monuments and you see it as lark or buzzard might see it—a bird's-eye view. There it lies, to the west, a tree-studded land of fields and farms, threaded by streams and, near Severn, by those dykes or ditches which are locally known as "rhines"; bounded by that great curve of estuary to the north-east, beyond which, if the visibility allows it, the wooded hills of the Forest make a dramatic horizon.

Not that you need restrict yourself to the viewpoints provided by the monuments to Tyndale (who was not, as it afterwards transpired, born at Nibley after all, but at Slimbridge, five or six miles off) or Lord Edward Somerset. Indeed, there are so many splendid viewpoints from which you may overlook the Vale that it might well claim to be better and more exclusively overlooked than any comparable region in the south-west. Unfortunately that is as near as most writers on Gloucestershire ever get to it. They admire the view from the Cotswold escarpment at Frocester or Uley Bury, Coaley Peak or Haresfield Beacon, Hetty Pegler's Tump or Stinchcombe, but they don't come down from the hills to see what it's really like. Thus it is overlooked in both senses of the word, and that is why this book has been written.

Before we go down into the Vale, however, it may be as well to survey it from one of the Cotswold outliers already mentioned, which, striking out from the great mass of oolitic limestone, command unparalleled views of river and spreading Vale.

The country immediately below the Cotswold escarpment is undulating, full of interest and variety, well wooded and intersected by many wandering roads, scarred by occasional quarryworkings, some recent, some ancient, exhibiting many different kinds of rock-formation. Beyond the narrow strip of Middle Lias is a wider strip of Lower Lias, after which we come across Carboniferous, Triassic and Silurian rocks in the broken, hilly country which gives way to the low-lying alluvial plain. At its extremities, the Vale flattens out into the Oxford Clay of Gloucester or breaks into the Bristol Coal Measures.

It looks peaceful enough down there: a country of easy prosperity, lush and self-forgetful, in strong contrast to the wide and windy shoulders of Cotswold with their grim reminders of the past and mortality in the shape of barrows and earthworks, with wide horizons, steep walls flanking straight roads, and hard-bitten fields falling to hanging-woods. The pattern of life down in the Vale has always been different. Its agriculture was, until recently, based upon dairy-farming on permanent pasture; so that its fields are small, with hedges instead of walls, and a large quantity of hedgerow timber. Much of this grassland has been ploughed-up in the last decade to meet the needs of the time, and this makes of the Vale a multicoloured counterpane, especially in autumn when you can distinguish the golden wheatfields from the silver oats, the dark green of meadow from light-green aftermath or yellow-green stubble. It looks peaceful enough. Yet the Vale has a history as rich (and as bloody) as Cotswold—a history which is not only local but national, even international. More important than any events, however, were the ordinary men and women who lived and worked, loved and died here, leaving each his or her own mark upon the face of the land.

As the inscriptions on countless tombs in village churchyards tell us, all flesh is grass. But though men and women die, their works endure and are everywhere apparent. The Vale has not always presented this jig-saw of fields and lanes, manors and cottages, woodland and parkland, arable and pasture. Once it was a forest—marshy, gloomy, dangerous. But that was long ago, and the men who made clearings in the forest for their settlements, and extended them to graze their beasts and grow their corn—those men are gone and forgotten by all but a few archæologists. Yet we ought sometimes to remember that it is to them and their antecedents that we owe our heritage. We may imagine ourselves very clever with our mechanical cultivators, our chemical fertilisers and agricultural research stations, but it is as well to remember, when our heads begin to swell, that all the pioneering work has been done for us. The country *we* inherit is already a garden, only wanting cultivation.

Before there were any men, there were rocks. And as rock-formations are the skeleton, the bony structure on which a country is built, we will briefly consider them before we discuss the arrival of man.

This Cotswold escarpment from which we are surveying the Vale is of Inferior Limestone Oolite. Behind it, to eastward, are the Cotswold uplands of Greater Oolitic Limestone. Below and before us, to the westward, is the gently undulating country of the Lower, Middle and Upper Lias. Between this lias and the alluvium of Severnside are a variety of rocks, with Carboniferous and Triassic preponderating and pockets or patches of Wenlock Shales, Upper Llandovery, Ludlow Beds, Old Red Sandstone, Dolomitic Conglomerate, Red Marl and Penarth Beds. Naturally, these varying strata have far-reaching effects on the fertility of the plant life, and on the distribution and living conditions of the human population of the Vale. They are best seen in the quarries of Cromhall, Damery, Alveston, Olveston and Almondsbury; the brickyards of Littleton and Over; the gravel pits at Frampton; and the cliffs at Aust and Fretherne. I have been told that the Vale of Berkeley has a greater variety of rocks and soils than any comparable area in England. Why this should be so I cannot say. It is not, as one might suppose, the result of extraordinary volcanic activity nor does it appear to be an outcome of the Great Ice Age, for the majority of the rocks are "sedimentary": accumulations of sand, grit, shells etc., in fresh or salt water. The Vale itself, of course, is a result of the persistent wearing away of rocks by running water—which is another way of saying it is in the Severn watershed.

Different rock-formations give rise to different conditions on the surface. For instance, the Old Red Sandstone of Sharpness, Tortworth, Kington, Kyneton Quarr, Milbury Heath, Gillingstool and Crossways produces sandy soils which are particularly good for rye at the lower levels. At higher elevations the soil formed is "grey and sterile and often boggy". On the whole, though, the Old Red Sandstone of the Vale produces a fairly good

3

agricultural soil. In her splendid book *A Land*, Jacquetta Hawkes describes this rock as "glowing with the remembered warmth of Devonian deserts". For those who know even less about geology than I, and who may be scratching their heads and wondering what deserts there are in Devonshire, it should be explained that "Devonian" is a term applied to a certain geological period early in our earth's history, between the Silurian and Carboniferous ages.

Of all these rock-formations, the most vital to our modern economy are the Coal Measures, near Bristol. They were formed in the marshes and brackish swamps in which, during the Carboniferous period, grew massive trees and ferns and thickets of giant horsetails whose diminutive descendants are still to be found on the margins of ponds and lakes. (I have seen them growing in the Wanswell Court moat.) In these great swamps of the Carboniferous period, life was vigorous and decay rapid. In them floundered massive amphibious monsters. Above them flickered gigantic dragon-flies. There was neither spring nor autumn, and the trees were mainly evergreen. The vigorous swamp life lived "above a tremendous accumulation of its own past". Then, in the succeeding geological era, the sea came in, to bury the swamp-forests many fathoms deep; and it was under this immense pressure that the coal began to form. Apart from coal, the Carboniferous period gave us that pinkish-brown, fine-grained pennant stone which is quarried at Winterbourne, and it is from the clays of the Coal Measures that bricks and pipes are made. Roadstone, derived from the Carboniferous Limestone Beds, has, at various times, been quarried at Chipping Sodbury, Wickwar, Cromhall, Alveston, Almondsbury, Elberton and Olveston.

One of the most curious rock-formations in Gloucestershire is Aust Cliff. Immediately above the Aust–Beachley ferry, it is about 150 feet high and a mile or so long. The base of the cliff is almost awash at high tide, but at any other time you can walk along the beach beneath it and examine the curious and beautiful stratification. The base is of Carboniferous Limestone, with Red Sandstone above it, and, above that, a layer of alabaster, like frozen candy or crystallised snow, which flakes off in lumps and is carried away by local children to be used as doorstops or to edge garden paths. I am told it is used in the manufacture of plaster of

Paris. Above the gypsum are the Keuper Red Marls, which predominate. Then a Tea-Green Marl; and, above that, the most curious of all these strata, the "Bone Bed". This is nothing less than a cemetery of prehistoric monsters. And it was from investigations on this very bed that the science of agricultural chemistry stemmed.

It was whilst he was helping Mary Anning excavate prehistoric reptiles from the cliffs of Lyme Regis that the geologist William Buckland, Dean of Westminster, had the notion that these remains might be rich in phosphates. By a lucky chance he soon afterwards met Liebig, the great German chemist, and together they came down to explore this Bone Bed at Aust. Amongst other bones they found those of ichthyosaurus and plesiosaurus, the last meal undigested within their fossilised ribs. "Most of the fossils were stained an unmistakable black with the indelible ink from the cuttlefish they had devoured," and ". . . there were boundless stores of coprolites, the undigested remainder of ancient meals." The English Dean and the German Baron straightway packed off specimens to Lord Playfair's laboratory in Manchester, where, after they had been ground and analysed, the fossil bones proved to be rich in phosphates. Buckland, who is supposed to have remarked on first seeing the Bone Bed, "I'll grind their bones to make my bread!" was certainly justified in the event, and soon afterwards Liebig published the suggestion (revolutionary at the time!) that agriculturists should use ground bones, fossil bones and the coprolites which occur in certain beds of lias to increase fertility. So the grinding-up of the bones of millions of bison slaughtered on the American prairies, and the nitrate industry of Chile, sprang from these investigations of a German chemist and an English dean at Aust Cliff.

Aust was once an island. It is actually a knoll, the stratification of which has been exposed on its western side by the action of Severn. But before Severn was born, Aust Cliff was an island, surrounded by a marsh or a brackish lake. Today it is surrounded by alluvial flats which make good pasture, both knoll and flats resting upon a solid base of Carboniferous Limestone.

So far as humankind is concerned, the story of the Vale begins in the Palæolithic period (the Old Stone Age), when there were men living on the gravel-terraces beside the Severn near Frampton. Specimens of their characteristic tool, the hand-axe, have been found there, and they may be as much as 200,000 years old! These, our first human inhabitants, were "primitive, hairy and stooped as they walked; they were chinless, yet they were truly human. They were nomadic hunters, and, with their crude weapons, had to fight for their existence against the mammoth, rhinoceros, wolf and bear, whilst they killed deer, ox, and other animals for food." I have been quoting from Dr T. A. Ryder's history of Gloucestershire. He goes on to describe the conditions under which the "River Drift" men lived. The climate was colder, the rivers and streams larger than they are today, and, owing to the cold climate, there would have been but little vegetation. When one considers what life meant for those primitive nomadic hunters, clad in a few skins, living dangerously, desperately, it is difficult to repress a shudder at their condition and prospects. Modern life, even at its worst, is a Utopia when compared with Palæolithic times.

Gradually the climate changed and became milder, and as a result the Vale became densely wooded, especially on the clay. Many new animals began to move into the district from farther south—from Europe, in fact : for in those times Britain was not a separate island. We have little trace of the human inhabitants of this period. They were primarily cave-dwellers, and the Vale is caveless. By an odd chance remains of animals of that period were preserved in a fissure of the limestone on Durdham Downs. They included wolf and badger, otter and weasel, mammoth and lion, rhinoceros and reindeer, lemming, bear and deer. Then, some nine thousand years ago, after Britain had been separated from the Continent, came Neolithic men, small of stature and long of head, to make their settlements and establish the beginnings of civilisation. They were an agricultural people, these Iberians, living more settled lives than their predecessors, domesticating animals and growing crops. They may have had some kind of belief in a life-after-death, too, because their burial systems were elaborate, and they buried their dead in long-barrows, with their tools and weapons beside them.

So far as I know, no long-barrows have been found in the Vale. It has even been remarked that prehistoric man preferred

6

the uplands, disliking the dense woods and danger from flooding. As evidence, some archæologists point to the great number of barrows still to be seen on the Cotswolds. But that is not quite fair. Although it is certain that early man disliked the heavy clays, it is unlikely that the gravels of the Vale would have supported thick forests, or, for that matter, been subject to flooding. R. J. C. Atkinson, of the Department of Prehistoric Archæology, Edinburgh University, who carried out an investigation on prehistoric earthworks between Whitminster and Frampton-on-Severn a few years ago, tells me that in his view parts of the Vale have probably been fairly heavily settled from Neolithic times onward. As for the absence of camp sites and barrows in the Vale, compared with the great number on the Cotswold uplands to the east, that is very likely due to the more intensive cultivation of fertile land, which has, over the centuries, obliterated surface traces of earthworks and settlement sites. "It is noteworthy," Mr Atkinson remarks, "that most of the gravel pits which have been opened near the Severn between Gloucester and Bristol have produced fair quantities of prehistoric and later pottery."

As Mr Atkinson's full report on his excavations at Frampton has not yet been published, he has very kindly sent me some notes and observations on his discoveries which will be of especial interest to archæologists. Most of the earthworks examined were Bronze Age. They were not known to exist until, preparatory to commercial exploitation of underlying gravel, the topsoil was removed from a large area. Indeed, the first two sites which Mr Atkinson examined had been so much damaged by mechanical excavators that it was impossible to give them a date. From their size and shape, the ditches surrounding these sites would seem to indicate that they enclosed barrows of Bronze Age date.

At the eastern end of the gravel pit already excavated, the western halves of two contiguous circular ditches were exposed. One of these had a causewayed ditch dug in a number of discontinuous segments. The other circle consisted of a narrow circular ditch about 70 feet in diameter. On its inner edge were two deep pits with very steep sides. These appeared to have been deliberately filled in with soil soon after they were dug (there's a mystery for you!). In the filling were fragments of Roman pottery of the first or second century A.D., which is probably also the date of the whole structure.

Now we come to the last and most interesting site, which was in a field adjoining the gravel pit, to the east. This proved to be a round barrow of the early Bronze Age, and once again there was something queer about it! The mound itself, though much ploughed down, was still discernible on the surface. Originally about 70 feet in diameter, it was surrounded by a circular ditch some 110 feet in diameter, 12 feet wide, and 5 feet deep, with a flat bottom. Near the bottom of this ditch was the crouched skeleton of an adult man! He was not accompanied by any of the customary grave-goods, although he was buried in early Bronze Age times soon after the building of the barrow.

The only feature of any importance in the central area was a small pit, a mere 2 feet in diameter, which was filled with tightly rammed fragments of a baked-clay structure, possibly a small oven or potter's kiln. Among these fragments were the sherds of at least five different beaker vessels typical of the early Bronze Age. (Incidentally, the people of this era and culture are usually known as the "Beaker" folk, their name being derived from their distinctive drinking-vessel, which was frequently buried with them.) Mr Atkinson sums up thus:

> "The barrow is remarkable, first for the absence of a central burial, secondly for the presence of that enigmatic pit and its contents, and thirdly because it appears to be of the 'bell' type, which has previously been recorded only once or twice in association with early Bronze Age remains. It is also important as one of the comparatively few early Bronze Age sites so far recorded from Gloucestershire."

Surely there is material here, not only for an archæological essay, but for a most unusual detective-story; the sort of mystery which Holmes would have revelled in, and solved, to the confusion of nit-witted Watson. Why wasn't there a burial in the central mound? What was the purpose of the pit full of fragments of baked clay? And what possible explanation could there be for the crouched burial in the ditch? Conan Doyle might have called it "The Case of the Vacant Grave".

In the absence of Holmes, we lack positive and startling answers to these enigmas. Perhaps Mr Atkinson will be able to throw further light on them when he publishes his complete—I was going to say "record of the case", but since this is a serious discussion and not a work of fiction, perhaps I had better say "investigations and discoveries".

That there are probably round-barrows in the Vale of which surface traces have been obliterated I am convinced. There were probably round barrows on the Carboniferous Limestone ridge between Tytherington and Thornbury, if one is to believe old quarrymen. Bill Curtis worked at Tytherington Quarries for most of his life, and he told me that, when they were working the Conyger field, the workmen came across a skeleton "all crouched up". From Bill Curtis's description of situation and skeleton, I should imagine this was quite probably a "crouched" burial of the Bronze Age. As far as Mr Curtis remembers, no one made any investigation of the site and remains. They had dug up so many skeletons thereabout, he said, that they didn't take much notice, even though the curious posture arrested their attention. Probably they were much more concerned when they came across the body of a new-born child, which was "discovered" to be the babe of a servant-girl working at one of the local big houses and suspected of being "on easy terms" with her employer. Taxed with it, the girl owned that the baby had died and that she had secretly buried it. Nothing was done about that either.

Returning to matters archæological, however, the Age of Bronze was followed by an Age of Iron. The Celts, who were the first blacksmiths, probably had their share in laying down the pattern of the Vale as we know it. They built the camp known as Brackenbury Ditches near Wotton-under-Edge; they rein-forced Uley Bury Camp; and, with their iron axes, they cleared large spaces in the forest for agriculture. It has been said that most of the Vale villages of today which are situated on knolls near the Severn or its tributary streams came into being under the Bry-thons (Celts, from which the word "Britons"). That, again, is debatable! It might equally well be said that in many cases they only displaced or intermingled with their predecessors. But the Celts certainly gave a fresh impetus to agriculture, and the cattle-tracks around their settlements, and their inter-village routes, winding and tortuous because they had to avoid obstacles which have long since disappeared, formed the basis of many of our country lanes. Indeed, many of the prehistoric tracks from Cotswold uplands to Severnside can still be traced, and Mr Norton of Coaley showed me where two such trackways crossed not far from his cottage near Coaley church. Many flints have been found hereabouts; so many, in fact, that some writers claim a settlement was sited here.

It was the Romans who created the most important road that the Vale has, or is ever likely to have. The Romans invaded Gloucestershire in A.D. 47. They marched over the Cotswolds, after overcoming the hilltop camps, into the Vale beyond. From the many Roman remains discovered here it would seem that they found it to their liking. From Glevum (Gloucester) at one end, to Abone (Shirehampton, Bristol) at the other, they made a road which has influenced developments and communications in the county ever since. A.38 is, in fact, the most heavily trafficked trunk road in the county. In 1938, when a traffic census was taken, the daily tonnage of vehicles using the road was between ten and fifteen thousand. Today it is greater still.

Nearly everyone who lives in Gloucestershire must know this Bristol–Gloucester road. From Almondsbury near Bristol, to Hardwicke near Gloucester, you are traversing the Berkeley Vale, for the road runs right through the heart of the region. Yet you could travel that road for years and know little of the Vale or gain any idea of its special characteristics. For traffic on this great thoroughfare is constant and rather terrifying: a perpetual stream of lorries, buses, cars.

Nearly all these vehicles are going through. They don't stop. They rush on to Bristol or to Gloucester: lorries, cars, charabancs full of trippers bound for Wye Valley, Cotswold, or Blackpool, or southward bound for Weston-super-Mare or Glorious Devon. And most of them are passing through country more interesting than any they are likely to see at their journey's end. A hundred yards from the noise, petrol-fumes and ribbon-development, you are in another country; another mile and you are deep in the country of the Vale. The scene is changed, the traffic of A.38 an unpleasant memory. Here are winding lanes and hedges, from which rise oaks and elms which, in summer, dapple the lanes with shade, and in autumn "drip in browns and duns", and in winter "thresh and ply" in the south-westerly gales. Here, too, are woods, remnants of the old forests or chases in which the local barons hunted deer. And fine old farms, with the bloom of time on them, set amid some of the finest dairy country in England. Miles of little orchards, with, here and there, at intervals, cottages—of half-timber and thatch in the Stonebench–Hardwicke–Frampton neighbourhood; of red-brick around Slimbridge and Berkeley; of limestone in the villages nearer the Cotswold escarpment. A few miles away from A.38, through tortuous ways, is the estuary of a great river, with a little-known, unique and fascinating life of its own. And you will also find—if you search for them, for they are often well-concealed—old manors, moated farms, delightful rivers and sluggish rhines, castles (though these are famous), saltings which harbour heron and wildfowl, lovely churches, friendly and remote old inns. I am not much of a drinker, but I must admit to a special delight in these fine old crusted inns of the Vale, where ancient men speak of the halcyon days of long ago, and tell tall tales of crops and storms and "gentry". The sound of their voices comes back to me as I write. Slow, deep, with long-drawn vowels, they have an expressiveness and beauty of utterance, a vigour and earthiness which is, to me, more satisfying than the honeyed tones of B.B.C. announcers.

Except their fine road from Glevum to Abone, the Romans left few really notable monuments in the Vale. There were, however, villas at Alveston, Tockington, Stancombe (under Stinchcombe Hill) and near King's Stanley. Camps can still be seen at Tytherington, Damery, Cromhall-Tortworth (Bloody Acre), Oldbury-on-Severn, Kingsweston, Elberton (Vineyard Brake) and Rockhampton; though it is probable that most of these are pre-Roman and that the Romans adopted them. More likely they were constructed, in the first place, by Iron- and Bronze-Agers, and one or two may even be earlier than that. There was a Roman burial-place at Newport on the Bristol–Gloucester road near Berkeley, at which there appears to have been a settlement of some kind. Coins and other relics have been found, and there is, near the lectern in the church at Berkeley, an inscribed tile, of "the century of Claudius Vitalis", which was found, with the bases of two Roman columns, when the church was restored.

Aust is also associated with the Romans. They worked a ferry from there, which is claimed to have been the terminal in a Roman vicinal or by-road, which branched off Acman Street and ran, via Kingswood and Durdham Downs (Bristol), to the Trajectus Augusti at Aust. There have been many disputes about this ferry by scholars, I believe; but then, disputation and scholarship seem to be inseparable.

The Camp at Bloody Acre is on the Earl of Ducie's estate—or what is left of it, for Tortworth Court and the grounds immediately adjoining were commandeered after the war, and converted into a prison. It is generally known as "the-prison-without-bars" because of its experiment in allowing prisoners a greater measure of freedom, but I shall have more to say about that later. Returning to this part of the Tortworth Estate still administered by the Agent, Mr Blair, we find, in Harris's Wood, on the hill opposite the Camp, a place called Lover's Leap. There is a legend about this place, which—like so many doubtful legends—has been celebrated in bad verse. I haven't been able to discover the author of this pathetic ballad, but a local schoolmistress, Mrs Smith, tells me that, soon after she came to Tortworth, and round about the turn of the century, she was shown this poem in manuscript by the old Foreman and Clerk of Works, John Groves of Charfield. It was written in a rather old-fashioned script, and being curious about it, Mrs Smith made enquiries in and around Tortworth—without success. It begins thus:

> *The Roman Camp on Tortworth Hill*
> *Stood high o'er Severn's sedgy plain,*
> *Proclaiming far the Conqueror's will*
> *To Britons in their own domain.*

There is altogether too much poetic licence here. In Roman days the plain was thickly wooded rather than sedgy. "The Conqueror" suggests William of Normandy. And the downtrodden natives (the *Dobuni*) were probably not so downtrodden either. They appear to have lived on fairly easy terms with the Romans, and may even have preferred them to their neighbours across the river, the savage and independent *Silures*. However, that Roman soldiers cultivated a vineyard on the slopes below their camp, and that below it, in the valley, was and is a stream, is not disputed, though most of our vineyards were made by the Normans. This vineyard was still in existence as late as the mid-nineteenth century.★

One day, goes the legend, a Roman officer with a working party surprised a "British" maiden who had come from the village at nearby Cromhall to fetch water from the stream.

> *The maiden, startled by the sound,*
> *Sprang to her feet in breathless fear,*
> *And, to a knoll with sudden bound,*
> *She leaped to scape the danger near.*
>
> *Next she stood up, and, with a frown,*
> *At once defiant and abashed,*
> *She eyed the foemen striding down*
> *Who roughly through the bracken crashed.*

★ This vineyard, of which the remains can still be seen, was situated on the steep wooded slope of a valley, facing south. The stone terraces are now overgrown by yews. Canon Ellacombe of Bitton described this particular site as "the most remarkable remains of a vineyard in Gloucestershire", adding that it was destroyed after a dispute between the rector and the owner respecting tithes. In a paper read to the members of Bath Natural History and Antiquarian Field Club in 1890, Ellacombe described the vineyard as follows: "The hill is a mountain limestone, and the soil seems to be shallow and stony. The terraces begin from the lowest level within a stone's throw of a small brook that runs through the valley. There are seven distinct terraces, divided from each other by walls a yard high—the distance from wall to wall being 12 to 14 feet. They vary in length according to the slope of the hill."

Lord Ducie, owner of the property, gave the following account of the Tortworth vineyard in 1887: "My late agent, still living, a very old man, has often told me that fifty years ago he remembered seeing a few wild vines among the bushes in the Vineyard. And in January 1882, calling upon William May, an old Cromhall labourer who had spoken to me of his recollections of the Vineyard, he told me how he had stolen grapes there as a child; they were, even then, out of cultivation and growing wild. He said: 'I do mind the Vines. They growed between the path and the brook—black ones. It were nigh about vower score 'ear ago, for I be now in the eighty-eights. My father told me as how one 'ear there were dree 'ogsheads o' wine made there.'"

On the subject of quality, Ellacombe quotes William of Malmesbury and Phillips, who, as recently as 1820, gave his judgment that some English wine "was quite equal to the Grave wines, and in some instances, when kept for 8–10 years, it has been drunk as Hock by the nicest judges".

Strange how she leaps upon that knoll in one bound, whilst the foemen have to stride *down* to it, crashing through the bracken! Apparently they had surprised her from a distance!

> *The British maid was tall and fair,*
> *Her stately limbs were tall and strong,*
> *And o'er her shoulders streamed her hair*
> *In waving tresses dark and long.*

Curiouser and curiouser! She is tall and fair, yet her tresses are "dark and long". The second "tall" is wasteful. If she herself was tall, you wouldn't expect her limbs to be short.

> *The warrior, holding back his band,*
> *Advanced to meet her where she stood,*
> *With contract bow and helm in hand*
> *He smiled away her frightened mood.*

> *"Fear not, I pray," he gently said,*
> *"No danger threatens thee, I ween,*
> *We search for water, my fair maid,*
> *'Tis sweeter now where thou hast been."*

> *Then, lifting up her earthen vase,*
> *He placed it gently on her head,*
> *And led her through the straightened pass*
> *To Cromhall, whence the maid had sped.*

After that Julius often strayed in the direction of Cromhall, just as—curiously enough—Wilbur was to do when, during this last war, U.S. forces were stationed at Tortworth Court. However, this Julius appears to have been less lucky than some of his successors. The maiden's old man got to hear about their meetings and, being British to the backbone, very much disliked the notion of his daughter receiving the attentions of Roman Julius. So that when a "British chief from Severn's bank" (a Silurian, from the Forest of Dean) sued for the lovely Olivia's hand—

> *The Sire in haste approved his suit,*
> *Nor cared to ask the maid's consent,*
> *But bore her off beyond pursuit, etc.*

And what does poor Julius do? Does he hasten after, like Young Lochinvar or Hickory Stern, to carry the lady off? He does not. Although—

> *The lover, maddened by her fate,*
> *Stalked wildly over hill and dale,*
> *With vengeance sword and deadly hate,*

nothing much seems to have come of it, because in the next verse he has only got as far as the big rock just across the valley from camp. It is now evening. He is alone. And, looking down on the place where they'd first met, Julius can scarce repress the starting tear . . .

> *In mournful gloom he viewed the scene,*
> *Cast down were all his hopes in life,*
> *No soldier's dreams as there had been,*
> *No glory now in arms and strife.*
>
> *The world was darkening round his youth,*
> *The Camp was dull, his comrades rude,*
> *Old Roman faiths were void of truth,*
> *Philosophy was false or crude.*
>
> *His fainting spirit craved for death,*
> *Till, brooding o'er his mortal woe,*
> *He drew one long and struggling breath,*
> *And plunged into the depths below.*

One would have thought Roman soldiers were made of sterner stuff! Personally, I should be less sceptical toward this legend if it had been Olivia who'd done the leaping, either because Julius had received marching orders, or because she discovered he had a wife back in Rome. As it is, this legend of Lover's Leap strikes me as being extremely legendary. At a guess I should hazard that the verses were the work of a local clergyman, *circa* 1850.

It was a day in late October when I was last in Tortworth Park. Approaching it from the Bibstone end, we had to walk through a miniature forest of rose-bay willow-herb. The plants were as tall as we, and their feathery seed-pods struck an appropriate autumnal note which was continued (or amplified) by the bright yellow withy-leaves which littered the ground near the brook. These had a lovely, luminous effect, like a carpet of gold. They shone with a lustre and intensity which made the leaden sky a poor thing by comparison. Such leaves as still clung to the trees were brightly coloured: warm scarlet, pale pink and yellow, dark vermilion, dull brown. Under the beeches it was like being in a cathedral, with the great smooth boles its pillars, and the branches curving to meet far above one's head, below fan tracery of the most delicate, regular and intricate kind. The light, filtered by a thin screen of scarlet, brown and yellow leaves, made one think of a cathedral, too: having the effect of stained-glass. Without thinking, you lowered your voice when you spoke, from a feeling of reverence and awe.

Harold Pember, the gamekeeper, who was with me, showed me what was left of a stone seat which a previous Lord Ducie had caused to be erected at "Lover's Leap" because he liked the view from there. It was in pieces at the foot of the hill. Mr Pember told me that twentieth-century vandals had recently broken up the seat and rolled the stones down the steep hill. "If I'd happened to be walking along that path at the time, I might've been killed," he complained. It was a strange way for them to express their thanks for the right to walk through this lovely park, I admit. But destructiveness and youth are inseparable. The same young men seem to have been actively employed on the decorative wall along the top end of the lake. They have pushed all the coping-stones off this wall into the lake, and I could wish Mr Pember had been behind them when they were doing it!

We climbed up the stiff slope to Bloody Acre Camp, which commands a wonderful view, both westward across the low-lying fields toward the Severn, and down into this wooded combe. Although it is grown over by fine beeches, they do not conceal its proportions or contours. The three separate ramparts and ditches are still there, and growing on them I saw the dark-green leaves of the stinking hellebore. Even at this dead season, the dark-green, spotted and serrated leaves were strikingly beautiful. They must be a lovely sight early in the year, when their pale-green blossoms cluster over these ramparts beneath the

16

beeches.* Among the decaying leaves which carpet the ground beneath the beeches grow many fungi. There was a form very like the common mushroom, I noticed, and another like a fragile toadstool of a tender, pastel-shaded pink, which might well serve as a fairies' umbrella. Another fungus which was to be found on stones among moss resembled nothing so much as tiny fragments of partly burnt blotting-paper.

Coming down from the Camp, we stopped at one point to look up the wooded valley, whose floor was the lake, to the elegant boat-house. Beyond it, the sloping lawns of Tortworth Court, complete the landscape and provide the focal point of the view. The lake, about half a mile long, fringed with reeds and speckled with wild waterfowl, is set quite perfectly to provide a mirror for the wooded hills, which rise on every side and were, at that time of the year, gorgeously apparelled. If I were a landscape painter I'm sure I should want to paint this scene. And I should want to paint it as I saw it then: the hill-slopes a glorious pattern of various colours, with individual trees standing out by reason of some subtle emphasis of colour (a particularly intense yellow, a blackish crimson, a lovely magenta, heavy bronze or golden brown), with the lake a placid mirror (flawed only by the wake of coot and wild duck) providing the last, refining touch by way of a liquid and romantic reflection.

About the Camp in Tortworth Park (which is actually between Falfield and Cromhall, and nowhere near Tortworth village), the Gloucestershire historian Samuel Rudder wrote in 1779:

"It is probable that the old road from Aquæ Sulis, or Bath, to the Trajectus at Oldbury,† and so on to the Roman stations in Monmouthshire, led through this parish of Cromhall, or a little to the southward of it; for there are the remains of a strong encampment in Tortworth Park, where it may be supposed the soldiers were posted to protect that road. That this was a Roman work is pretty certain from some coins which have

* A curious thing about this plant is that snails assist in the distribution of its seeds. Attached to each side of them is a fleshy band called the "oil-body". This is eaten by the snail and the seeds stick to its slime, to be scattered at "a snail's pace".

† Whether this Trajectus was at Aust, Oldbury or Sheperdine has been disputed. I can only say that Aust seems the most likely.

been found, and from a tesselated pavement sometime since discovered there, about eighteen feet long and fifteen broad, composed of small cubical bricks or stones of various colours, and set together with a strong cement in a very curious order and regularity."

There is another Roman Camp at Rockhampton, not far from the Severn estuary, which comes to mind, perhaps because it is so utterly different from Bloody Acre. The latter is grown over by fine beeches, which give the place an almost ecclesiastical atmosphere. Rockhampton Camp, which has only one vallum, overlooks the Severn, is very exposed, and is not very easy to find without Ordnance Map and compass. Its smallness and difficulty of access seem to have discouraged archæologists, for I have not been able to obtain a full report on the site.

I well remember my first visit. The Camp is clearly shown on the Ordnance Map, with a field-path to it from Rockhampton churchyard. I found the stile on the south side of the churchyard all right, but of a footpath there was no sign. No doubt there had been one once. But it had long ago grown over, and I had to guess my way. You can imagine what happened. I was soon involved in difficulties: climbing gates, jumping ditches, crawling under barbed wire, searching for a place to squeeze through the hedge. Coming to a stiff hill, I toiled up it, tripping over restharrow which grew plentifully there, only to find, on reaching the top that I'd climbed the wrong one. Down I staggered to a gate at the bottom, where I found (so strange a thing is Fate!) a couple of enormous mushrooms. Then I began to climb up the hill to the Camp. It was rough going, for the side of the hill was steep and much overgrown and it was a very hot day. I remember noticing a superabundance of scabious; and I remember, too, that I was very short of breath by the time I reached the top. Sitting down to rest on the side of the vallum, I had a marvellous view not only of the camp but of the great sweep of Severn to the west. It is a fine vantage point, and it isn't difficult to see why it was chosen for a camp. In the central area I noticed a bit of marshy ground which may once have been a spring or well.

There is a local legend that a battle was fought somewhere hereabout, and I was told that the sexton often finds piles of bones when digging in the churchyard, though whether these are battle casualties or plague victims is difficult to say. There is also, in Rockhampton, a well which is attributed to the Romans and called the Pennywell. Years ago, local people depended on it for their drinking-water, and its water is still supposed to be beneficial for the eyes. However, there are so many of these wells about, most of them associated with some particular saint, all supposedly good for eye-trouble, that I'm afraid I didn't seek out the Pennywell. Near the well, and running under the Eastwood ridge, is an ancient trackway which the local people refer to as "the Roman road".

Returning to Cromhall: there used to be on Anchoret hill not far from Bloody Acre the ruin of an anchorite's cell. Here lived the wise man whom the Monks of Bangor consulted before they went to meet St Augustine. The story is well known. So much so that I thought at first to omit it. But it belongs to the Vale, and there is always the chance that some readers are not aware of it, so here it is. . . .

When he came to England, St Augustine found that there were, already, Christian churches in the West and in Wales. They had survived from Roman days, and it was these Celtic churches that sent missionaries into Ireland. They were, however, too independent to please Augustine, for they did not acknowledge the Pope, and their ritual and observance was peculiarly their own. In their monasteries the scriptures were studied and preachers trained. They had their bishops and their hermits, one of the wisest of which dwelt on Anchoret hill.

Augustine, being properly appointed Archbishop of the English, did not much relish these independent churches on the western fringe of his domain. So he invited the leaders of the Celtic church to meet him at "Augustine's Oak", on Aust Cliff,★ to urge them to unite with him in the common task of converting the pagans. His primary purpose, however, was to get them to

★ I am quite aware that this is in dispute, and that a Bishop of Bristol has claimed that the meeting took place at St Augustine's Priory at Bristol. In either case, it has to be admitted that Cromhall was a long way out of the Celts' way, and looks extremely inconvenient for them. However, the whole thing is so misted by time that one story is probably as good as another.

acknowledge his supremacy and change their ritual and customs to accord with the practice of Rome.

At that time Bangor, in Wales, was a famous seminary. It sent a deputation of monks to meet Augustine, but lacking confidence, they decided at the eleventh hour to consult the hermit of Cromhall. Coming to his cell, they asked him for his advice, and he told them: "If Augustine is a man of God, follow him."

"But how shall we know whether he's a man of God or not?" they asked.

"Our Lord said, 'Take my yoke upon you, and learn of Me, for I am meek and lowly of heart.' If, therefore, Augustine is meek and lowly, he has taken upon him the yoke of Christ and offers the same to you. But if he is stern and haughty, he is not of God, nor are you to regard his words."

He went on to advise them how to put matters to the test. They should arrive at the conference late, some time after Augustine and company. If, after they had kept him waiting, Augustine rose patiently from his chair to greet them, they should listen submissively. But if he showed his impatience, and hurt pride forbade him to be pleasant with them, they would know he was not from God; that he was merely an ambitious priest.

They put it to the test, and Augustine remained seated, annoyed and affronted by their lateness. At once the Celtic priests accused him of pride and intolerance, and contradicted everything he said. He appealed to them, saying that he would allow them a measure of independence if they would, firstly, administer baptism in the manner of the Roman church, secondly, keep Easter at the time appointed by Rome, and thirdly, join with him in preaching to the English. They flatly declined; whereupon Augustine lost his temper and told them that if they wouldn't help him preach to the English, they should die at English hands.

The story is significant, for it demonstrates how the hermit's wisdom showed up Augustine's lack of humility and unchristian desire for vengeance. It also shows how his unworldliness led him to put absolute values before practical realities, with the result that much needless bloodshed and suffering followed. However, to such a man (and such men are not, even now, quite extinct) right is Right. There is no such thing as compromise.

Whether the Celtic churchmen subsequently blessed or cursed him, I cannot discover.

Strangely enough, Aust has another legend, less well known, which also concerns pride and humility, but has a different ending. It is told in Bigland's Collections (1786) thus: King Edward the Elder, lying at Aust Clive, invited Leolin, Prince of Wales, then at Bethersley (now Beachley), to a conference about certain matters which were in dispute between them. Leolin refused to cross the Severn, however; whereupon Edward, despite his greater power, crossed the river to Leolin, to hold the conference on the Welsh side. This so moved Leolin, ashamed now of his suspicion and false pride, that, before Edward's boat reached the Beachley shore, he leapt into the water and embraced the keel, saying, "Most wise king, your humility has conquered my pride, and your wisdom triumphed over my folly. Mount that neck which I have foolishly exalted against you, and enter into that country which your goodness has this day made your own." And so, taking the English king on his shoulders, he carried him ashore.

CHAPTER II

RISE AND DECLINE OF THE HOUSE OF BERKELEY

THE Roman legions left Britain in A.D. 410, and a dark age followed: an age of tribal warfare, plundering and strife. Here and there Romans may have stayed on in their villas, pockets of peace and culture in the general chaos, but they were not destined to remain in peace for long. Soon the Saxons were invading the East Coast and spreading westward. And although the Britons held on to the Cotswold forts, their last bulwark against invasion for some years, the Saxons were eventually too much for them. By that time, the movement had become more in the nature of a vast migration from the shores of the Baltic to the island of Britain, than a military invasion or conquest. At the Battle of Dyrham, in A.D. 577, the West Saxons defeated the Celtic princes, and all the land between Cotswold and Severn lay open to the invaders.

Some of the defeated Britons fled to the Fretherne–Arlingham peninsula, around which Severn crooks a benevolent (or tyrannical) arm. They were making for the Severn crossings at Newnham and Priding, and it may have been on this day that Unla Water got its name. Unla is a contraction of the Saxon word for misfortune.

The Britons were familiar with the crossings and able to cross the river in safety, but their pursuers had never seen Severn before. Later in this book I shall have more to say of the dangers of Severn for those unfamiliar with her. For the moment it is enough to point out that Unla Water, where it runs under the north bank of Arlingham, is perhaps the most dangerous reach of all. Even at low tide it is a maze of currents and whirlpools, and it was here that the Saxons, emboldened by their success on the battlefield, tried to cut off the enemy by swimming across Severn. Most of them were drowned. Then, as now, Severn was not a river to be trifled with.

Because the Saxons were pagans, they replaced the early Christianity of the Romano-British period with the worship of Thor and Woden. Destroying Bath, the Aquæ Sulis of the Romans, they began rapidly clearing the forest of the Vale for their settlements. Usually their settlements were beside a stream: a family or group of families making it their own. These settlements have influenced the subsequent development of the Vale, and the Saxons have even been blamed for its under-development because, loving privacy and family life and distrusting strangers, they sited their villages away from the Roman roads.

Saxon village-names persist to this day, as in Tortworth, Arlingham, Frampton, Coaley and Falfield. Indeed, more than 80 per cent of Vale villages were Saxon settlements. Usually Saxon names describe the economic or geographical features of a place (e.g. Rockhampton), or celebrate some particular individual (Mangotsfield). Each of their villages had its leaders, who represented it at the Hundred Court, consisting of five men from each of twenty villages. Thus the Hundred was our first important administrative unit, and you might even say the Saxons were the first to introduce into England a form of democratic government.

These Hundreds persisted long after the Hundred Court had gone. But they survived as a geographical rather than an administrative entity. As late as the early seventeenth century, John Smyth, steward and historian of the Berkeleys, wrote a fascinating account of the Hundred of Berkeley. And he still called local folk "hundreders", using the term with a special affection which suggests that, even then, there remained a real sense of unity and common identity within the Hundred. When Smyth writes of "We Hundreders" the phrase has a sort of tribal ring, something of the quality of an invocation.

Smyth was steward to the Lords of Berkeley from 1584 until his death, and there is little doubt that he was a good servant. He did not live at Berkeley, but at Nibley, under the Cotswolds. Here he married a widow in comfortable circumstances and settled down to what seems to have been an active, happy life of service. His worldly affairs prospered. So much so, that he has been accused by some of feathering his own nest. That may be only gossip, for the Berkeleys appear to have been sincerely grateful for his services, and may well have been generous. His labour of love during the latter part of his life was upon the Berkeley Manuscripts. These consist of a series of biographies, the *Lives of the Berkeleys*; *A Description of the Hundred of Berkeley, and of its Inhabitants*; and a catalogue of *Men and Armour in Gloucester-shire, in 1608*. This manuscript remained in the Muniment Room of Berkeley Castle for 250 years, until it was at last printed, under the editorship of Sir John Maclean, in 1885. It contains much of value. Smyth's biographies of the early Berkeleys have provided the basis for much that follows, and his *Description of the Hundred of Berkeley* is most entertaining. Here he turns from the great men of the *Lives*, to the common folk, their work and customs, proverbs and pastimes, dialect and superstitions. Listing words and phrases which are common in, if not peculiar to, his Hundred, he writes:

"So natural is the dialect of pronouncing *y* between words endinge and beginninge with consonants, that it seems drop-pinge from the air into our mouths. As: *John y Smith; Sit y downe; Come y hither; Well y said, my Tomy; My moll is a good y wench; Come y my sweet y will y!*

"The *v* is frequently used instead of *f*. As: *vethers, varthinge, vire,* and *vat*. G is substituted for *c*, as in *guckowe* (cuckoo), *grabs* (crabs), *guckold* (cuckold).

"*Thicki* and *thucki* mean this and that. As: *Don't y go thucki way*."*

Nearly all his comments apply to the dialect as it was commonly spoken within living memory. But as a result of compulsory education, it is now only to be heard from the lips of old people. The local proverbs which Smyth also quotes were of their time, and, so far as I know, have been quite forgotten. Here are a few examples:

"He's like an Aprill shoure, that whets the stone nine times an houre" (of a lazy reaper).

"He seeks for stubble in a fallow field."

* Other examples of local dialect quoted by Smyth are *wenchen* for wenches or girls, *shard* (or *shoord*) is a gap in a hedge, *shoon* are shoes.

"When wheat lieth longe in bed, it riseth with an heavy head."

"He mends like sowre ale in somer" (*viz.* Goes from bad to worse).

"When Westridge (wood) is motley, 'tis time to sowe barley."

"He that will thrive must rise at five:
But he that hath thriven may lye till seaven."

And this one, with Smyth's personal comment thereon:

"All the maids in Wanswell [a hamlet near Berkeley]
May dance in an eggshell."

This seems to imply that there are no maids in Wanswell: that all the young women are wantons. But Smyth comments: "I holde this a lying proverbe at this day; *it slandereth some of my kindred that dwell there.*"

"An head that's white, to maids brings noe delight: or: An head that's gray, serves not for maydens play;—In which state *my* constitution now stands."

John Smyth was not a local man. He came from Lincolnshire. But his wife (the good widow) was from Cowley (now Coaley), under the Cotswolds, and was thus a true Hundreder. One presumes that it was she who supplied him with much of his local material. At any rate, he has a comment to make on one of the local proverbs: "*He is as mild as an harnet!* was a proverb as frequent with my wife as the chiding of her maides."

Although Smyth was three years younger than Shakespeare, and outlived him by a quarter of a century, he never mentions his name. On the face of it, this seems to dispose of the theory that Shakespeare was at one time at Berkeley Castle as a tutor, or connected with the Lord Berkeley's Players. But it is not conclusive. Gloucestershire is a long way from London, and Smyth may not have had a high opinion of the stage. Or there may have been a personal reason for the omission. Shakespeare's two Gloucestershire justices, Shallow and Silence, may have been sly caricatures. And satire may not have been appreciated in the "Hundred".

The Berkeley Hundred was not, of course, the Vale; it included Cotswold slopes and a chunk of the hilltops. Nevertheless, Smyth's description of it is worth quoting:

> "This Hundred seems soe evenly devided, by one part thereof standing high in the wolds and the other in the vale at the foote of those hills, that it is not easily discerned whether of the two is the greater part: By reason of which scituation, many hundreds, even thousands, of springs breake forth at the sydes, knees and feete of those hills, begettinge divers delicate small Rivers, neither knowinge want of water in sommer, nor so increasinge their channell in winter that the trade of clothinge which heere aboundeth is either in drought or wett wether hindred: a principall cause of the multitude of Tuckmills and fullingemills which heere abound."

You may not agree with me, but I consider that that's a very pretty statement of fact; a sensible, civilised and even elegant piece of writing.

Smyth himself was a Christian, but no puritan. He loved country games and jollifications, and describes them with infectious gusto. Church-ales, wrestling and dancing all find a place in his *Description*. That he was no spoil-sport is evident from a letter he wrote to his son, in which he remarks:

> "I like well, in this my decrepit age, to walk in somer-time on Sundaies after Evening Prayers with my wife to Hodley's Green between our two houses, and there to behold my neighbours' children and servants, with yours and mine own, to run at Barley-breakes, dance in a ringe, and suchlike sports as they like best."

He also describes stow-ball, a game which (according to Strutt's *Sports and Pastimes*) was somewhat like golf, though it has also been described as like rounders. Of this he writes that

> "the downes or hilly playnes of Stintescombe, Westridge, Tickruydinge and others . . . doe witnes the inbred delight that both gentry, yeomanry, rascallity, boyes and children doe take in a game called stoball. The play whereat each child of 12 years old can (I suppose) as well describe as myselfe: And

not a sonne of mine but at 7 was furnished with his douball stoball staves, and a gamester thereafter."

In almost everything he wrote John Smyth left the mark of a vigorous, humane and likeable personality. If some of the proverbs he records are crude, what of it? They were crude people who made them, living vital, earthy, industrious lives of intimacy with soil and season. They do not seem to me so immoral as the suggestive and tittering smut turned out by the society writers of a later time.

Very early in the Berkeley MS. comes the story of Earl Godwin and the Lady Abbess of Berkeley. By Godwin's time, the Berkeley Convent had grown very wealthy, holding most of the land in that neighbourhood. And though Godwin was already a rich man, he coveted these lands, and devised a plot to win them from the church. Visiting the convent, in company with his nephew, "a very proper and beautiful yonge gentleman", he pretended that the nephew was sick, and left him in the Abbess's care. Now, this young gentleman was very far from being sick. He appears to have been a lusty and licentious fellow, whose quality Godwin knew full well. Before he left him, Godwin had given him "pretty ringes and fine girdles" in order that he might the better tempt the Lady Abbess and her nuns to share his bed. Smyth writes:

"Hee therefore beinge gladly and willingly entred into this course of libidinous pleasure, (for that the way downe to hell is easy); the Devill thrust out Pallas, brought in Venus, and made the church of our Saviour . . . a very stewes." In short, the nuns found the proper young gentleman quite irresistible. "And when"—to quote Smyth again—"as many of their bellies bare out bigge and round, this youth, beinge by this time over-wearied with conquest of pleasure, getteth him gone. . . ."

On hearing from his kinsman of the scheme's success, off went crafty Godwin to the King to tell him that "the Lady Abbess of Berkeley and her Nunnes were great with childe, and commonly prostitute to every one that would". The king made enquiries, discovered that the first part of the allegation, at any rate, was true, and (as is commonly the case) assumed that the second part must be true also. Whereupon Godwin suggested that, when he was disposing of the place, the King might bear in mind the services of his faithful servant. The King did.

That is how Smyth tells the story, and there is a curious coincidence which may be said to support it. Godwin is known to have bought a manor at Woodchester, and to have given it to his wife *because she would not eat any of the produce of his Berkeley property*. Might not this be because she knew how it was obtained?

Smyth's pedigree of the Lords of Berkeley begins with Harding, "sonne to the king of Denmark". This Harding is supposed to have come across with William the Conqueror, and to have been rewarded by William for his help at Hastings. Upon the Norman Conquest, Smyth comments in grandiose terms:

> "The Crowne was taken up by Duke Harrold, sonne to Earl Godwin: whereof scarce possessed before William Duke of Normandy urged a resignation. Howbeit, Crownes, once assumed, are not accustomed to bee layde downe by papers or parly: the Sword (that prince of weapons) must be Arbitrator between theis potent Competitors. . . ."

But Smyth's pedigree rests on a faulty base. It is more probable that Robert Fitz-Harding, reeve of Bristol and a rich merchant, who was granted the manor of Berkeley in 1153, was the son of one Harding, a Bristol magistrate in the time of the Conqueror. This Harding, says William of Malmesbury, was "better used to whet his tongue in strife than to wield his arms in war". Robert Fitz-Harding was, like his father, a financier and merchant. It was he who founded the Monastery of St Augustine at Bristol, now Bristol Cathedral, and when the Empress Matilda and her son Henry (later to be Henry II) were living at Bristol Castle, Robert Fitz-Harding was their friend and supporter, ready to put his great wealth at their disposal. So, when Henry came into power, it was only natural he should do something for the man who had been his friend. What he did was to grant Fitz-Harding the manor of Berkeley, with an undertaking to build a castle there. Roger de Berkeley, the former lord of Berkeley, was turned out, partly because he had refused to pay his rent to the King, but chiefly because in the recent troubles he had supported Stephen. The actual charter of grant to Fitz-Harding is of interest, but it makes curious reading today:

"Grant from Henry, Duke of Normandy, Count of Anjou, to Rodbert Fitz-Hardinge of the Manor of Bitton and a hundred librates of land in the Manor of Berkeley, with all liberties and customs, with Tol, Them, Soch and Sache, Belle and Burghiet and Infanckenethef, to hold by service of two mewed hawks, with an undertaking to build a castle at Berkeley according to the taste of the said Rodbert."

Meanwhile, Roger de Berkeley, who regarded himself as the rightful owner of Berkeley, had retired to his other castle at Dursley in what the Victorian romancers used to call high dudgeon. (There is a local legend that Roger did not go to Dursley, but, taking to the woods, became a sort of local Robin Hood.) This Roger continued to harass Fitz-Harding, whom one imagines to have been a shrewd but peaceable man, to such effect that Fitz-Harding asked the King to intercede, and matters were eventually settled in the approved manner of the time—by a marriage; in this case, by a double marriage. A marriage contract was signed by Roger de Berkeley and Robert Fitz-Harding, whereby Maurice Fitz-Harding took in marriage the daughter of Roger, whilst Roger's son married Robert's daughter. Presumably the respective sons and daughters were not consulted!

Robert Fitz-Harding continued to live at Bristol. It was his son Maurice who went to live at Berkeley Castle, and, after his father's death, began to call himself Maurice de Berkeley. Thus began one of the most remarkable associations between family and locality in county history. From Maurice onwards, it is impossible to separate the history of the Vale from that of the Berkeleys. One of the remarkable things about them is that although they were constantly involved in treasons, rebellions and regicidal conspiracies, none of the lineal barons perished on the scaffold or the field of battle. Perhaps that original strain of shrewdness in the Bristol merchant stood them in good stead. The third lord, Robert, was excommunicated, it's true, because he'd sided with the barons against King John. Moreover, his castle and lands were confiscated. Some of the estates were subsequently restored to him, but not the castle or the town of Berkeley, which reverted to the family by way of his son, Thomas.

The next in succession, another Maurice, entertained Henry III at the castle, so it would seem that the pendulum had swung in their favour once more. In his time it is recorded that the "household and standing domestical family consisted of 200 persons and upward". Maurice III seems to have met with the nearest approach to a violent end. Having taken part against the two Despencers, he was imprisoned at Wallingford by Edward II and died there. By an irony of fate, Edward II was to end his life as a prisoner in Berkeley Castle, where he was undoubtedly murdered.

It would take too long to go into details of Edward's unfortunate association with the Despencers and his final overthrow by Queen Isabella, Prince Edward and Mortimer. But early in 1327 the unhappy Edward was in prison at Bristol. A plot was discovered which aimed at his deliverance from captivity and escape to the Continent, and at this the authorities panicked, and consigned him to a safer place from which there could be no escape.

The story goes that Edward was taken from Bristol to Berkeley by night; hurried along the swampy paths of Severnside without sufficient clothing for the chilly spring air, and crowned, in mockery, with a crown of twisted hay. His gaolers ordered the King to shave off his beard as an effective disguise against recognition, and after he had agreed to this indignity, Sir John Maltravers and Sir Thomas de Gournay (who seem to have been as rascally a pair as any in history), brought him cold, muddy water in a rusty helmet, to shave with—at which Edward is said to have burst into tears.

He arrived at Berkeley on April 5th, Palm Sunday, and was received by that Lord Thomas whose father, it will be remembered, died in prison at Edward's command. It is often contended that this Lord Thomas Berkeley was a humane man; so much so that he was ordered to go and stay at his manor at Wotton, to be out of the way; and that no sooner was he out of the way, than Gournay and Maltravers began their work. They had received from the Queen a cryptic message, which was so ambiguously worded that it might have been regarded as a death warrant or not. Its actual wording was *Edwardum occidere nolite timere bonum est*, which can be construed either as: "*Do not kill Edward; it is good to have fear*" or as: "*Do not fear to kill Edward: it is a good thing.*"

Maltravers and Gournay had no doubt that the latter was the correct meaning. So, with Lord Berkeley out of the way, they put putrid carcases in the dungeon beneath Edward's chamber, and to further encourage ill-health they allowed him no rest and no proper exercise. But Edward stubbornly continued to live. And then, giving up hope that he would oblige them by dying by "natural means", they decided to murder him. The business was done during the night of September 22nd, 1327, when the towns-folk of Berkeley slept. But so terrible were the King's cries that "many a one awoke, and prayed to God for the harmless soul which that night was departing in torture". In an attempt to regularise the affair, Gournay and Maltravers summoned wit-nesses from Bristol and Gloucester on the following day. They could find no outward signs of violence on Edward's body and concluded that he must have died of a seizure. He was probably stifled with a bolster. It is terrible to think that this was the King who, during his captivity and whilst waiting for the end, wrote these beautiful lines:

> *On my devoted head*
> *Her bitterest showers*
> *All from a wintry cloud*
> *Stern Fortune pours.*
> *View but her favourite*
> *Sage and discerning,*
> *Graced with fair comeliness,*
> *Famed for his learning:*
> *Should she withdraw her smiles,*
> *Each grace she banishes,*
> *Wisdom and wit are flown,*
> *And beauty vanishes.*

It is wryly amusing to read Smyth's account of this episode. He, who worshipped the Berkeleys, obviously wants to believe that Lord Berkeley was innocent. But apart from being Steward of Berkeley, Smyth was a historian, and his scruples would not permit of any distortion of the facts. When Lord Berkeley had been brought to trial he had defended himself by saying that he had been away from home and ill at the date of Edward's death;

so ill, indeed, that he had lost his memory of the events of that time. But Smyth points out that Lord Thomas cannot (as he stated) have been ill at his country house at Wotton, because the account book of his steward there does not note his arrival until *September 28th*. Furthermore, even if his lordship had been sick, he cannot have been very much so, for on the day following the murder he sent personal letters by the hand of Gournay to the Queen, to the young King Edward III and to Mortimer, giving them the news.

Edward's story did not end with his death, for it was then that the question of where to bury him was raised. The Abbot of St Augustine at Bristol, and the priests at Kingswood and Malmesbury, were all asked to take the body. They all (to their shame) refused, because they did not want to affront the Queen. And then one braver than the rest came to the rescue. Abbot Thokey of Gloucester came down to Berkeley and, demanding the King's body, conveyed it to Gloucester in his own carriage. Here it was received by the monks in procession and buried near the high altar. It is good to know that Abbot Thokey's courage did not go unrewarded. Edward's death was soon regretted, and the common people began to flock to Gloucester to pray at his tomb and to express contrition for being, even though indirectly and passively, responsible for his murder. Naturally the Abbey benefited from the offerings of these pilgrims, and much of the present cathedral was built from money received from this source. Truly, "from evil cometh forth good".

Thomas, the fourth of that name and tenth Lord Berkeley, is one of the characters in Shakespeare's *Richard II*, wherein he is represented as meeting Northumberland and Bolingbroke just outside the castle. His part in the play is *not* a meaty one. He is, in fact, merely a messenger from York to Bolingbroke, who, after the latter refuses to accept him as such, is dismissed contemptuously in the following terms:

BOLINGBROKE: *I shall not need transport my words by you:*
Here comes his grace in person.

This scene, by the way, is laid in "the Wilds of Gloucestershire". Bolingbroke and Northumberland meeting, the former asks:

The Vale of Berkeley from Cotswold Escarpment near King's Stanley

BOLINGBROKE: *How far is it, my lord, to Berkeley now?*
NORTHUMBERLAND: *Believe me, noble lord,*
I am a stranger here in Glostershire:
These high wild hills and rough uneven ways
Draw out our miles, and make them wearisome.

Presently they meet up with Percy, and Northumberland enquires of him:

NORTHUMBERLAND: *How far is it to Berkeley? and what stir*
Keeps good old York there with his men of war?

PERCY: *There stands the castle, by yon tuft of trees,*★
Mann'd with three hundred men, as I have
heard . . .

This was the Thomas, Lord Berkeley, who precipitated a prolonged and vicious family feud which ended in the last "private" battle fought on English soil. As a result of this feud between Berkeleys and Lisles, Berkeley Castle was from time to time taken, lost and retaken, and the town of Berkeley half-destroyed. Finally, in 1469, the young Viscount Lisle—last of his line— challenged his contemporary, William, twelfth Lord Berkeley, to settle the issue by a battle on Nibley Green, not very far from where the Tyndale monument now stands. They were each of them to be followed by their own retainers, whom they were to lead into battle. But Lord Berkeley cheated. He secretly obtained the services of several hundred Forest of Dean men, outnumbering the forces of Lisle, who was himself one of the first casualties. There is a local tradition that Lord Berkeley ambushed the Lord Lisle in Michaelwood Chase, and that Lisle was shot in the face by an arrow aimed by a Forest of Dean man called Black Will, who afterwards finished his lordship off with a dagger. Lord Lisle's followers were routed, many were killed. According to an old lady with whom I discussed the battle of Nibley Green, Michaelwood is haunted by the ghosts of Lisle's men, and sometimes, after dark, the rides echo with the clash of armour and the cries of

★ Apparently they were on the Cotswold escarpment, most likely in the neighbourhood of Stinchcombe Hill. Berkeley Castle is also mentioned by Hotspur in *Henry IV*, *Part I*.

3★   33

Fifteenth-century tomb of James, 11th Lord Berkeley, and his son
in the chancel of Berkeley church

the dying. When I last visited Michaelwood it was certainly echoing with the impact of steel on wood, for they were felling the trees. But I should not care to go through Michaelwood alone after dark. It has an atmosphere. Although much whittled down by felling, it still possesses something of the dignity of the ancient forests, a little of their awe and secrecy.

Lord Lisle's attempt was not the last to threaten the Berkeley estates. The next threat came from Robert Dudley, Earl of Leicester. Accompanying Queen Elizabeth on her tour of the West in 1573, he persuaded her to break her journey at Berkeley and to hunt Lord Henry Berkeley's deer in the Castle Park. His lordship was away at the time, and, taking a very unsporting advantage of his absence, the Queen and her favourite slaughtered no less than twenty-seven stags in one day. On arriving home and being told of this wholesale butchery, Lord Henry was justifiably annoyed. Tactlessly, he gave expression to his annoyance. Whereupon the Queen sent him a message to say that he'd better be careful, or the earl who had plotted against his deer might plot against his *castle* or his *life*. It is unlikely that his lordship complained again.

It seems strange that, despite their power and wealth, the Berkeley family seldom distinguished themselves or produced great men. For centuries they were involved in history without ever really *making* it. The truth is that nobility of character and high seriousness of purpose do not appear to have run in the family. Most of them were all too evidently the descendants of a Bristol merchant who had financed a king. One quality they did possess, these Berkeleys of the fifteenth, sixteenth and seventeenth centuries, and that was shrewdness. Their predecessors had been land-grabbers, who enclosed any land they could get their hands on, and they, in turn, consolidated and protected these possessions.

Their shrewdness was apparent in their marriages. Few Lords of Berkeley before the fifth Earl appear to have married for love. Indeed, they were not usually allowed to choose for themselves, their wives being selected by their fathers whilst they were still in the nursery. One writer expresses it acidly in these words: "In the art of wedding money to money, the Berkeleys of the Middle

Ages could have given points to the most dexterous marriage-broker of the East." In those days marriages could be registered provided both parties had reached the age of seven years, and such marriages would remain valid if, when the youth was fourteen and the girl twelve, they confirmed the arrangement. In the course of two centuries, no less than five marriages in the direct line were contracted between parties averaging less than eleven years.

Thomas, first Lord Berkeley, derived a regular income from the buying and selling of wardships and marriages. As a contemporary might now speculate in stocks and shares or real property, this Thomas, Lord Berkeley, speculated in marriage portions and dowries. One Lord Berkeley was actually contracted to marry before he was six. Maurice, third Lord Berkeley, was a husband at the age of eight, and a father before he was fourteen. And he was by no means exceptional. Some of the youngsters who succeeded him were quite astonishingly precocious.

Much of the shrewdness of the Berkeleys seemed to desert them after the first Earl. Thereafter the predominant tendency seems to have been uncontrollable lust—or, if you prefer, an excessive romanticism. Of course they were not unlike other great families in this. But it is strange that their practicality and shrewdness should suddenly leave them—and leave them so utterly to the mercies of the "tender" passion. This may be said to have caused their downfall. Though for long they continued to be a power in their own locality, it was a waning power, with the sins of the fathers coming home to roost with the children. At Berkeley itself you will come across old people who, perhaps because they saw service on the Berkeley estates, still have an enormous respect for the Berkeleys. But in London, after the first Earl's time, the name of Berkeley was too often associated with scandalous propensities for it to be respected as its antiquity and feudal power deserved.

The first Earl Berkeley appears to have been a shrewd and businesslike man, for he was associated with the East India Company and the Council for the Foreign Plantations, was a founder-member of the Royal African Company, and Governor of the Levant Company. A memorial of his association with the East India Company used to be exhibited at the Victoria and

Albert Museum. It was a silver tea-pot, and the inscription ran
as follows: "This silver tea pott was presented to the Committee
of the East India Company by the Right Honourable George
Lord Berkeley of Berkeley Castle, A member of that Honourable
and Worthy Society, and A true hearty lover of them, 1670."

A writer has described Berkeley Castle in the Earl's day as a
cross between Haworth Parsonage in the Brontës' time, and
Wimpole Street in Mr Barrett's. But it is possible that he did less
than justice to his lordship, for it is certain that John Evelyn came
there, and surely he would have avoided a home that was "sombre
and austere, overladen with a dreary sanctimoniousness". This
writer blamed the Earl for his children's misdemeanours, claiming
that it was the repressive atmosphere of their home that made
them so wild and reckless. Certainly, the Earl's three daughters
gave London something to talk about. One of them, Elizabeth,
was fond of jewels, and much liked by the King of France. Another, Mary, who married that dissipated character Lord Grey of
Werk, seems to have been the lover of Monmouth, both before
and after her marriage to Lord Grey. She fell in love with Monmouth, it seems, at their first meeting. He reciprocated, and, in
the spring of 1671, Earl Berkeley thought it prudent to send Mary
into the country. Monmouth, however, who was his father's son
in this at least, was no laggard in love. He discovered her whereabouts and followed her. Disguising himself as a pedlar, he tried
to slip into the house by the back door, but was frustrated by the
vigilance of a faithful old steward—or, if you prefer it, infernal
busybody!—who sported the unlikely name of Zachary Gee.
Eight years later, when she was the wife of Lord Grey, Mary and
Monmouth once again became intimate, and, her husband discovering the fact, she was given "but one night's time to take
leave, pack up, and be gone".

Not that Lord Grey was in any position to play the outraged
husband, for he was in the middle of an intrigue with Mary's
younger sister, Henrietta, then little more than a child. He did
not take long to make his intentions known to her, and Henrietta,
for all her youth, does not seem to have been behindhand. For
more than a year, this girl and her brother-in-law carried on a
clandestine love-affair under the Earl's nose, seeing each other

almost every night, without him ever suspecting anything amiss. For two delirious days, presumably during the temporary absence of mother and father from the Castle, this shameless pair lay hidden in an inner closet of Henrietta's bedroom, without either food or drink, subsisting on love and a few sweetmeats. Inevitably it could not go on for ever. One day Lady Berkeley came across a note from Henrietta to Grey. It was only a short one, but its implications were plain enough, and a very terrible shock it must have been to Henrietta's mama to discover the truth about her. On being taxed with it, Henrietta and Grey went down on their knees and pleaded forgiveness, vowing never to offend again. But their repentance was of short duration, for Lord Grey soon afterwards abducted the girl. Too angry and outraged to consider the ensuing scandal, Lord Berkeley charged his son-in-law with "conspiracy", and the case was brought before the Lord Chief Justice in the summer of 1682. Macaulay describes the opening of the trial in these words:

> "A scene unparalleled in our legal history was exhibited in the Court of King's Bench. The seducer (Lord Grey) appeared with dauntless front, accompanied by his paramour. . . . The old Lord Berkeley poured forth reproaches and curses on the wretched Henrietta. The Countess gave evidence broken by many sobs, and at length fell down in a swoon."

It was a terrible come-down for the proud Berkeleys. But it may be that this particular generation was *too* proud, and—as that vindictive old proverb has it—"pride goeth before a fall". The Earl had no notion of the consequences of his action. He did not realise that, in a trial of this kind, nothing would be sacred. Not an imaginative man, he failed to understand that in such a trial it was really the house of Berkeley which was being tried, and the family honour which would suffer. Indeed, Henrietta's lies in the witness-box were so blatant and so shameless that the Lord Chief Justice reproved her in words which, one imagines, the gossips of the time memorised for frequent repetition. He said: "You have injured your reputation, prostituted both your body and your honour, and are not to be believed."

Although Lord Berkeley won his case, matters did not end with the verdict, for his daughter flatly refused to go back with him. In his temper, the Earl shouted: "Hussy! You *shall* go with me!" After which there was a fight in court between the two factions, both aiming to carry off Henrietta by force. Swords were drawn and the situation was looking ugly when the Lord Chief Justice came back into court, restored order, and "for her better safety" committed Henrietta to the custody of the Marshal of the King's Bench Prison.

In the end it did not greatly matter, because soon afterwards Lord Grey got mixed up in the Rye House Plot, and when he fled the country (in the company of his wife's seducer, Monmouth) he took Henrietta with him as his mistress. If all these shifts, seductions and stratagems resemble the plot of a scandalous period-novel, I'm sorry, but cannot help it. For to dress the facts in the language of respectability would be to misrepresent them. One of the most incredible features of the whole affair is that, despite her husband's obvious preference for her younger sister, despite his lies and pretences, and despite her temporary infidelity with Monmouth, Mary, Lady Grey, continued to love her husband. Indeed, so great was her love for this apparently worthless profligate that, after his death, nothing could induce her to remarry.

The fact that the fourth Earl and his wife had not set them a very good example may have had something to do with the peculiarities of the fifth Earl Berkeley and his sister, the lovely but dissolute Lady Craven. Both were subjects of the most scandalous gossip. And it must be admitted that both deserved it. Of the two, perhaps Lady Craven was the more outrageous. But then, she could afford to be. She was pretty, intelligent and extraordinarily vivacious. Her brother was reputedly ugly and rather stupid.

In her youth, Lady Craven had the itch to write plays—in which, of course, she duly appeared. They were very bad plays, but it is a vice one can understand—and pity. All her ladyship's vices were not so innocent. Vanity was her chief trouble. She knew she was pretty, and she couldn't resist making the most of it. Her conquests were many and varied, and her attitude to marriage was, even in the scandalous eighteenth century, regarded as somewhat "peculiar". Apparently she saw marriage as a sort of cloak of respectability, under the cover of which one could take as many lovers as one chose.

An amusing story is told of her good-natured and conspiratorial relations with her servants. It appears that her ladyship sometimes slipped her Irish butler a guinea to seal his lips, and on one occasion he went straight off to the nearest tavern to spend it, whereupon his tongue was so loosened by the drink that he told his fellow-roysterers the very secret he had been paid to keep. When she heard of it, Lady Craven sent for him with the intention of dismissing him from her service. But when she reproached him for his indiscretion, the butler told her the fault was her own for giving him a guinea, because "Had you not given me the money," he said, "I would have remained sober. But I'm just like a hedgehog, my lady—when I'm wetted upon, I open at once."* This so amused her ladyship that she hadn't the heart to sack him, so she let him off with a caution.

When her first husband died, Lady Craven decided to become the Margravine of Anspach, which, in due course, and after being for some time the Margrave's lover, she did. For her sake this poor nitwit of a German princeling ceded his principality to the King of Prussia for an agreed sum of money, only part of which was ever paid. Thereafter the Margravine often chose to call herself the Princess Berkeley, a title which had been conferred on her by the Emperor of Austria. She became a legend in her own lifetime, and never lost her amorous interest in, and for, men. Even in her sixties, when she was living in Marseilles, there were scandalous rumours in circulation about her being the lover of one of her servants and, at the same time, contemplating intimacy with the King of Naples.

Whilst the notorious Lady Craven was, to quote the *Whig Club*, "acquiring a reputation for unblushing profligacy", her brother, the fifth Earl Berkeley, was living with a succession of mistresses, before the last of them, a Gloucestershire butcher's daughter, made him fall in love with and marry her. Berkeley's system until he met Mary Cole was a popular one with the profligates of his day—never to keep a mistress too long. When

* I have never seen this particular weakness on the part of hedgehogs mentioned in books of natural history. It may not be an accurate observation, of course. Or it may be that nobody else has cared to mention it.

they began to grow familiar, and the novelty wore off, he would hand them a liberal cheque and show them the door.

The Earl's courtship of Mary Cole is unusual enough to make a good story. At the tender age of seventeen, Mary had come up to London to stay with one of her sisters, Susannah. There is no evidence that Mary was not a chaste young woman at this time, but there is plenty of evidence that Susannah was a whore. In fact Susannah's apartment was provided for her by a rich "protector". Anyway, a few days after Mary arrived, the two girls were interrupted at supper by two ruffians, who tried to drag Susannah out of the house to carry her off to a sponging-house, swearing that nothing less than a hundred guineas would induce them to leave off. In the midst of this terrible scene, Mary fainted away.

When she came to herself, it was to discover that a nobleman, having heard the girls' cries from the street, had come in to see what it was all about. Mary entreated him to help her sister; he hesitated, failing to see why he should pay so much money out of mere kindness of heart. In desperation, Mary promised him that if he would relieve them, he might do what he would with her. And the fifth Earl responded by paying down the money and relieving her of her virginity. "I have been as much sold as any lamb that goes to the shambles," was how Mary herself expressed it.

It is doubtful if the Earl realised at first that in Mary he had met his match, for the truth was that Mary wasn't quite such a simple country girl as she appeared. Finding that her lover was indolent and impractical, she took over his household and business affairs, so that before very long the Earl found that Mary was not, as his other mistresses had been, a luxury, but a necessity. And besides, the Earl was in love with her. Perhaps he had never really been in love before. Certainly he had never met a woman of Mary's calibre. For Mary was an exception among women, in that she knew what she wanted. She wanted to be Lord Berkeley's wife, and she wanted her sons to inherit. Unfortunately, it was not until she was the mother of four of his sons that Mary could induce his lordship to make an honest woman of her, and that, to put it mildly, led to certain complications. So jealous was he for the honour of his wife and four firstborn, that Lord Berkeley tried to legitimise them. He did this by forging an entry in the Berkeley Marriage Register which purported to prove that a clandestine marriage had pre-dated the birth of Mary's eldest son. Unfortunately he carried out this forgery so clumsily and in the face of so much contrary evidence that it led to that incredible mix-up, the Berkeley Peerage Case.

For all his faults, no one could truthfully call the fifth Earl a contemptible husband—once he'd decided he wanted to be married! He never in his life exhibited so much animation in a cause as he did in this matter of legitimising his first four children and trying to prove his first marriage. I write "first" marriage, because he did marry Mary Cole properly and undoubtedly in the end, and her two sons Moreton and Grantley were born in wedlock. In the normal way, of course, Moreton would have inherited. But that was not the Earl's intention. He wanted the first-born of Mary Cole's sons to be Earl of Berkeley. That he used all manner of means, including perjury, forgery and misrepresentation, to achieve his object, may not be held against him by broadminded people, for it is evident that he repented, bitterly, his wrong to Mary Cole; and tried, in the only way he knew, to mend matters. He knew that desperate situations call for desperate remedies, but the remedy he chose to apply was not so much desperate as disastrous.

Not by any means a dramatic or heroic individual, the fifth Earl's life contains the material for a Shakespearian tragedy—or comedy, I'm not sure which! Even his death has a peculiar, legendary quality about it. It happened at Berkeley, after an accident in the Park, when he was attacked by a buck in the rutting season. (Shakespeare would surely have made much of this, drawing parallels between the young buck and the reformed rake.) Although he was in his sixty-third year, his lordship was still a very strong man, and contrived to grasp its horns and prevent it goring him to death. Ten times he threw that buck to the ground. And ten times it recovered and attacked him. Then, feeling his strength ebbing, the Earl called out to his son Henry to kill the animal. Henry was armed only with a knife, but after some fumbling he contrived to thrust a knife into the buck's throat, after which it bled to death. But the Earl was never the same man again, and to the end his mind was troubled by fits of conscience. According to the Countess, during the last week or so before he died, he kept crying out in a terrible voice, "Retribution!" To us this seems too melodramatic, too early-Victorian, to be true. But in those days life itself may have been more melodramatic than it is today. I am tempted to think it was.

As it happened, the Earl's efforts proved not only unavailing but fatal for his family. His eldest son was never able to prove his legitimacy. And Moreton, who might have claimed the title, did not do so because it would have meant admitting that his elder brothers were illegitimate, his mother a kept woman, and his father a liar, perjurer, forger and rake. Some commentators have deemed Moreton's delicacy strange, to say the least, in view of the fact that all these matters had long ago been brought to the public notice and a committee of peers had decided that the so-called "first" marriage at Berkeley was a fraud. I do not intend to be quite so cynical. Moreton appears to have been a quiet, blameless, self-effacing sort of man who, if he never did much good, at any rate did no harm either. If he wanted to believe in his father's uprightness and his mother's virtue so desperately that he chose to do so at the cost of an earldom, let us respect him for keeping the appropriate commandment and his own peace of mind.

Moreton's younger brother, and the second son born legitimately, was called Grantley, and the Hon. Grantley Berkeley was, as a young man, what was then known as a "Corinthian". That is, he was a dandy, a sportsman, and even an author. One of the Bulwer Lytton crowd, he was tall and heavily built, handy with his fists or a riding-whip, and inclined to be "dangerous". As a writer of the period puts it, "One of the drawbacks of walking with Berkeley was his liability to knock you down if you disagreed with him."

At first he, like his brother Moreton, supported his brothers' claims to an earlier marriage at Berkeley. Of course that implied forgoing his right to the title if Moreton died, and this Grantley found increasingly difficult to do. For a time he was sufficiently friendly with his elder brother (later Lord Fitzhardinge) to enlist his support as a candidate for Parliament, in which he duly took his place as member for West Gloucestershire. He did not distinguish himself as a parliamentarian. Nor as an author, though some of his writings were lively enough. *Berkeley Castle* was the title and subject of his first novel, a pretentious and inflated historical romance which, considering that the family and their country seat had recently been the subject of a peculiarly outrageous scandal, could not be described by the most benign of reviewers as "timely" or "appropriate".

One at least of the reviewers was far from benign. That was Dr Maginn, editor of *Fraser's Magazine*, who saw the book as an excuse for a broadside of invective on the Berkeleys, past and present. There was really no reason why Maginn should have been quite so offensive, but that he enjoyed cutting up Grantley's novel cannot be doubted.

"Mr Grantley Berkeley," his review began, "should have been among the last people in the world to call attention to the history of his house. . . . There can be no indelicacy in stating that Mr Grantley Berkeley's mother lived with Mr Grantley Berkeley's father as his mistress, and that she had at least one child before she could induce the old and very stupid lord to marry her. All this is set down in the Journals of the House of Lords. Why, then, under such circumstances, bore us with long panegyrics upon the purity, antiquity and nobility of the Berkeley blood? Why torment us with a book vilely written, and without any other end, object or aim, but to prove that the Lord of Berkeley was a great man once upon a time, and that if there was a Lord of Berkeley who could prove that he was legitimate, he would be a great man again."

This is not merely critical. It is insulting, challenging and in extremely bad taste. But worse follows.

"Of the Berkeley family in general it may be said that not one of them was in the slightest degree distinguished. . . . We shall not go farther than this very stupid book before us. . . . He fixes his tale in the days of the War of the Roses, and in that war, when all the honourable, or the hot, blood of England was up—when the flowers in the Temple Garden had set every bosom in a flame—in those days the Berkeleys were carrying on a lawsuit among themselves, and skulking like cowards from the field, to appear as beggars before whatever faction ruled the Court. They were 'beating smooth the pavements between Temple Bar and Westminster Hall' while York and Lancaster fought for the throne of England; and here we have a descendant of theirs writing a book about the days of those spirit-stirring and gallant wars, in which he describes the great men of his lineage lying quiet in their halls, locked up for fear of bailiffs—*a dread which, we rather imagine, has extended to some of their posterity*—and actually has the impudence to put into the mouth of such a skulking laggard as the last Lord Berkeley of his line some impertinent observations upon the King-maker which 'renowned Warwick' would have most illiberally recompensed by a kick.

"In fact we do not recollect anything in our history about the Berkeleys except that one of them was considered the proper gaoler for Edward II; that another, if Horace Walpole is to be credited, proposed to George I to kidnap his son when Prince of Wales and ship him to South America. Of honourable actions, we do not, at the present writing, remember anything."

Maginn might have remembered that it was the novel which was under criticism, not the Berkeleys. His reference to Grantley's mother and father is cruel, to say the least, and the Hon. Grantley, as might be expected of a Corinthian, did not fail to respond to it. Three days after publication, he arrived at the office of the pub-lisher with a riding-whip. Maginn was absent, so Grantley con-tented himself with thrashing the publisher. He then went home and challenged Maginn to a duel with pistols. Maginn accepted; the duel was arranged; and, after three shots had been fired, Maginn was slightly wounded. The Hon. Grantley's accounts of the duel differ widely and are probably equally truthful. At first he said that Maginn had come padded, with instructions from the publisher to kill him. Later he told it differently, claiming that Maginn, pleading poverty, had tried to beg off and also to borrow a few pounds off him on the promise that he would give his next book a good notice. In 1865, when all the people concerned were dead and therefore no longer able to deny it, Grantley gave an even more curious account of the duel. He alleged that he had really challenged Maginn, not because of any review, but because Maginn was trying to seduce Letitia Landon, the poet and novelist, who had appealed to Grantley to rescue her from his advances. Like his mother and father, Grantley was no lover of the truth for its own sake.

Yet one must not be too hard on the Hon. Grantley. For Fate played with him as a fisherman plays a pike. Having quarrelled with his elder brothers and made it clear that, on Moreton's decease, he would lay claim to the earldom of Berkeley, he waited impatiently for his ailing brother's death. But he was doomed to disappointment if he thought he would father a line of earls, for his two sons both predeceased him, leaving no issue, and *still* Moreton obstinately clung to life. In his old age, Grantley became an almost pathetic figure, glad to be recognised by one of his old acquaintance who might be disposed to listen to his tale of woe. He finished his career as a club-bore, dying, in 1881, in his eighty-second year. Moreton, who for so long had upheld his mother's honour and stood between Grantley and the title, followed him a year or so later.

It is perhaps too much to claim that the Berkeley Peerage Case finished the Berkeleys as a great family. That it was the *beginning* of the decline, however, can scarcely be denied. Today the castle at Berkeley is empty. The Berkeley Square property was sold early in the '30s. And although there are still Berkeleys living in the Vale, some of whom still play a significant part in local activities, it is not unfair to say that, as a family of great power and possessions, hereditary lords of the castle and manor of Berkeley, their history is over, their day is gone.

What would John Smyth have thought of this decline of a great house? It is certain that, although he might lay some blame on the uneasy times, his shrewd mind would have fastened on the salient weaknesses of some of the subsequent Berkeleys. Perhaps he would have compared them, unfavourably, with their ancestors. Very certainly he would have had something bitter to say about the failure of the barony and the dispersal of the estate, for in Smyth's eyes the continuity of those two was a sacred trust. But we must remind ourselves that Smyth was, after all, only a Berkeley steward, and one suspected of "feathering his own nest" at that. For my own part, I am sorry there is no Berkeley at Berkeley Castle. They were there for so long that they must have seemed, to many, one constant in the quicksands of changing times. The castle, it is true, still stands; but it is a shell only, without life, empty, closed and deserted; waiting—for what, or whom?

CHAPTER III

NORTH OF BRISTOL

ON fine days Almondsbury "Tump" is a favourite rendezvous of Bristolians. And no wonder! For it commands one of the loveliest vistas in South Gloucestershire. There is something magical, something breath-taking about that sudden revelation as you turn the corner by the Swan. You have struggled up through the city suburbs—through Cheltenham Road and Gloucester Road, with their crowds of shoppers; past Horfield Common and the Barracks, along that rather dreary Filton Road; past the sprawling mass of the B.A.C., with maybe a glimpse of the Brabazon or Britannia on the runway of the airfield; through Patchway, facetiously known as "Little Wales"—to emerge on the edge of this valley, spreading, like a patchwork counterpane to the great silver bow of Severn.

Although the height above sea-level is not great (about 275 feet), the view is a splendid one. Below and beyond, to west and north, lies the Vale—a mosaic of meadows, orchards and corn-fields, with occasional hamlets and villages and narrow twisting lanes: the whole liberally sprinkled with trees which, here and there, cluster into coppices and woods. Most of the fields are in grass, for this is still dairying country—some of the best in the county. The villages and hamlets are small, with a tendency to hide inside a fringe of trees. There's Woodhouse and Ostbridge, Awkley and Pilning Street, Northwick and Redwick, Elberton and Olveston, Tockington and Ingst. Thornbury is hidden by the bulk of Alveston Down, with its Tumulus and its hanging woods. On fine days this view, dramatised by the majestic sweep of the river, cannot fail to thrill and invigorate. However often you pass through it on that main road, even though the route becomes wearisome with repetition, I do not think you could ever grow tired of that sudden spread of vale from the edge of the plateau of lower lias at Almondsbury.

From here to Alveston, the main road (A.38) is near the edge of this plateau or ridge, which from time to time gives widespread views to the west. The hamlet between Almondsbury and Alveston is appropriately called Rudgeway. It clusters about A.38: a sprawling, uneven place, with some modern bungalows, a group of stone-built cottages and an interesting farmhouse or two. Although it has been gutted by the main road, it still has considerable interest, even charm.

To return to Almondsbury. The old village is, of course, below the plateau, on a tongue of carboniferous limestone which extends from Thornbury, and well away from the main Bristol–Gloucester road. Looking down on it from the tumpy green by the hospital, you see the haphazard cluster of roofs and gardens, orchards and winding roads, all dominated by that peculiar herringbone spire of the church. Alcmund, father of Egbert, King of Wessex and later England, is supposed to have lived, died and been buried here, to have given the place its name, and to have built a church. In those days Almondsbury was part of the Kingswood Forest, and the Severn much nearer than it is today. In the Middle Ages it possessed a monastery, and one of its monks still haunts the village, according to Mrs Ledger. She tells me that she first heard of the ghost in 1924, when she came to live here. Someone told her it was the ghost of a Madam Green. And it was supposed to haunt the garden of her house and the nearby road on moonlit nights. But although she often looked out for it on moonlit nights, Mrs Ledger saw no sign of it. And it wasn't until some six years had passed that it became active. Then a number of stories of its appearance began to circulate. A villager saw it twice and was so frightened that "he vowed never to walk along that road again after dark". A young man and woman were also scared, the lady claiming to have seen the very buckles on its shoes.

Mrs Ledger's husband often saw it, and "sometimes it walked beside him, like a tall lady in a flowing veil. We had," she says, "a boy lodging with us who used to laugh at my husband and his ghost, until (one morning) he met, as he thought, a friend outside and actually spoke to him before he realised that it was no living person. At dinner-time he was still scared, and all he could say, ruefully, was: 'I met it this morning all right!' " At that time local people so feared the ghost that few cared to walk around that corner after dark. Mr Ledger still believes absolutely that there is a ghost, and that he saw it. It is now identified with a monk who was murdered near the ancient monastery, the site of which abutted on the Ledgers' garden.

The story of this monk may throw some light on the phenomenon for students of the occult. It seems that Abbot Barry of Bristol had come to Almondsbury on a visit when he met, begging for food on Almondsbury hill, a former monk. He took him to the monastery, where the fellow apparently ran amok, killing one of the Abbot's men. He would have killed more, only the alarm bell was rung and the people of Almondsbury helped to secure the monk from further mischief. It is curious that some of those who saw the ghost described it as a grey lady, for at Aust, not very far away, there is a Grey Lady of some renown, who has made several appearances recently. And Over possesses a White Lady who, on one occasion, frightened the local band, who dropped their instruments and ran.

In 1572 a terrible frost occurred at Almondsbury, and a man, his wife and three children were frozen to death on Woodhouse Down. They were weavers on their way to the North. Having crossed the Severn by ferry, they had walked to Almondsbury, where they were given food and a sixpence by a Mr Jamieson and sent on their way. In the morning they were found in a heap. The man was lying on top, frozen stiff. He had stripped off his outer clothing to cover his wife and children, but although they were not dead they never recovered.

Alan Tarbat describes the church of St Mary as "a rum piece of garishness". Other writers disagree. It is cruciform, a mixture of Norman and Early English, with chancel, transept, clerestoried nave of four bays, north and south aisles, north and west porches and a central tower which leans slightly to the south. Above the Norman porch is a priest's chamber, the stairs to which are lighted by a charming miniature window. In this chamber, priests who visited the church would sleep. It still contains the chest which once held ornaments and plate belonging to the Brokenboro' Chauntry, which arrived at Almondsbury via Gaunts Erdcote and the Chapel of St Swithin at Over. But the chest is now empty. A chalice and 40 ounces of silver were stolen from

48

it in 1148, and the rest of the contents were used to finance repairs to the church.

There is a magnificent Renaissance tomb with effigies of Edward (Lord of the Manor of Over) and Katharine Veele, with a humble and appropriate epitaph to the effect that all flesh is grass. There are also windows to Bishop Grey, who hid from the Bristol mob at nearby Knole Park after he had preached against the Reform Bill (1831), and to Charles Richardson, the designer of the Severn Tunnel. Knole Park is the local Great House. It is mainly Elizabethan, though the octagonal tower on the east side is said to have existed before the house was built, being used as a look-out. From it can be seen five counties in clear weather. The site of Knole Park is a fine one. On the summit of a hill previously occupied by a Roman outpost, it commands a fine view of the Vale. Once it was the seat of the Chester Masters family; now, like so many of our English country houses, it is a school. There was for long a small dark room down some steps from the buttery called the Bishop's Cellar, and it was here that Bishop Grey hid from the mob shouting for his blood, whilst the servants stood by with muskets brought back from the Peninsular wars.

There is an interesting road from Almondsbury Tump through Knole Park, Over and Compton Greenfield. Strictly, it is beyond the southern limit I have already set myself, but Over and Compton Greenfield may well claim to be part of the Vale, and anyway I am determined to write of them, so (with your permission) we will now take that road afoot—as a companion and I did one summer afternoon recently.

It was the first time George had been to Almondsbury. And he was so thrilled with the place that he tried to dissuade me from the walk I'd planned through Over and Compton Greenfield to Hallen and Henbury. He pleaded that it was very pleasant here, that there was a café nearby and also a pub; that the day was too warm for walking, and surely it would be better if we concentrated on exploring Almondsbury itself. After all, he reminded me, there was plenty here to interest us. Hadn't I said myself that there were Roman entrenchments which had probably been a link in Ostorius' western defences? And the church, too! Surely it wasn't fair to rush a chap away before he'd had a

4   49

Thornbury Castle: South Garden Front, showing oriels and tower

chance to see everything. He particularly wanted to see the Norman doorway and font. (Incidentally, it is surprising how many churches in this part of the country have Norman doorways and fonts. These two features seem to have outlasted all others. Or perhaps subsequent churchmen have considered these features the only ones worth retaining.) The seven-hundred-year-old chancel, too, with vaulted roof and finely-carved bosses; was he to be prevented from seeing that? But I had been here before, so I could afford to be adamant.

We took the road to Over.

For a while this road gives splendid views of Vale and river. Then it dips, the trees close in, and when you emerge in the neighbourhood of Knole Park, the views to north-west are obscured by ribbon-development. Between detached Desirable Residences you snatch glimpses; and that is all.

At the top of the hill, a turning on the right leads right up to Knole Park House, very large and white and rather bare on its flat-topped hill, on which may still be traced faint evidences of the vallum of an ancient British camp, which was later a Roman outpost. Not far from the house, and inside the vallum of the camp, live Mr and Mrs Tritton. Their charming house, which has been adapted from what used to be coachmen's quarters, commands splendid views of Vale and Severn. But, beyond their lawn, the ground suddenly drops sharply to the south-east, and this has been terraced for use as a vineyard. Here Mrs Tritton has been experimenting with various types of vines, to discover which are most suitable for outdoor cultivation in this part of Gloucestershire.

Vineyards used to be a feature of this part of the county in the Middle Ages. You still find southerly slopes in the neighbourhood of great houses called "Vineyards". And although it may be centuries since vines grew there, one can often trace the terraces on which they were grown. I know of three such "Vineyards"—at Rodway Manor, Mangotsfield; at Elberton; and in Tortworth Park. There were probably more, but Mrs Tritton's vineyard at Knole Park is not legendary or historic but real. Already there have been several grape-harvests, from which Mrs Tritton has made wine which experts have declared comparable with those of the Rhine and Moselle. She has thus proved, first, that grapes can be grown on terraces out-of-doors in this part of the country; and, second, that good wine can be made from them.

Before we leave Knole Park, there is a story about it which may amuse. The leading character is Princess Caraboo, who was found wandering in a brilliant Oriental costume on the highroad nearby, in the year 1817.

She spoke a language which nobody could understand, but as she made signs indicative of distress, she was taken to Knole Park, which was then the home of a Mr Worral. With great difficulty she contrived to tell her story. How she was the princess of an Eastern country, and had been captured by pirates whilst she was walking in the Palace Gardens. She was taken aboard their ship, but when she saw the shores of England, she had jumped overboard and swum ashore. Ever since then, she had wandered the roads.

Naturally, Mr Worral, being an English gentleman, did not doubt her story. The English have always been a gullible race, easy victims of the tall story. Remember Trinculo's remarks on discovering Caliban:

TRINCULO: . . . *A strange fish! Were I in England now (as once I was), and had but this fish painted, not a holiday fool there but would give a piece of silver; . . . when they will not give a doit to relieve a lame beggar, they will lay out ten to see a dead Indian!*

Believing the princess knew but little English, Mr Worral and his friends spoke openly in her presence of the little tests they would apply to check her veracity. Forewarned is forearmed! The princess was always ready for them. Two of her achievements, in particular, served to reinforce their belief in her. She could swim like a fish, and she was an excellent archer.

Locally, the princess provided a real sensation. Indeed, so proud were the Worrals and their friends of their Princess that they sent a sample of her handwriting to Oxford University—to a young man who, in later life, became Archbishop Whately. He was cynical, obviously regarding it as a hoax, and sent it back with the comment that it was written in the Humbug language.

Shortly afterwards, "one of those who had been so forward in bringing public attention to the princess" wrote a letter to *The Times* claiming that a specimen of her writing had been sent to the University of Oxford, which had pronounced it to be the writing *of no known language*!

A few days later, a young local woman happened to come into Mr Worral's kitchen where "Caraboo"—as she called herself— was idling away the time.

"Why, it's Mary Baker!" she cried. "However did you come here? And in that funny dress!"

And without blinking, "Caraboo" replied to her in tolerable English, with a Devonshire accent. For Mary Baker she was, the daughter of a Devonshire cobbler from Witheridge.

On being reproached by Mrs Worral for her deception, she said calmly: "It was very kind of you, ma'am, but if you will recollect, I never *asked* you for anything." Which, of course, was perfectly true, but not very satisfactory to the Worrals.

On one side of the road is Patchway Tunnel, with its red clay. Opposite is the entrance to Cattybrook Brickworks, between a pleasant avenue of trees. The quality of Cattybrook bricks is exceptional. Various types and colours are made, including Blue, Dark Red, Yellow, Brindle, Purple, Grey, Brown, Ripple, "Catty-rustic", Autumn Shades, Golden Brown, Cotswold Grey, etc. Fry's factory at Somerdale is built of Cattybrook bricks, so are the offices of the Imperial Tobacco Company at Bristol, Portishead Generating Station, and the Severn Tunnel. The story of this brickyard is not uninteresting. It was discovered in 1862 when the Patchway tunnel was being made. The contractor who was building it, being struck by the quality of the clay excavated, tried the experiment of making his own bricks. The venture succeeded. And when Charles Richardson, builder of the Severn Tunnel, saw the quality of the bricks produced, he determined to use this clay in the bricks for his tunnel. He leased a few acres and built a small factory in 1865, and from this the present Cattybrook Brickworks has developed. Those who like statistics may be gratified to know that 76,400,000 bricks were supplied from here for the construction of the Severn Tunnel. Geologists may be surprised to learn that *coprolite* (a formation which originates from the dung of prehistoric monsters) in the clay is a headache to modern brickmakers.

Over is a diminutive roadside hamlet, with a couple of charming cottages and a large mansion which had the misfortune to be occupied by H.M. forces during the war. Through tall iron gates we saw a moss-grown driveway and, at the end of an avenue, an imposing and ornate gateway with a clock minus hands and a rather bogus-looking tower. Strands of ivy drooped over it, so that it possessed just the right degree of forsaken and decaying grandeur to make it romantic. Even in full daylight it looked somewhat unreal, a scene stolen from one of the Gothic novels or a backcloth for one of those lurid and nearly forgotten seventeenth/eighteenth-century dramas. I think Rex Whistler would have liked that gateway. It might have provided an entrance to anything. One could imagine it at night, with the moonlight falling on it: the strands of ivy casting strange, disturbing shadows; an owl hooting from the nearby elms; and maybe the White Lady of Over taking her midnight constitutional.

Over Court was the home of the Cann-Lippincotts. During the war it was commandeered, however, and since then it has stood empty. The deer park, too, has lost its fallow deer since it had to be ploughed up. Behind the Court rises Over Hill, on top of which is a large circular entrenchment. From a tumulus nearby, two skeletons were excavated in 1650. One of these skeletons was that of a man of unusual stature, a veritable giant, and it was assumed by the all-too-credulous excavators that this was the skeleton of Offa, builder of Offa's Dyke. The "view" from here is locally famous.

Not far from Over we met the main road at Cribbs' Causeway. Half a mile along it, on the road to Redwick and Severn Beach, is Easter Compton. It straggles along beside the main road, with its chapel, pub (the Fox), cottages and council houses, whilst the week-end traffic races through it to Severn Beach and New Passage. The sexton told me that until recently they called it East Compton, but the older form was revived by the local M.P., Mr Robert Perkins. Compton Greenfield, the sister-village, lies a mile away across fields, as quiet and untroubled as Easter Compton is noisy and petrol-tainted. Between them, the church of All Saints stands amid carpet-smooth meadows. Its fourteenth-century tower and lichen-grown stone roof look over one of the neatest and prettiest little churchyards we've ever seen, though George (always critical) said he didn't care for the modern notion of calling graveyards "Gardens of Rest". He said it was just another bit of bourgeois complacency.

Two great families have connections with Compton Greenfield: the Berkeleys and the Grenvilles. The Cornish Grenvilles owned the manor for two centuries, then it passed into the hands of Thomas, Lord Berkeley, who had improved the family fortunes after a period of deflation. After he died, in 1361, his wife held for life the manors of Beverstone, Tockington, Over, Compton Greenfield and Kingsweston. All of these, except Beverstone Castle, are in the Vale.

It is perhaps significant that the manor of Compton was acquired, in the middle of the fifteenth century, by the Canns of Bristol. Significant because they represented a new and powerful class. They were Bristol merchants—the bourgeois *nouveau riche*.

William Cann was a strong supporter of Parliament during the Civil Wars. Oddly enough, his wife Margaret was the sister of Robert Yeomans, an equally strong Royalist. Yeomans (Bristolians may remember) was executed in Wine Street, in 1643, for attempting to admit Prince Rupert into the city. But either Margaret didn't share her brother's loyalties, or else she and her husband must often have disagreed, for in 1648, when William Cann was Mayor of Bristol, he publicly proclaimed the abolition of the monarchy. His son Robert must have taken his politics from the distaff side of the family (or maybe he'd seen which way the wind was blowing), for in the year his father died he was knighted *for his services to the Royalist cause*! His grandson married Elizabeth, daughter of Thomas Chester of Knole Park. It is a very long shot, but within the bounds of possibility, that they first saw each other in this church of All Saints, Compton Greenfield. However, we mustn't go rambling on about matters manorial, for we haven't quite finished with matters ecclesiastical yet.

All Saints has a very fine Norman doorway which now forms the inner entrance in the south porch. It is twelfth-century work, with an exquisitely carved and remarkably pure design. To quote the Rev. L. S. Tull, it is "deeply recessed and richly adorned with rings of various designs, consisting of dogtooth, zig-zag and key-patterns". Whilst we were looking round the church, we were joined by the sexton who, with great pride, showed us the new electric-lighting system. Seeing the old candelabra we had assumed that the church was still lit by candles. But he showed us where electric lights had been skilfully installed in the roof corners.

"We leaves the old candelabra up," he said, "because it shows you how things used to be. And apart from that, they looks sort of *fitting*, as you might say."

Then he took us outside to show us the amusing drop-weight stile in the lych-gate, a curious but efficient arrangement which is very necessary at Compton to keep cows out of the churchyard. Despite the stile, there are times when the cows get in. "Last time some calves got in we'd an awful time of it," he assured us. "We did drive 'em here, and they did run there—in and out of the yews and sweetbriar. And o' course, we had to stop 'em eating the yew, because it gives 'em the belly-ache."

I asked him if he had any opinions on yews in churchyards. Did he believe (a) that it was because long-bows were of yew, but since it was dangerous for cattle, the only safe place to grow it was the churchyard; or (b) that the connection was older, and that yews were one of the ancient death-symbols, with a place, perhaps, in Druidic lore.

"Well, I don't know about that," said the sexton, "but they'm one's work to keep trimmed."

We left him ringing the bell for evening service, crossed two fields, and rejoined the Hallen Road. To our left rose the curiously named Spaniorum Hill. For long I cherished the hope that this had some connection with Spain. I had visions of a swarthy, helmeted Don atop of it, looking with a vengeful eye on Bristol to the south-east. But it was an idle dream. Spaniorum has nothing at all to do with Spaniards. Its derivation has caused doubts, but none of the theories put forward favour Spain. The first theory is that it derives from *Span* (Middle English, meaning "stretch" or "extent"), and *ora* (Old English for "a bank"). This looks all right, but I think anyone who has climbed Spaniorum Hill will agree with me that "bank" is somewhat inadequate.

Another theory is that Spaniorum was a Roman outpost. A third that it is based on the Latin *spinus* or blackthorn. Since the hill was once famous for its blackthorns, this doesn't seem impossible. But since we were neither etymologists nor archæologists, George and I did not pursue the subject farther.

Spaniorum Farm (which is also a cider-manufactory) squats beside a rhine, the first we'd seen that day. That was because we had kept to the foot of the hill-slopes. If we had approached the Severn we should have seen any number of them, fringed with rushes and sedge, brooded over by friendly willows, as they dither across the meadows and marshland to Severn.

Of the walk from Spaniorum farm to Hallen I shall say little, except that it is bordered on the left by Berwick Wood on the slopes of the hill, and on the right by extensive and complex underground storage tanks for petroleum. It wasn't that the installations were ugly, or that they spoilt the scene. They nullified it. And they reminded us that we were near Avonmouth, with its granaries, factories, smelting and chemical works. Hallen and environs is not really in the Vale of Berkeley. It has the look of a place which is doomed. Behind its inn, the King William IV, is a large old building which, the landlord told us, used to be a brewery. In those days the King Billy brewed its own beer. But, alas! no longer. Situated as they are, Hallen and Henbury are ripe for development. And there are some who will say, the sooner the better.

Not Clem Hignell, however! Clem lives at Norton Farm, just outside Henbury, near a place called Botany Bay; but he used to farm at Aust. He is getting on in years and crippled with arthritis, but he is still "very alert in mind, with white hair and a ruddy face, quick piercing eyes, usually wearing well-cut riding breeches and white canvas gaiters" (so Bristol journalist and artist Charles Thomas tells me). Clem recalls the old days with a vigour that brings them alive for us. For instance, he remembers when, sixty-eight years ago, the Severn came inland as far as Hallen. Only for a few hours—but salt-water got into the wells and spoilt the water, and many cows and pigs were drowned. And he remembers when, some forty years ago, Severn Beach was isolated for three weeks. Hearing that I was writing a book about the Berkeley Vale, he wrote me a letter which I cannot do better than quote, for it sums up the recent history of this locality, its transition from pleasant countryside to city suburbs.

"I have lived", writes Clem Hignell, "near the Severn nearly 70 years and could tell you a lot about the Local History. For instance there was, up to 50 years ago, a Fishing industry all along the shore from Avonmouth to the New Passage. Some of our pastimes were Rabbiting, Duck Shooting on the shore Morn and Even, Birding on winter nights with a Lantern and Net (a Clap Net held between Lantern and hedge, with a beater the other side of the hedge), Pidgeon Shooting, Fox Hunting, Ratting with Ferrets, etc. Working men used to go down and help the fishermen clean the nets on Sunday mornings during the Sprat season, taking home as many Sprats as they liked. They used to catch so many sprats at one time that farmers used to lend their Horses and carts to help haul them to Bristol. If they couldn't sell them, they would tip them in the Quay. But Avonmouth Dock finished the Spratting.

"One time a Derbyshire man came to this district as a carter. The locals didn't like him, so, when he was ploughing and had marked out his ground for a strike out, first thing next morning they moved his Pegs into a half-circle and got him in a muddle. When it got around, the locals carried his Plough a quarter of a mile and hung it high up in the Poplar trees across the entrance to the Farm Drive. On another farm the Carter was a bad Ploughman, so the locals carried the Plough and slung it up in an apple tree between the Field and the Road, and the Owner let it stay there till he wanted to use it, and had a good laugh about it.

"Of course there was always a poacher about. One well-known to me was seen to put down a wire for a hare during the day, so one of the men got some Tar and put it on the hedge (nearby). Later on he went to the pub and there was the Poacher sat down with his cup. Presently up he gets and goes out. Half an hour later he came back, and sat down. Before long someone said how it do stink of Tar. Each one looked at another, and then the Poacher looked down and saw his trousers and coat, and didn't he swear!

"The first policeman we ever had was a Welshman and he

caused some fun for the locals this way. . . . Another poacher used to watch for Taffy to go strolling by when he knew Taffy was about, and Taffy would get mad and say 'All right, Chibby, I will get you one day.' Anyhow, Chibby found a Hedgehog that day, wrapped it up in Paper, put it in his Pocket, and went home when he knew Taffy would be about. 'Ha, ha! Chibby, now I got you! What you got in that pocket? Come on, hand it over.'

" 'Oh, no!' says Chibby. 'If thees want it, take it out thee-self!' Taffy dives his hand in to get what he thought would be a couple of Rabbits and soon withdraws it with blood spurting out of it. He never did catch Chibby.

"A local custom was that if a man got on the Booze and knocked his wife about, the locals would get a sheaf of Straw and fix it up at his front door to show the neighbours he had been 'thrashing'. They used to spend a week at a time digging Badgers out, or trying to, in Berwick Wood. There would be a lot of drink about at such times, I can tell you!

"Great sport was had at low tide Congering by parties before haymaking, getting Plastered in mud and having great fun and a good bag of Congers to take home. Some farmers adjoining the shore used to put down wire-netting and catch a nice lot of Sand Dabs (small flatfish), and they are lovely cooked fresh out of the Severn for Breakfast. This really was a lovely Place to live 50 years ago before Avonmouth became Dock Town.

"When the ferry-boat used to ply between New Passage and Portskewett and they got good company down at the New Passage Hotel waiting to cross, the Captain would say: 'Can't cross today. Too rough. You must wait till morning.' Then a good night was had by all. Perhaps the Captain was in league with the Landlord. I wouldn't know.

"On June 18 there were the Waterloo Races on Aust Wharf and a Pleasure Fair. This was a general holiday and looked forward to far and wide. You see, it was the end of the Winter season and the Farmers and their men used to grind their Scythes and get the other hay-making tools ready in the morning, then go to the fair. The Booths ran the whole length of the Wharf on the East side of the road, and great doings were had. After the Fair, people really got to work. Drank plenty of cider and ate plenty of good food—it would frighten you to see the men at work 50 years ago. I knew one man, a real old-timer, would drink 4½ gallons of Cider between daylight and dark, day after day. He worked piecework. I knew another man who would drink 2 quarts of cider from a wooden bottle without taking the bottle from his mouth. When the Severn Tunnel was being built the Navvies would get in the Cross Hands (Redwick) and have a booze up. When they got merry they would vie with each other who would pay for the most quarts and tip them up, and the Beer would be over the soles of their boots sometimes. At those times they didn't bother to unlace their boots, simply ran a knife down the laces and put in a fresh pair next day.

"Cheerio.

"Clem Hignell."

After that, I feel, anything I may write will be merely anti-climax, though it may be necessary to add a few words of explanation about Clem's "clap-nets". In these days of bird protection, the barbarous old custom of catching, cooking and eating small birds has died out. But until fifty years ago, in Gloucestershire, catching hedge-birds with a clap-net at night was a profitable (if uncivilised) sport. The idea was for the beater to poke about in the hedge on one side, and so startle the small birds (thrushes, blackbirds, finches, hedge-sparrows), which would fly out of the other. Then the clap-net, which was often an old length of lace-curtain fastened to two long poles, was clapped together to net them. When the birds were taken home in their hats, mothers and wives would pluck and bone them, and the resultant flesh was made into a pie. Blackbirds and thrushes were best liked. But even sparrows were eaten. I wonder what the modern housewife would think of hedge-bird-pie? Most young women would flinch from plucking and cooking small birds today, I fancy. Poverty and long families did not leave much room for squeamishness in those good old days.

It must be admitted that I do not care for Severn Beach. Many years ago, when I was very young, it used not to be so.

Perhaps my tastes have changed. Maybe I have grown more critical. Ah, well. There it is. Severn Beach, I no longer love thee!

Possibly the time of year (late autumn) was at fault, or the recent rains; or it may have been the plague of daddy-longlegs which seemed to have descended on the place (they were everywhere—flying into your face, getting up your sleeves, hitting you in the eye); or the fact that the road was up for the installation of drains. Anyway, the result was that I felt like a character in a Graham Greene novel. I was depressed, bored by the seedy bravado of the place. Cynical about its pretension to be a seaside resort. Repelled by its tin shacks, side-shows, and converted buses. It seemed to me that the gaiety of Severn Beach was a veneer, like cosmetics on the face of an old hag. In places it was peeling off— a broken window mended with cardboard, rusty pipes, cracked concrete—to reveal the sordid reality.

Even the "Beach" seemed a bit of a sham. Beyond the strip of unconvincing shingle is mud, sticky, slimy Severn mud; and beyond that the water of the estuary, thick, grey-brown and sinewy with current. Beyond that again, to the south, are chimneys—of the factories on the Chittening Trading Estate, toward Avonmouth—of the factories of Newport, down the estuary. It wouldn't be so bad if Severn Beach didn't put on so much bright paint and dress itself in quite so much corrugated iron. The Severn is a great river, perhaps the greatest in England, and its mud has a fascination all its own. But its estuary does not favour "seaside" resorts. It is not, and cannot be regarded as, a plaything. It is, indeed, rather dangerous. Sometimes it breaks loose and wrecks some of the entertainments which at Severn Beach cluster along its shore. Maybe that is why they possess that temporary look, as though their owners had said: "Well, the river may knock this down next winter, so it'd be silly to put too much into it now."

Many will disagree with me, I have no doubt. They will say that it is convenient as a week-end place where you can bring the children. Or that it is an easy cycle-ride from Bristol. Or that I am beyond appreciating the adolescent joys of the fun-fair and the "Blue Lagoon". They will be right, of course. It is all prejudice on my part. Prejudice against what seems to me a painted gaiety and a pitiful illusion that this is seaside and that the gravel is sand.

I asked Margaret Brooks, who lives at Severn Beach and is

herself a writer, what she found attractive there. She had to admit that she had never found Severn Beach itself very alluring; "but the walk along the sea-wall to New Passage and beyond is lovely at all times—especially in winter or early spring when there are very few people about." Margaret Brooks told me that Severn Beach used to be a great place for salmon fishing. Four generations of Mark Britons plied their trade from the sea-wall farm which has now become uninhabitable. They fished the Salmon Pool between the shore and English Stones: the same pool which caused trouble during the building of the Severn Tunnel.

English Stones is the site of an old ferry—a ferry which once played a tragic part in history. The estuary here is about two and a half miles across. English Stones accounts for a little more than a mile and a half of it, and Lady Bench for another half-mile. The actual river-channel, called The Shoots, is only 400 yards across and 80 feet deep. And the Salmon Pool accounts for the rest. At low water English Stones and Lady Bench are exposed. That is the setting, and a sombre one it is. Here is the story.

It was during the Civil Wars, when the Roundheads were pursuing a party of Royalists, led by Charles Stuart. The boatmen were Royalists, so they ferried across the pursued with alacrity, and then took their time about returning. When they did return, the pursuers forced the ferrymen to carry them across at the point of their swords.

But instead of rowing the Roundheads across to the other side, at Portskewett, the boatmen landed them on English Stones, just as the tide was turning. The tide rises swiftly here, and it is the highest tide in Europe. All sixty of the Roundhead cavalry were drowned. When he heard of this callous trick, Cromwell abolished the ferry, which was not used again for a hundred years.

Between Severn Beach and New Passage is the Pumping Station for the Severn Tunnel. This rather ugly building is responsible for pumping up many thousands of gallons of spring-water every day from the tunnel, which here underlies the estuary at a depth of 50 feet below rock bottom. Here, too, is to be found the only true shingle beach in the county, which consists of material excavated from the Severn Tunnel and "dumped" here. On or near it grows the sea-aster, which is, indeed, common beside Severn, and Townsend's cord-grass (of which more later). Until 1931, this bit of shingle was the home of the lovely Yellow Horned Poppy which is often found on shingle-beaches. I remember seeing it in flower among the pebbles of Porlock beach, lonely and windswept, and apparently independent of soil. Sea-holly and samphire have both been reported from here, but the sea-holly has now disappeared, having failed to weather a particularly disastrous storm.

Local history hereabouts is measured as B.S.T. and A.S.T.—before and after the building of the Severn Tunnel. That is not surprising, for the tunnel completely altered the fabric and economy of local life. Before it was made, the estuary was crossed by a ferry-boat from New Passage to Portskewett, and the place was often crowded with people waiting to cross. But the tunnel meant the end of the ferry-boats. And when the Severn ferry was revived to meet a new demand for carrying across motor vehicles, it was the Old Ferry which was revived, from Aust to Beachley.

All the older people of the neighbourhood have memories of the building of the Severn Tunnel. And no wonder, when you remember that it took ten years in the making and provided work for 3,628 men. Its engineer and originator was Charles Richardson. But it was completed under the direction of Sir John Hawkshaw after what must have seemed almost insurmountable difficulties. It is an epic, the story of the building of this tunnel under the Severn estuary. I wish I could do it justice, but I'm afraid I have neither the space nor the qualifications for more than a very brief outline.

The first shaft was sunk in 1873, but it wasn't until 1877 that the G.W.R. proceeded with the work. In 1879, at a critical point in the tunnel's construction, a disaster occurred. The Great Spring broke into the workings and flooded them. If workmen had not been warned in time, this would have made history as a great tragedy. Fortunately, they *were* warned; but even so it was disastrous from a constructional point of view. At this stage T. A. Walker of London became the contractor and Sir John Hawkshaw was called in to assist Charles Richardson. When they inspected the workings, the scene was one of utter desolation. In the following year larger pumps were installed, but even these only just held the water. Then, in the summer of that year, a diver called Lambert showed great heroism in going down in darkness through water and debris and, after one unsuccessful attempt, closing the iron door and screwing the valves to exclude water from the workings. A strong wall was built to cope with the spring-water, but in the next year (1881) there was more trouble when water burst in from the Salmon Pool. Two years later, in the October of 1883, the Great Spring again burst in, helped by a tidal wave. At this time the workings were in a worse state than they had been in 1880.

In December of 1883 the Great Spring was finally conquered. It was diverted to a line parallel with but underneath the tunnel. In the spring of 1885 the tunnel was finished, and in April of that year Sir Daniel and Lady Gooch (and presumably a driver and fireman) made the first railway journey through. The tunnel cost £1,806,248 to make, and it still costs quite a lot to keep dry.

I was told that the man I ought to meet was Archie Powell. He could tell me all about the old days at New Passage, the farmer who was my informant assured me.

"Are you sure of that?" I queried. For although I was familiar with the name of Archie Powell, I knew it as that of the biographer of W. G. Grace, the author of many articles about local history, and one of our best-known Bristol journalists.

"Sure of it?" said my farmer. "O' course I'm sure! Why, bless your heart, he use' to work on one of the ferry-boats. He was cook, or steward, or summat. I can't tell 'ee exactly. But you go and see 'n. He'll tell 'ee all about it!"

And he did.

He told me that he'd been both cook and steward on the ferry-boat *Christopher Thomas*, named after a famous Bristolian and soap manufacturer, in 1884. He'd only been a lad at the time, and had lodged in an attic in the New Passage Hotel. He would never forget those Saturday evenings when the tunnel was being built. The long room of the New Passage Hotel would be packed —with navvies from the workings and with "ladies" from Bristol. The amount of beer consumed must have reached astronomical figures. Sometimes there would be disputes over certain of the "ladies", and feelings would run high. But the M.C. of the evening would order an adjournment to the field opposite before it came to blows. There a ring was formed, the two men stripped to the waist, and, being unleashed, set about each other until one of them had to "give best". Then the crowd returned to the hotel, the combatants shook hands, and the entertainment continued.

Oliver Norris was a sort of uncrowned king of the district, Archie Powell told me. He was a farmer and landowner, and had been the first contractor for the Severn Tunnel. He was a bluff and hearty old chap, always known as *Looky* Norris, because of his frequent injunctions to "Looky here!" and "Looky there!" The Norris family stood high in the local hierarchy. Oliver's brother, Charles, lived in a house near the pier and owned the salmon fishing. And there was old John Norris who kept the village store, and was a leading Methody, with a truly terrifying *Amen*!

After the ferry service was discontinued, the *Christopher Thomas* was sold to an African company for use on a west coast river. She finally came to grief at the mouth of a river out there, being stranded so high on a mud-bank that she could never be got off. This was many years later, and by that time the former ship's cook was director of a Bristol newspaper. One day a letter came to his desk. It was from the manager of the African company which had purchased the *Christopher Thomas*, telling of its end, and asking if anyone remembered the vessel at Bristol; and, if so, what was its history. "It was rather a coincidence," Mr Powell mused. And when you consider the improbabilities involved, it was more than that. If a writer of fiction used such a device, he would be "unconvincing" and "improbable", his "machinery" would "creak", and he would be consigned to the outer darkness for intruding such a cheap "trick". Yet, you see, these things do happen! Perhaps not often, as Gogol remarks at the end of his story *The Nose*, but they *do* happen.

It may be a surprise, even to local people, to know that "talkies" were first invented in this neighbourhood. The inventor was Harry Grindell Matthews, famous in his day as "The Death-Ray Man". He tried for a time to interest British film producers in them. But it seems they had too much capital bound up in silent pictures, and anyway they thought the talking-picture idea was a monstrosity. Grindell Matthews did most of his work at Pilning, and the first full-scale experiments took place in the ballroom of

Almondsbury and the Vale of Berkeley, from Almondsbury hill

the New Passage Hotel. Ten years after Matthews (who was born at Winterbourne Court and educated at a Dame's School at Alveston) had abandoned this idea, the Americans took it up. The British film industry had had a golden opportunity to lead the world in the new medium. They had thrown it away, and have ever since been trying to catch up.

Most of the land adjoining the estuary hereabouts is marshy. Without its rhines, much of it would revert to unproductive and worthless swamp. Nowadays these rhines are the responsibility of the Drainage Board. Anciently they and the sea-wall were kept in order by H.M. Commissioners of Sewers, who were headed by the great landowners, Berkeley and Poyntz, Chandos and Throckmorton. In or about the year 1600, H.M. Commissioners received the following letter from the yeomen of Redwick, near New Passage.

> *To the Right Worshipfull Commissioners of Sewers.*
>
> *May it please you to understand that whereas the Countrie after the Great Flood cam downe into John Hortts Orchard in Redweek, and there cutt a great slewes to let forth the water and never since made up sufficiently to defend the same, but ever high tide wee your poore supplyants, being dwellers there, bee greatlye damnified and almost un donne therebye.*

The charge for repairs amounted to £4.

New Passage is to my mind a much pleasanter place than Severn Beach. It is not dotted with week-end chalets, nor does it possess any counter-attractions (save, perhaps, the New Passage Hotel) to Severn shore. Nevertheless it has its disadvantages. An old mill with a tall chimney is crumbling away into ruin alongside a gout, and there is a firing-range nearby which, when in operation, prevents walkers from following the sea-wall. That footpath along the sea-wall from New Passage to Aust is worth following. It is country typical of the estuary. Beyond the sea-wall are the New Grounds, or Warth, and here you will find little heaps of stranded seaweed and the feathers of seabirds where in summer cattle are grazed. Beyond this, there's a lower level of coarser grass on ground recently reclaimed from Severn and still underwater in heavy tides. It has a different flora from that of the

5* 65

Compton Greenfield

Warth, usually light-green with a bluish or brownish tinge. Beyond that, again, is the shore, shelving down to a lovely chocolate-brown or purplish mud. In this mud grows the coarse Dutch (or Cord) grass, first introduced to this part of Severnside by Squire Fust of Hill.

This cord-grass spreads with amazing rapidity. It is the quickest and most effective of colonisers for reclaiming land from mudflat: a tough, tussocky plant of a pale-green colour, growing about two feet high and sending strong roots down three feet or more into the mud. In his book *Rivermouth*, Brian Vesey-FitzGerald has this to say about it:

> "Cord-grass is, I am sure, the world's finest natural mud-binder. It spreads because seeds or pieces of rhizome are carried by the tide to new areas of mud and pioneer plants develop. It grows very quickly, and within two years, under favourable conditions, a circular colony several feet in diameter may develop from a single plant. These new colonies gradually coalesce and so form a new meadow. . . . Cord-grass retains considerable silt in its stiff stems, and this raises the level of the mud rapidly, so that the grass can advance farther seawards almost all the time. It is in fact a landwinner."

Which is all very true, but Severn basket-fishermen hate the sight and sound of it. It menaces their off-shore fisheries; drives away the salmon; silts up or diverts the channels from their pools and basket-weirs.

The mud of Severn is not as other mud. Some say it is healthy, that it has considerable curative qualities. Others shudder at the sight of it and say it haunts their dreams; that it looks as though it harbours every germ in creation. To me it suggests the pure primeval slime, from which life first emerged so-many-billions of years ago. It has a curious fascination, being at once repellent and inviting. You feel an irrepressible urge to wallow, and an even stronger disinclination to break its smooth unctuous contours. Those who think that things like worms and flies, snakes and toads, spiders and mice ought to be exterminated to save them annoyance, will probably dislike Severn mud and wish it might be replaced by nice clean sand. How annoying for them that this disgusting Old Man River should choose to deposit its sand in the middle, to confuse navigation, whilst depositing only mud on its shores, where its rich sliminess turns the stomachs of sentimental countrygoers. Such sentimentalists should be warned that the Severn estuary is not for them. It has not yet been, and perhaps never will be, completely tamed. Sometimes it changes its course slightly and, carving a few acres from one shore, adds them to another. In some ways, perhaps, it is just as well that Severn *is* contrary. If the river were tamed and its shores sandy, this grass-grown sea-wall and lonely Warth, these ditches and rhines, harbouring wild duck and heron, moorhen and coot, might be replaced by tin shacks and converted tramcars. For, strange as it seems, sentimental people who shudder at the sight of Severn mud do not seem to object to corrugated-iron and advertisement hoardings. Their noses quiver in horror at the scent of pig-manure, but petrol fumes evoke no shudders, perhaps because they are so familiar they aren't noticed.

This stretch of mud between the New Passage and Aust is known as Northwick Oaze, taking its name from the nearby hamlet of that name. The last time I walked this way with George, we picked several mushrooms on the sea-wall. There were none on the Warth. Perhaps the presence of salt discourages them. There is a ditch on the landward side of the sea-wall, and George and I flushed a heron and three mallard from it in the space of less than a mile. Hereabouts the sea-wall wanders inland. Or rather, one should say, the estuary has retreated from it, leaving many acres of Warth. The sea-wall is simply a grassy mound with a footpath on top of it.

Down by the saltings among the stones we saw numbers of wagtails, jerking about with great animation, in addition to ringed plover and dunlin. Nearer Aust there were a small flock of goldfinches which flirted ahead of us on the sea-wall path, feeding on thistle seeds. They would perch in a mass on a couple of large thistles and gobble until we came up to them, when they would be up and off to the next clump of thistles. We pursued them in this way for about a quarter of a mile until they left the foreshore and went inland. Where Cake Pill Gout runs into the estuary, the footpath turns into the main road. On this open ground beside the estuary and alongside the main road, near Aust, cars collect in their hundreds on sunny days and people picnic on the Warth. There is great profusion of litter. Cigarette cartons, toffee papers, paper bags and ice-cream tubs abound. Here, among the fragments of paper and cardboard, I found the sea-aster growing. The plant had crept into a small ditch to hide, and so had escaped being picked or trodden-on.

There is little doubt that Aust was used for trade even before Roman times. Some of the earliest invasions came by way of Severn, and there is a strong probability that Phœnician or other traders came here to barter goods to the native inhabitants. An exotic female figure with a crescent-shaped head-dress which was found at Aust is now in the British Museum. It is probably a representation of a goddess. Other figures have been found here, which suggests that even in the Bronze and Iron Ages there was a certain amount of international trade.

Aust ferry is known as the Old Passage, and it has been identified as the Trajectus Augusti of the Romans. Today it is a busy motor-ferry, crossing to the Beachley peninsula below Chepstow. The Severn is only about a mile wide at this point, though it soon widens out again into what looks like a great inland lake—on calm days! I remember such a day, in July, when the river above Aust was calm as a mill-pond. Tide was at the full, so that it appeared in all its glory. And from across the mile-or-so of shining water at Aust, the hamlet of Beachley, near Chepstow, looked extraordinarily inviting. Away to westward of Beachley Point, the rocky little island of St Tecla, or St Twrog, looked isolated and romantic. This island can be reached at low water by wading through the mud at Beachley; and as it has a navigation light within the two remaining walls of its ancient chapel, Mr Palmer, the lightkeeper of Sheperdine, has to go down every week to see to it. He told me that St Tecla or St Twrog (for no-one seems very certain which of those names is the right one) is a small and not very attractive place, nearly covered with slippery seaweed. But on that July day, as I remarked, it looked romantic. That, no doubt, was a result of the blue distances and shining Severn. Facets of the gently rippling water glittered like brief diamonds, whilst across it moved a stately procession of cloud-shadows. But there are times when the island of St Tecla or St Twrog (the former being the name of a local saint, murdered in A.D. 47) is far from romantic, and I do not envy the hermit who once lived there. I am told the island still contains the saint's holy well.

In the early part of the nineteenth century, when the Old Passage was a busy ferry, the ferry-boats appear to have sunk, with loss of life, at distressingly frequent intervals. On September 1st, 1839, the boat *Dispatch* went down in mid-channel. Captain Whitchurch, the master, who was making the crossing "against his judgment", went down with it, as did his son, a boy, and nine or ten others, as well as five horses and two carriages. Only a dog escaped, by swimming ashore. Four years later, Captain Whitchurch's other son went down with another Passage boat, which was also lost with all hands.

Above Beachley on the far side of Severn are Sedbury Cliffs, the counterpart of Aust Cliff and once joined to it before Severn cut its channel between. Above Sedbury Park is Tidenham, whose mediæval tower has been a landmark to sailors for centuries. Behind and beyond, the shadowy hills of Dean provide a fitting and dramatic horizon.

On that particular July day, I remember, we sat on a large pebble on Aust beach, with the cliff at our backs. And whilst I smoked a leisurely pipe, George watched the cars go bumping down the pier to the ferry, and the ferry-boats crossing. A small sailing-boat, probably from Thornbury Sailing Club at Oldbury Pill, suddenly appeared out of the north-east, tacking into the wind. The white sail skimmed the water like a strangely shaped sea-bird. It came towards us, then tacked away toward the mouth of the Wye, and was soon lost in the blue haze to westward.

Aust village is a good half-mile from the ferry, behind a sheltering hill. It is a small place now, just a group of cottages, a church and a few scattered houses and farms, grouped loosely around the Boar's Head, outside which a notice warns motorists that this is positively the last tavern they'll meet with this side of the ferry. The church is well-sited, with a backing of trees, on rising ground. It has a bold fifteenth-century tower, but the interior appears to have been "restored". However, the graceful font is worth noticing, and so is the sixteenth-century stone pulpit with its carved symbolism. A pleasant avenue of limes flanks a path through the churchyard, but the path did not look much used. It wasn't overgrown. It just looked unused. And I remember it struck me as curious that, of the two ways to church, the majority of churchgoers appeared to favour the less interesting, more prosaic one. Perhaps the majority always do! At any rate, it is a characteristic of Severnside. Natives of the Vale will do anything to avoid publicity, or making, as they term it, a "poppy-show" of themselves. They are true Saxons, most of them: slow of thought and speech, unwilling to obtrude themselves or their affairs, not very interested in things outside their own locality.

At the Boar's Head, we got into conversation with Hugh Clare, whom we found presiding over the bar-parlour from what he humorously refers to as his "pulpit", a tiny semicircular bar. He told us that in the old coaching days, when travellers to Wales were brought here for embarkation by ferry, Aust possessed no less than five inns. It had then at least twice its present-day population, and was *en route* for the shipment of Irish cattle. One of its five inns was on Aust Cliff, and, after the landlord had been warned that it was unsafe, it collapsed, along with a portion of cliff, into the river. Passage House, now a farm, was another inn. The Boar's Head, so far as he was able to discover, was at least three hundred years old. Before he had it, it was kept by a retired sea-captain.

"And how long have *you* kept the Boar's Head?" George asked him.

"Twenty-six years. I'm a Northcountryman myself. And I used to be an engineer before I became an innkeeper."

I asked him if he'd become completely absorbed by the village life.

"Good gracious, no! I'm still a stranger here, really. You need three or four generations of residence behind you before you're regarded as a local man here."

Then he asked me the question I always dread answering.

"How old do you suppose I am?"

I tried to hedge. "That's not easy to say. And anyway, I'm not much good at guessing ages."

"Try!"

"Well, then—sixty-five."

And I waited for the reaction, not without nervousness, for my honesty in this matter of age-by-appearance has been known to give umbrage. To be honest, I had thought Mr Clare might be around seventy, but I gave him the benefit of the doubt.

"I'm eighty-one," he said.

I looked, and what was more, felt, surprised. Hugh Clare is a splendid advertisement for the Aust air, still a fine-looking man with his waxed moustache and small imperial.

When I asked for his frank opinion of the local people, he showed himself to be no mean observer, for he said: "I believe that climate plays a great part in forming character and outlook. As you know, Aust village is nearly a mile from Severn, sheltered by hills on two sides and therefore mild and relaxing. So it's not surprising that the village people tend to be complacent among themselves and indifferent to strangers. They haven't much curiosity and they aren't very friendly to outsiders. But there's a deep sympathy for and understanding of neighbours whom they've always known."

From a corner of the bar a man spoke up: "I don't agree with you, Mr Clare." This was Mr Norris, whose salmon fishery is not far from the ferry. Mr Norris is the grandson of "Looky" Norris, already mentioned, and very well known locally. His weir of "putchers" has been long in the Norris family. Putchers, by the way, are the smaller openwork baskets which, arranged in tiers, or "weirs", act as salmon traps.

"Had a good season?" I asked.

"Quite good," he said. "Can't grumble."

"Some salmon fishermen have told me it's been a bad year."

"Not for me."

"Do you think the catch has fallen off much in recent years?"

"We-ell, it certainly isn't what it was once. And, of course, it varies in different parts of the river from year to year. Down here it's been pretty good. Very good at the beginning of the year. But it dropped off later. One chap, fishing down below, tells me he's had the best season for years."

This was something of a surprise for me, because elsewhere I'd heard nothing but grumbles. It may be that the fishery down-river had benefited from being below the mouth of the Wye, which, despite bad pollution in recent years, is still a fine salmon river. Wye salmon would turn away from the estuary a little below Aust, and this might account for the variation of catch. But there are many other factors involved: wind and tide, the shifting channel and movement of sand and shoals, river-pollution, and the spread of cord-grass (over which salmon will not swim). All these affect the quality of the catch.

I should have liked to ask Mr Norris many more things, and to have had Hugh Clare's opinion of the proposed new suspension bridge over the Severn from Aust Cliff to Beachley, which will have a central span of 3,300 feet, and will be one of the longest suspension bridges in the world. But time, tide and buses wait for no one, and we had to go.

From Aust the pleasant inland road crosses Old Splott Rhine to Red Hill, and then branches off to Elberton and Littleton-on-Severn.

Elberton has a gabled manor which was the birthplace of that remarkable Quaker, Joseph Sturge. A man of character and principle, Sturge was at first a farmer. But when his religious scruples prompted him to refuse service in the militia, his sheep were driven off to pay the fine. As a corn factor, he wouldn't sell his barley to brewers, for he didn't hold with the manufacture of liquor. Then he began to take an interest in the slave-traffic. Going out to the West Indies, he bought a plantation and proved that sugar could be grown without slave labour. His work helped to hasten the emancipation of the slaves, after which he went to work on plans for their education. Sturge's house in Hyde Park was an international meeting-place, and he was an ardent worker for peace. In fact he was one of the deputation sent to the Tsar of Russia by the Society of Friends to try to stop the Crimean War.

East of Elberton village, on the western edge of Alveston Down, are the remains of a small Roman Camp. By a lane to the secluded church is a fine great chestnut, and higher up, in the woods on Vineyard Hill (*et seq*), there is a huge wild-cherry tree.*

Littleton-on-Severn is another quiet place among orchards and meadows. It has a brickyard near the Severn which employs most of the local people, and a church which possesses some interesting features but was largely rebuilt in the last century. There are some tiles here which came from Thornbury Castle, some of them showing the arms of its builder, the Duke of Buckingham,

---

* In his *Saxon Charters and Field Names of Gloucestershire*, G. B. Grundy refers to "Bear Wood", Elberton, as a survival from the time when the brown bear was still to be found in this country.

others with the badge of Essex, the Stafford knot, Bohun antelope and the fiery axle of the Woodstocks. Despite its name, Littleton is more than a mile from the estuary, on rising ground.

Olveston is a large village with a richer history than Elberton or Littleton. Here the Denys family lived in a castle or fortified manor, of which little remains. Strangely little is known of this place and its great family. Few ancient buildings of a comparable size remain so poorly documented. What is left of the castle is grouped around Olveston Court Farm. A fine gateway with traces of a drawbridge is all that remains, except for traces of a great castellated wall, running alongside the dried-up moat. No one seems to have the faintest notion how or when it was destroyed. Considering that, in the Middle Ages, this was one of the principal domains in the county, with its tilting-ground for knightly tournaments and jousts, it really is extraordinary that so little is known about it. The dimensions of the place are considerable, and in its day this castle must have dominated the surrounding country. There are local yarns of ancient battles between the lordly factions of Olveston and nearby Tockington, but they are far too hazy and unsubstantial for one to put any faith in them. The fact that, from time to time, cannon-balls have been dug up nearby suggests that the place was at one time besieged. And it is possible that, the siege being successful, it was destroyed. Nevertheless, Olveston remains a mystery which smarter brains than mine must unravel.

Olveston village has an "air", a personality which the smaller places lack. In the church are some interesting tombs—one of them fourteenth-century—if you are a tomb-lover and inscription-reader. And there are a couple of fifteenth-century brass portraits of Morys Denys and his son, Walter, showing them on their knees in armour and tabards. Olveston used to be on the road from London to Aust ferry, according to my friend Richard Leakey, the schoolmaster at Tytherington: and he tells me that it was the birthplace of Dr Basil Harwood, the hymn-writer (see *Hymns Ancient and Modern*). Coming down to fairly recent times and less exalted personages, Teddy Duffety, a well-known gipsy, used to live on Olveston Green. He was honest as the day, a remarkable fiddler and a keen pugilist. A farmer who had known him told me about the time Teddy fought another gipsy, John

Locke: "It was a real scrap, hell for leather, with bare fists and no nonsense about resting in-between-whiles. They fought solid for three hours, and only finished when they couldn't stand up. Both of 'em had to be taken to hospital, and Teddy was crippled for life as a result. Neither of 'em were ever the same again. They half-killed each other."

In the Bodleian Library at Oxford there is a rare old black-letter tract, with a rather lengthy title:

> *Fearful Newes of Thunder and Lightning, with the terrible effects thereof, which Almighty God sent on a place called Olvestone, in the County of Glocester the 26 of November last.*
>
> *Having prefixt before it, a short discourse, concerning two other admirable accidents, that soone after ensued. Truely related by P. S. And dedicated unto the Kings most excellent Maiestie. At London printed by G. Eld, for Frauncis Burton, 1606.*

It is the earliest publication in which the *County* of Gloucestershire is mentioned, and was the work of an Olveston schoolmaster. This is how he describes the storm: "The morning of the aforesaid day being lowering and sad did yet, a little after eight, begin to smile. . . . Before nine there came up a strong wind from the west, bringing up a most dark mantle that overspread the whole heavens." Thereafter appeared a rainbow, which in turn was followed by a great darkness and a frightful hailstorm which left the ground more than six inches deep in hailstones. Then did the wind make "a terrible rattle", and there were "feareful flashes of lightning, and soon three or four claps of thunder louder than ordinary. Whereof," P.S. comments smugly, "I took occasion to talk to the gentlewoman of the house and her young plants which (being five sons with the son of a friend) sat at table with us, to this effect: That the atheists of the world, and such as did not know, acknowledge and fear God had great cause to be terrified . . . but such as did truly fear God, they need not be appalled or dismayed." The worthy schoolmaster was so pleased with this little lecture that he was soon repeating it to his class. Unfortunately, it was interrupted by the jangling of the church bell. And when our schoolmaster sent out a boy to see what was wrong, he came running back to report that the steeple was on fire. Olveston church had been struck by lightning!

A little way along the road past Olveston Green is Tockington, a sleepy little place of no great beauty, huddled around a tiny green and a war memorial, with a Nonconformist chapel, a pub and a mill nearby. The trouble with Tockington, a local man told us, is too many dogs. "'Tis all dogs here!" he grumbled. "You can't step a dozen yards without 'em getting under your blessed feet."

Talking to a man who was hedging and ditching here one day recently, I asked him if the farmer he worked for still made his own cider. "Oh, ah," he said. "What's it like?" I asked. "Oh, all roight, s'know . . . *if thee canst stick it!*"—and he pulled a face. He was a youngish man, with an open, innocent, weatherbeaten face. Unlike most of the younger men, he spoke a rich, earthy dialect, and seemed to derive as much pleasure from speaking it as I did from listening to it.

A Roman villa was discovered on the Tockington Park Estate in 1787 and excavated exactly a century later. In 1821 Tockington was in the news on account of a very curious occurrence: a fall of snail-shells of the species *Felix Virgata*. They fell "like a great shower, which continued upwards of an hour, and . . . the earth's surface was covered near six acres, three inches deep", according to *Felix Farley's Bristol Journal*, the leading Bristol newspaper of that time.

Climbing the hill from Tockington to Old Down, there are old quarry workings to the right, with parkland and woods. At the top of the hill is an unenclosed common, and from there, on a day last summer, George and I branched off by the lane to Lower Hazel. Hearing crackling sounds from the gorse which borders the lane, we thought it was on fire until we stopped to investigate. It was the sound of the seed-pods bursting, scattering their seeds quite a distance away from the parent plant. In this way gorse solves one of the great problems of the vegetable kingdom (the distribution of seeds at a distance from parent) without dependence on any fortuitous agency. Other plants depend on birds eating their fruit, thus distributing the seeds in their lime; or on the wind carrying them, as in the case of dandelion and willow-herb; or on animals or birds which, coming into contact with seed-heads, carry away some of the seeds, which are specially adapted to cling to them by fine fairs or tiny hooks. Gorse is independent of these. When its seeds are ripe, the seed-pod bursts and vomits them out.

The hedge banks were full of flowers, and my companion and I commented on their profusion and on the fact that so few people nowadays have sufficient curiosity to identify them. A man with a couple of small children had passed by, and the little girl had said: "Daddy, what's the name of this flower?" Irritably, the father answered: "How should I know! Some sort of weed, by the look of it. Don't *dawdle*, Mary!"

As a matter of interest, George and I noted down the names of such wildflowers as bloomed freely here. There was lady's-bedstraw and St John's-wort, wild mignonette and ragwort and yarrow. Shell-pink flowers of the lovely lesser-convolvulus looked up from the grass, and white trumpets of the greater-convolvulus topped the hedge. There was red dead-nettle in the ditch, blackberry blossom, and a few last dog-roses in the hedge-row, which was also a riot of traveller's-joy. All these contributed to the rich and mellow scent which hung in the warm air and lulled the senses like the garden of Proserpine. Down in Lower Hazel (haunted Hazel, if we are to believe old accounts) the odours were even more heady, consisting of new hay and privet-bloom, rose-blossom and honeysuckle. The very insects reeled and droned about as though drunk with nectar and the scent of high summer. It reminded me of a book I'd recently read by Sylvia Townsend Warner, who complained that whilst people use their eyes when travelling they seldom use their noses—at any rate in an æsthetic sense! Perhaps we should cultivate our noses more, develop our sense of smell, which, with centuries of neglect, is in danger of atrophying. One might even, to make an entirely new approach, write a guide-book of smells, analysing and cataloguing each place's distinctive odours. George examples: "Clearwell, a place of contrasts. Near the church jasmine makes the air most fragrant, but a few yards past it our nostrils are assaulted by the vigorous and racy smell of pig. The bar-parlour of The Flower Pot is compounded of a most curious mixture of stale beer and kippers, wood-worm and geraniums." He thinks one might use as one's title "Nosing round Gloucestershire" or "a Nose on the Mendips" or even "Down the Vale with a Sniff".

It *could* be done. The trouble is that smells are so transitory. Roses fade and honeysuckle withers, and though pig-manure may last a little longer, it, too, will not stand the test of time. Smells are very much things of the moment. Nothing affects us quite so immediately or profoundly, but on the other hand, odours are unreliable, varying much with wind and season. Nevertheless, it ought to be put on record that we found those lanes around Lower Hazel to possess a very rich and mellow "bouquet" on that particular July day.

We did not see that female apparition of which a startled Hazel resident of long ago said that—"as side-steppered he, so side-steppered she". I rather wish we had, for it might have cured George's scepticism. But we did see the Quaker's Burial Ground, dated 1656, with small headstones clustering round a sundial making a scene of quiet serenity. How different the scene and smell when we reached the main road near Alveston. A.38 was buzzing with cars, malodorous with petrol-fumes. It is a fine road, with some splendid views of the Vale; but to the walker and cyclist it is a headache. Coaches flash past, loaded with gaping and sweet-sucking sightseers in transit to Wye Valley or Cotswolds or Weston-super-Mare. Cars, lorries and vans pelt along in a constant stream. Here and there are outbreaks of ribbon development, horrible little snack-shacks and main-road pubs. They are inevitable, being parasitic on the traffic. They flaunt their gaudy invitations to catch the eye of motorists speeding by to somewhere else. They don't belong at all: are a sort of over-dressed gipsy, clamorous and cajoling, trying to divert the attention of coach-drivers and cycling-clubs. Absurd to grumble at them (though George does!). They are a sign of the times, an indication of the power and bad taste of that huge rootless urban civilisation which our cities have fostered and equipped with wheels.

To the passing motorist, modern Alveston means ribbon development, a caravan factory, and The Ship. The latter, a fine old coaching-inn which has kept up with the times as regards comfort, is well known to local sportsmen. In Tudor days it was a village hostelry, deriving much passing trade from the coaches and wagons which carried merchants and merchandise northwards from Bristol. Part of the original building still survives. It is the gabled wing to the left of the porch. Now a lounge and writing-room, it was formerly the inn kitchen and bar parlour (adapted for the use of "commercials" in coaching days, and known as the Travellers' Room). Here you will still find great oak beams and an open kitchen hearth; and the cupboard beside the chimney has Elizabethan oak-panelling. Underneath this room is a cellar known as the Smugglers' Den. Leading from it, no one knows where, is a blocked passage which seems to support the old tradition of this inn's connection with smuggling. Many a cargo of contraband was secretly run up the estuary in olden days, and the Ship's cellars would have been a wonderful hiding-place.

With the stage and mail coaches came a new prosperity for the Ship. Alveston was the first stage out of Bristol, and travellers used to wait in the small room to the left of the front porch, listening for the sound of the guard's horn. The courtyard would be a place of great activity, in those days; full of the clatter of postboys, shouting of ostlers, and horses' hooves. This same yard still echoes with the sound of hooves and hunting-horn on the Boxing Day meets of the Berkeley. There's always a good crowd to see them move off.

The Ship at Alveston has seen many famous cricketers, for the adjoining field has long been the home of Thornbury Cricket Club. W. G. and E. M. Grace, Wally Hammond and Gilbert Jessop have all played here, and left behind legends of mighty drives and sixes over adjoining buildings. Another event which always brings visitors to the Ship is Alveston Flower Show, held in August each year in the field behind the Jubilee Hall. It started, in 1888, with a display of vegetables on two wagons. Since then more than £6,000 has been collected for charity at Alveston Flower Shows.

Alveston was a settlement in the Stone Age, from which the tumulus near Vattingstone Lane dates. The name of the village probably derives from "Alwih's Stone", which may have been one of the megalithic stones on Old Down which were recently dispersed. Only one remains, and that is the Kissing Stone above Lower Hazel. The manor of Alveston belonged to King Harold, and it was here (according to legend) that Fulke FitzWarren turned the highway through his hall, so that he could press his hospitality upon travellers. There is also a record that William Rufus hunted here. Some of the old field-names are worth reviving. *Sweet Waterings*, for instance, and *Forlorn Hope*; *Nine Elms, Galloping Ground, Summer Gates, Cuckoo Pen, Briarlands, Silver Hill, Lark's Lane Field*, and *Orchid Leaze*. *Merry Heaven*, a corruption of Merlin Haven, is a reminder of falconry. *Old Lippiatt*, or Leap-gate, reminds us of the gates used for rounding-up deer in the forests—gates by which they could enter but not leave, except by jumping. *Flash Stocking* was not, as some might suppose, a resort of spivs, for both spivs and nylons were unheard-of when the name was given. More likely it was a place where a tree-trunk (or "stock") bridged a ford (or "flash").

Although extensive ploughing has caused many casualties among the wildflower population, I am told that the autumn-crocus and ladies'-tresses are still to be found hereabout. So is dyer's-greenwood, which yields a good yellow dye, and is very likely a survival from the days when the village was closely connected with the Gloucestershire cloth-trade. Teazles were grown locally, and so were other plants which yielded dyes. Tanning, carried on at Rookery Farm, was another local industry.

Fine views of Vale and Severn are to be seen from the Kissing Stone, from the cricket-pitch on Old Down, and from Milbury Heath. Between the Ship and Milbury Heath, on the right-hand side of the road nearly opposite Little Abbey, is all that remains of a prehistoric camp. It is scarcely perceptible now, because the field, which is now a meadow, has been repeatedly ploughed-over, until the rampart is marked only by an undulation of the ground.

The new church at Alveston is of little interest, but the old church, near Rudgeway, although it is partly ruined, has much of value. Battlemented tower, walls and bellcote on the gable of the nave are fourteenth-century. Work has recently been carried out on the old wall-paintings, and there is a curious carving in a round doorway which may be Saxon. Colonel Thomas Veel, the Royalist, is buried within the Laudian altar rails.

It is unfortunate that modern roads have destroyed the character and grouping of Alveston village, for it was formerly a most attractive little place, lying beside the ancient Ridgeway and the high downs (it is 342 feet above sea-level). But although the requirements of heavy traffic have to some extent spoilt it as a place, Alveston makes a good base for ramblings and excursions. The Ship is a Trust House. Need I say more?

CHAPTER IV

THORNBURY AND OLDBURY

ANOTHER writer* has called Thornbury "Queen of the Vale". The title is an apt one, for although it is only a small market town, Thornbury has dignity and character, and its happy combination of spaciousness and bustle, historic interest and accessibility make it a pleasant centre for seeing the Vale. As a place, it is very much more alive than Berkeley, with a vigorous life of its own, an easy relationship with Bristol, and intimate connections with the surrounding countryside.

The Plain at Thornbury is a real centre, a rendezvous, the axis around which Thornbury life revolves. High Street is the shopping centre, where Swan (kept by my old friend Frank Turner) and White Lion face each other intrepidly but never fight! Other inns are the Royal George, the Barrel, Plough, Queen's Head, Wheatsheaf and Exchange. Joe Pavey's saddler's shop straddles across the High Street approach, and there is a nice little antique shop. Beavans' drapery store occupies what used to be the old Market Hall in High Street, a building which in spite of the conversion of ground floor into modern shop premises for the benefit of Thornbury ladies still retains some architectural interest. There is also and inevitably a cinema.

Thornbury is not, like some of your country towns, a matter of one street and a few alleys. St Mary Street has some curious corners and old walls which in summer sprout stonecrop and snapdragon. Then there's John Street, and Saw Mill Lane, Pullin's Green, Horse Shoe Lane and Rock Street, Chapel Street (which contains the Cossham Hall, named after Handel Cossham, the locally famous mine-owner who was born here), and Castle Street which leads on from High Street to church and castle. . . . However, no useful purpose would be served by enumerating *all*

* R. P. Beckinsale in *Companion into Gloucestershire* (Methuen).

the streets of Thornbury. Enough to say that my list is far from complete.

In the words of Leland, the town is set "almoste upon an equalle grounde, being large to the proportion of the letter Y, havinge first one long strete, and two hornes goyne out of it. There hathe been good clothing [trade] in Thornebyry, but now Idelnes much reynithe there!" The idleness was, of course, consequent on the decline of the woollen and cloth trade in this part of the world, as a result of new methods of manufacture and competition from mills in the North-country. Not only Thornbury was involved. Berkeley, Dursley, Stroud, Eastington, Cam and Wickwar were all dependent on the cloth-trade, and of course the Cotswold towns were almost wholly dependent on fleeces. When the manufacture of Cotswold broadcloth came to an end in these towns of Southwold and Berkeley Vale, so did their development. Dursley and Cam, Stroud and Thornbury have since developed other manufactures, but Wickwar has dwindled from a town with its mayor and twelve aldermen and a grammar school, to a sleepy village with only a parish council. Berkeley, too, has languished. And for many years Dursley and Stroud, Cam and Eastington had a lean time of it. That is why these places possess a distinctive character. They flourished mightily in Elizabethan times, and much of their building dates from those boom years. Then came a depression, which prevented their development and saved them from the dreary architectural styles of the nineteenth century. Now that they are recovering, they have acquired a rash of council-houses on their outskirts.

Another severe blow to Thornbury's pocket and prestige was when it lost the coaching trade from Bristol to Gloucester. That was in the eighteenth century, when a new turnpike took a short cut east of the town, a course still followed by the main road (A.38) instead of bringing traffic straight through it, as formerly. This by-pass saved Thornbury's character, but at the cost of remaining a "backwater".

Thornbury Castle is not so well known as Berkeley, and for a very good reason. It was never completed. There was a castle of sorts here in the time of Edward II, but in those days it was held by the Earls of Gloucester. The present castle was begun by that great courtier Edward Stafford, Duke of Buckingham. It was in

6 81

Aust Ferry

1510 that he obtained Henry VIII's permission to impark 1,000 acres at Thornbury, and Leland, in describing the effects thereof, remarks that "the inhabytants cursyd the Duke for the lands so inclosed". Naturally they did, since the land "imparked" was probably their common grazing land. But, although there is little doubt that Thornbury folk "cursyd" Buckingham, it is doubtful if they had the courage to do so publicly, for he was then one of the King's favourites.

Still to be seen on the castle gateway is the old inscription: "Thys gate was begon in the yere of our Lorde God MDXI, the ij yere of the Reyne of Knge Henri VIII by me, Edw. Duc of Buckyngham, Erll of Herforde, Stafforde, and Northampton." Ten years later, when Buckingham met his end, the castle was still far from completed. The story of his downfall is variously told. One version tells how Henry VIII grew jealous of him, perhaps because he had expressed some shadowy claim to the throne in the event of Henry leaving no heir—always a sore point with that monarch. There is another version, in which Buckingham is made the victim of his uncompromising pride and of Cardinal Wolsey's jealousy. It is said that Wolsey's enmity was aggravated by an incident when the Duke happened to hold a basin for the King to wash his hands in, and Wolsey took the liberty of dipping *his* fingers into the water. This was too much for Buckingham. He had no objection to holding a bowl for the King, but he was damned if he'd play the lackey for an upstart churchman, the son of a butcher! And he threw the contents of the basin over the Cardinal's feet. At this, Wolsey was heard to mutter that henceforward he would "stick to the Duke's skirts". Some took this to mean that he would hound him down, and the tale must have been in general currency, because when he heard of Buckingham's execution, the Emperor Charles II commented: "A butcher's dog has killed the finest buck in England."

Those are two, admittedly romantic and simplified versions of the Duke's demise. The first is the more likely, for only a short time before Wolsey apprised the King that Buckingham was ambitious for the throne, the Duke had given the Cardinal a cup of gold as a New Year's gift. And Wolsey's suspicions do not appear to be entirely unfounded. Indeed, Buckingham, like Macbeth, seems to have been the victim of an ambition swollen out of all proportion by the predictions of an oracle, in this case not three Witches on a Blasted Heath, but a monk called Nicholas Hopkins, of Hinton Charterhouse, near Bath. According to Hopkins, Buckingham was to be a king and father of kings. Whether the monk's intentions were purely mischievous or well-meaning, foolish or crafty, one cannot say. But it is certain that his predictions paid him good dividends, for the Duke made a number of cash payments to his "ghostly father" at Hinton.

Buckingham's credulity was fatal. That it was an integral part of his character and not just an offshoot of his vanity is shown by his respect for, or fear of, gipsies. Instead of punishing them, as did most landowners, Buckingham encouraged and rewarded them. And some of them adopted his name in gratitude. Buckingham is—or was—a gipsy family-name hereabouts. Buckingham's accounts for June 10th, 1519, show a payment "To certain Egyptians at Thornbury, 40s." It is doubtful if the Duke's encouragement of Egyptians would have endeared him to the yeomen and traders of Thornbury, especially as he had confiscated the commons of the former to provide himself with an estate.

In Shakespeare's *Henry VIII*, Buckingham is arrested in an anteroom of the Palace. In point of fact he was at Thornbury, watching the growth of his castle, when the summons came. He went to London, and there appeared before his peers in Westminster Hall. He was unanimously convicted of high treason, and executed on Tower Hill. His farewell speech—in Shakespeare's play—concludes thus:

> . . . *You few that loved me*
> *And dare be bold to weep for Buckingham . . .*
> *Go with me, like good angels, to my end,*
> *And, as the long divorce of steel falls on me,*
> *Make of your prayers one sweet sacrifice,*
> *And lift my soul to heaven. . . .*
> *Heaven has an end in all: yet, you that hear me,*
> *This from a dying man receive as certain:*
> *Where you are liberal of your loves and counsels,*
> *Be sure ye be not loose; for those you make your friends*
> *And give your hearts to, when they once perceive*

The least rub in your fortunes, fall away,
Like water from ye, never found again
But where they mean to sink ye. All good people,
Pray for me! I must now forsake ye: the last hour
Of my long weary life is come upon me.
Farewell:
And when you would say something that is sad,
Speak how I fell.

Thornbury Castle is utterly unlike Berkeley. The latter was built for the business of defence, and its keep is, or was, its most important feature. Thornbury was to have been not so much castle as palace, with the emphasis on comfort, pleasure and style; but the north side was never begun and no single side was finished at Buckingham's death. How the dispossessed farmers and yeomen must have exulted at this sudden eclipse of their lord and master! But it did them no good, for their lands were never restored to them, and the manor of Thornbury became a royal demesne until it was regranted to Lord Stafford, Buckingham's eldest son.

The castle at Thornbury was never completed, for succeeding owners were too poor to carry on the work that Buckingham had begun. Despite its machicolated walls and eyelets, Thornbury is really more mansion than castle. As Sir James Mackenzie writes, in his *Castles of England*, the effect is as though a house had been built within a castle. The façade of the house, with its range of superb oriels and bays, has been described as the best piece of English domestic architecture of the period. The great tower, which dominates the building, is dated 1514. There are even a few rooms remaining of an older manor-house, most of which Buckingham had pulled down.

Four years after Buckingham's execution, Henry VIII and Anne Boleyn stayed at the castle for ten days, when an outbreak of plague prevented them going on to Bristol as they had intended. To them came the ambassadors of Bristol Council, bringing presents of oxen (for the King), and gold (for the Queen). One feels the indelicacy of thus standing on the dead body of an old enemy—and friend. Rightly the castle should have been haunted by Buckingham's ghost; but it wasn't, appar-

84

ently, for Henry and his new queen do not appear to have been rendered uneasy.

Very near the castle is Thornbury's other architectural pearl, its church, with a very beautiful and lofty fifteenth-century tower which can be seen for miles, with open parapet and high buttresses carved with clinging animals and adorned with pinnacles. It is a noble church, with two Norman doorways and a spacious and graceful interior.

We must return to the Plain to see Thornbury life, and for one of the best views of the town's many-gabled rooftops, clustering companionably together, every one a different shape, striking a different pitch, rising and falling, sharp and oblique, rusty-red and lichened. Yet, for all that seeming chaos of angles, Thornbury's roof-tops make a pattern which is perfectly harmonious and accordant. They express the character of the place, a fact which was once pointed out to me, with pride, by a notable Thornbury personality, the late G. R. Millard, who used to be chairman of the parish council, magistrate and county councillor, as well as secretary to the South Glos. Internal Drainage Board. His office was just across the way, and he took me across to it to show me some old Minutes of the Commissioners for Sewers.

No, these records are not dull! They are even exciting. For Sewers and Drainage in this part of the world don't necessarily mean drainpipes and manhole-covers; they mean rhines. And rhines were what I wanted to find out about, for without them the Vale would lose much of its interest and nearly all its value for agriculture. Before there were any rhines, this land near the Severn was boggy, unhealthy, sour and unproductive. If there were no rhines today, the meadows would revert to marsh, agues and fevers would increase, so would herons and wild-fowl, whilst farmland would deteriorate. It is the business of the Drainage Board to keep the rhines in good repair. This is no small job, for sedges and reeds have to be kept under reasonable control by cutting, which is termed "ridding the rhines"; and periodically they have to be cleaned out, which is called "mudding out". Until fairly recently this was done by manual labour. Now it has to be done by machinery. Unfortunately, the use of machinery necessitates a clear bank. Which means that the willows which used to border the rhines, leaning drunkenly over them with their great twiggy heads, and contributing much to the individuality and beauty of the flat-lands near Severn, have had to be cut down. Thousands have been slaughtered in this way, and for this reason, in the past decade.

Observing that my features were expressing alarm and despondency, Mr Millard said: "I know it's a pity, but what else could we do? We were sorry they had to come down, and if there'd been any other answer . . . But it was forced on us by necessity. Even if we could have got enough labour, and the men were willing to do the job, we couldn't have afforded it with rates of pay what they are nowadays." The old, old story. Everybody wanting more for doing less, and the quality of the work having to suffer in consequence. Not that the mechanical dredger isn't efficient. I am sure it is. But those withies were part of the Berkeley Vale.

I was curious about the originators of rhines. Who first made them, I asked. Mr Millard thought that whoever made them were the first farmers of the region. Most of the land must have been partly under water before the sea-wall was built and the rhines made. When the Commissioners for Sewers were appointed, about 1583-4, land drainage had fallen into disrepair. Everyone wanted to dodge the responsibility of keeping the sea-wall and rhines in good order; millers were a nuisance (because in order to get a good head of water they dammed the rhines and frequently flooded adjacent land); farmers blamed the landowners and each other; landowners did likewise, and farming suffered. The Commissioners were appointed by Queen Elizabeth, and they included "Lords—Barkley and Chandos; Knights—Nicholas Poyntz, John Tracie, Thomas Porter and Wm. Winter; Esquires —Thomas Throckmorton, Pawle Tracie, Henrie Poole. John Hickfoorde, William Owldsworth", etc. They were served by a jury, and their commission was to "survey, reform and peruse all the walls, dytches, streames, banks, guttars, shewards, gowtes, calycs, brydges, trenches, mills, myldams, fludgats, powndes, lockes, hebbings, weres, and other impediments, letts and annoyances from Kyngrod* to Barkley, which, by the rage of the sea, flowinge and reflowinge, have byn or are impayred or hurte."

* The Kingroad was Avonmouth.

A typical entry in the minutes of that period reads:

Conygers   Item.   Wee finde a defaulte in the sea walle at
Throughe   Conygers throughe, of the length of 12 perches and is
to be repayred by the L. Barkley's Charge and will
cost 26s. 8d. by our judgement. . . . And to be performed before All Saynts.

From the beginning it is obvious that there are certain trouble-
spots. Cowhill Pill was one. This was the joint responsibility of
Lord Stafford and Mr Champneys. But although "Mr Champneys is and hath been alwaies redie for his part", Lord Stafford
was *never* ready for *his*.

Oldbury Mill was another annoyance. This was always a
subject of controversy; never out of the news. Either the "wether
gats" needed "repayring", or the "cutt is not donn", or the
millers let in overmuch salt water, or else they make themselves
a nuisance by "penning and stoppinge-up the freshe, regardinge
more of their owne pryvat gain than the common profitt of the
countrey". In 1606 the inhabitants of Kington petitioned the
Commissioners, complaining that 200 acres of their land was
subject to flooding as a result of the vile machinations of Oldbury
millers. And on April 27th in that year, the Commissioners actually met at Oldbury to examine the cause of the trouble: a mill,
at the end of Oldbury Pill, near the site now occupied by the
Anchor. They decided that the water should not be penned above
a certain mark, that the gates should be repaired and "hanged
flapwyse", and that the "fludgats be reformed". Fines or "paines"
were to be "forfected" by the owners, Sir James Harrington and
Lady Stafford. The latter was made responsible for repairs, but
she appears to have been as obstinate as her late husband. Eventually, nothing having been done to reform the floodgates, the
miller was haled to Thornbury for "corporall punishment".
Let's hope this taught *her ladyship* a lesson!

There are some humorous examples of imperfect scholarship,
and some very revealing pleas for help, among these minutes. In
1607 a petition was sent to the "Right Worshippfuls Comy-
shoners of Shewers" by "your worshipps poore subpliant to
command Edward Macham". This petitioner asked for assistance
in "makeing upp 27 perches and better of the sea-walle

cleane brooke and cutt downe", and his pathetic document concludes:

"I humbly beseech you therefore that you wilbe pleased to remember mee and my poore estate having nothing in the world left to releeve me and my poore brother but my lif in that thing and hit left to mee greatly indebt by my father and in so doeing I shall be bound dayly to pray for your worships long lif and health.

Edw. Macham."

The word pill (anciently *pyll*), which in the southern part of the Vale describes the creeks or tidal inlets of streams into the Severn, is not common throughout the county. Above Arlingham such tidal inlets are called sconces, and rhines are sometimes called moats.

In olden times there was much trouble with the pills or sconces, for during exceptionally high tides salt water from the estuary would rush through them to flood the meadows beyond. Nowadays this is prevented by a tidal flap. When the tide is out, pressure of fresh water behind the flap keeps it open to permit outflow, but when the tide comes in it is kept shut by pressure of the salt water without, thus preventing sea-water flooding the rhines. One unfortunate result of this contrivance is that, whereas Oldbury cottagers used to be able to go down to the rhine with a garden fork and spear a few flounders for breakfast, they can no longer do so, since the flatfish are excluded with the salt water. However, that is perhaps a small matter compared with ruined crops and waterlogged meadows.

Since 1930 the Commissioners of Sewers have been replaced by the Drainage Board, which is democratic. The more you pay in drainage rate, the more votes you get. Voting is by post. The Board controls 200 lineal miles of rhines. And I am told that nearly 20 per cent of this area would be capable of greater crop-production if it were better drained.

A few doors up the street from the council offices is the office of a firm of solicitors. Mr F. H. Burchell of Thornbury has worked here for sixty-three years. He is a mine of information about the personalities of Thornbury in Victorian days. He remembers Thornbury Mop, the spring hiring fair, to which folks seeking employment came with a bit of ribbon or an emblem of their trade in their hat. There would be roundabouts on the Plain, and stalls of all kinds spread halfway up the High Street. But some of the residents objected to the Mop, and it was excluded from the streets. For a time it was held in the yard of the Royal George, and then it ceased for good and all. Among the "characters" of that period, Mr Burchell remembers Rebecca Harvey, who used to carry on a little laundry business in Castle Street. She was also caretaker of the church, and would send two or three of her laundry-women to church every week to do the necessary clean-' ing. Mrs Harvey was the last official pew-opener. Every Sunday, morning and evening, she used to sit just inside the church door in the first seat. She knew all the regular churchgoers by sight, of course. But when a stranger or visitor came through the door, she would jump up from her seat, curtsey, and lead the way to a pew. She carried on her duties until shortly before her death, since when there has been no official pew-opener. Another Thornbury "character", who was before Mr Burchell's time, was Mrs Curtis, caretaker of Thornbury Castle, then unoccupied. This lady had her coffin made and kept it by her, sometimes showing it to visitors to the castle. She used it as a repository for apples, because "they kept so well there", and it had been made so long and received such hard wear before her death, at the age of seventy, that it had to be repaired for her burial.

Sir Algar Howard of Thornbury Castle also has memories of some of the old stalwarts. Tom Ashcroft, the mason, was one. He was a first-class mason and the best-known poacher in town. "When he was not putting up walls, he was out at night with a long-net," says Sir Algar. "I remember I thought I'd like to learn something about poaching and asked if he would give me a lesson. . . . We met up at Milbury Heath about 10 o'clock at night and started to put the nets down, but he got so excited about it that I think the rabbits must have run away before we got there." The farmers of those days were individualists, no two alike. There was "fat old George Wherrett, with his long, drip-ping moustache, mutton-chop whiskers and suit of check. Stout when I first knew him, he got fatter and fatter. When he used to go to Bristol market on a Thursday, he used to fill the cart. George was well known in the town as a horse-dealer." Sir Algar

Howard's father, Sir Stafford, was very interested in temperance reform. This, according to his son, was not without its disadvantages. For it was a habit of Sir Stafford's to employ reformed drunkards as butlers and footmen, in order to keep an eye on them. Needless to add, this was not always a satisfactory basis for efficient service.

Thornbury's literary associations are not extensive, though Horace Walpole came here in 1774 and met with a cool reception. He wrote to his friend, the antiquarian William Cole, about it:

"From Berkeley Castle I went to Thornbury, of which the ruins are half ruined; it would have been glorious if finished. I wish the Lords of Berkeley had retained the spirit of deposing till Harry the 8th's time. The situation is fine, though that was not the fashion; for all the windows of the great apartment look into the inner court, and the Prospect was left to the servants. Here I had two adventures. First I could find nobody to shew me about. I saw a paltry house that I took for the sexton's at the corner of the Close, and bade my servant ring and ask who could shew me the Castle. A voice in a passion flew from a casement, and issued from a Divine: What! what! was it *his* business to shew the Castle! go look for somebody else! What did we ring for, as if the house was on fire? My poor Swiss (servant) came back in a fright, and said the Doctor had sworn at him. Well, we scrambled over a stone style, saw a room or two glazed near the Gate, and rung at it. A damsel came forth and satisfied our curiosity. When we had done seeing, I said, 'Child, we don't know our way, I want to be directed into the London road; I see the Duke's Steward yonder at the window, pray desire him to come to me, that I may consult him.' She went; he stood staring at us at his window, and sent his footman—I do not think courtesy is resident at Thornbury. As I returned through the Close, the Divine came running out of breath, and without his beaver or band, and calls out, 'Sir, I am come to justify myself; your servant says I swore at him; I am no swearer, Sir.—Lord bless me! (dropping his voice), is it Mr Walpole?'

" ' Yes, Sir, and I think you was Lord Beauchamp's Tutor at Oxford, but I have forgot your name.'

" 'Holwell, Sir.'

" 'Oh yes.'

"And then I comforted him, and laid the ill-breeding on my footman's being a foreigner; but could not help saying, I really had taken his house for the Sexton's.

" 'Yes, Sir' (said he), 'it is not very good without; won't you please to walk in?'

"I did, and found the inside ten times worse, and a lean wife suckling a child. He was making an Index to Homer; is going to publish the chief beauties; and had, I believe, just been reading some of the delicate civilities that pass between Agamemnon and Achilles, and that was what my servant took for oaths. . . ."

A humorous impression of Thornbury in 1857 is conveyed in verses written above the pseudonym "Clodpoll", printed by Mr Presley of Wotton-under-Edge, under the title of *Letter from a Gloucestershire man to a friend in Bristol*:

> *While my hand's in I'll zay a word or two*
> *'Bout our old Town, zo dearly loved by yoo.*
> *Zence you last zeed'n there's been many a change;*
> *And zum on 'em you wool conzider strange.*
> *A Draper's Shop now stands where stood the Crown;*
> *The White Hart's closed and zoon wool be pull'd down;*
> *The anshunt Lower Pump it zeems is gwain*
> *Zoon to be moved to middle of the Plain!*
> *As vor the Upper Pump I can't now zay*
> *Whether they'll muv thuck too, or let'n stay:*
> *But be it as it wool, 'tis not much matter,*
> *Pervided that we gets zuffishunt weatter.*
> *The church and th' old Cassul be not muv'd*
> *But boath on 'em be very much impruv'd.*
> *Our strits be lited up in splendid style*
> *And Gas illumes th' church droo ivry Ile.*
> *The House where Dan'l Pitcher use' to stop*
> *Is turned into a vamus chinee shop*
> *Wi' two gurt winders, deccarated up*
> *Wi' many a teapot, basin, dish and cup.*

And so on, detailing with great exactness all the recent changes in the Thornbury of that time. The dialect in which it is written is not accurate, but at least it gives a faint idea of how Thornbury talked then.*

When I have told cottagers that I was troubled with occasional attacks of asthma, they have sometimes advised me to drink snail-water for it. A recipe for this is to be found in Mrs Gore's old manuscript cookery book, dated 1718. Here, for the benefit of readers with jaundice, colick, or consumption, is this sovereign old remedy:

Thornbury Snail-Water

"*Take a peck of garden snails* and wash them in a great bowl of bere, then make the chimney very clean and pour out ½ a bushel of charcoles, sett them on fire and when they are kindled throly then make a hole in the middle of them and pour in the snails and water among them and lett them roast *so long as you hear them make a noise*, then take them out with a knife and coarse cloth. Pick them and wipe all the green froth from them very clean, then put them in a stone morter and bruise them shells and all. *Take also a quart of earthworms*, slice and scower them, salt them, wash them and beet them to peices in a morter haveing the pot ready on which the lymbeck must stand, put in it of angellico and salendine each 2 handfulls, then the snails and worms, then a pound of rosemary flowers and of agrimony, bearsfoot, dock roots, bark of barberry-tree-

---

* Local dialect still includes the following: *quist*, wood-pigeon; *oont*, mole; *drough* (pron. "druff"), gout or drain; *bange*, lie out in sun; *spreathed*, sore; *dag*, smallest of a litter; *withywind*, wild clematis; *tissick*, tickling cough; *brivet*, nosing into things, as *ferret*; *bedwind*, convolvulus; *tellet*, loft; *gamut*, play the fool; *cag-mag*, chatterbox; *scrage*, scratch, tear; *daddocky*, rotten; *quomp*, depressed. "It do stink whoopings!" is a phrase I have heard, and it is very expressive if not exactly precise. In a recent *Bulletin* of the Society of Thornbury Folk I was interested to find some of the old call-words which were used to call home cattle and poultry. Among other words were *Chook, chook!*—calling pigs to their food. My grandfather, who used to rear pigs, always used this call, and indeed his nickname among the urchins of the parish was "Chooky Wilshire". *Het* or *Hoit* were horse calls. *Coop, coop, coop* is still in almost universal use to call hens. *Dil, dil* or *widdy-diddy* are for ducks. Many different calls were used for calves, including *goge, boss, rap-rap* and *suck*. These are the very roots of language, onomatopeia that may well be remnants of the speech of the prehistoric Beaker Folk.

wood, sorrel, bittany each 2 handfulls, of rue ½ a handfull, of fennigreg and turmerick each 1 oz., of saffrom beeten to powder the weight of 6d., *then pour in three gall. of the strongest ale large measure*. Lett it stand covered all night in the place you still it, then put to them 3 oz. of cloves beeten and 6 oz. of hartshorn grated or filed."

Two spoonfuls to be taken two hours before meals. After which, I suppose, you wouldn't want the meals! Undoubtedly it is a wonderful remedy, but for my own part I prefer to remain asthmatic.

Before we leave Thornbury, some mention should be made of Mr Tidman's hen. This worthy fowl helped to gather funds for the missionary work of the Congregational Church, and, after her death, was celebrated by a tombstone bearing the following inscription:

December 21st, 1869.

Here lies Tidman's Missionary Hen,
Her contribution's four-pounds-ten;
Although she's dead the work goes on,
As she left seven daughters and a son
To carry on the work that she begun.

SO BE IT.

This memorial was first erected at Thornbury, but later removed to Falfield by the Rev. W. Dove, when he moved from the one place to the other. I trust the poor fowl's remains were also removed.

There is no straight road from Thornbury to Oldbury-on-Severn. They straggle and wander, these lowland lanes, through Moreton and Kington and Cowhill. So that any routes but field-paths tend to be circuitous. There *is* a short-cut across the fields to Oldbury, but having enticed you a mile on the way, it deserts you, fades away and leaves no sign. George and I walked that way last August, taking the path left of Thornbury church which skirts the outer battlements of the castle, beyond a strip of marshy ground which may once have been the moat. A little way along this path we got a good view of Thornbury Castle over a cornfield, its great tower, above the battlements, dominating the more domestic and peaceful manorial buildings; the church tower keeping it company, contributing additional force and dignity.

Having lost the footpath, or rather, the path having lost *us*, we were soon wandering across fields in the general direction of Oldbury, hoping for the best, though (in the case of George) fearing the worst. Eventually we struck the Kington–Oldbury road near Churnmead Farm, and followed it half a mile to the Sheep-wash (as it used to be called), where white posts on the sides of the road betoken a rhine. This is Oldbury Rhine, though elsewhere it would be called a brook. Its channel is not, perhaps, a natural one. In ancient times when this country west of Thornbury was marshland, the brook probably sprawled and straggled all over the place. But at some remote time it was canalised, and so it is a rhine, even though it is a freshwater brook first and a land-drain second. This is the stream whose estuary makes Oldbury Pill. But between the Sheep-dip and the Pill it traverses many an orchard, for Oldbury-on-Severn is a village among orchards, mainly of apple-trees, much of the produce of which will be made into cider.

Chapel Road takes us to Oldbury cross-roads. All along this road are charming cottages among the apple-trees, with jasmine or clematis over the door, neat lawns and roses lining the pathway, periwinkle in the hedge, and hens round the back-door. Liking the place and envying its inhabitants, I remark to my companion on Oldbury's self-sufficiency. It has a little general shop, two pubs, a church and a chapel; it is near the Severn estuary and is on a bus route (two days in the week). What more, I ask, could a man desire? I am told, pretty promptly, that a man might desire nothing more, but that a woman would not be so easily satisfied.

The cross-roads by the chapel might be regarded as the centre of Oldbury. To the left is Pullen's Green, the Anchor, Oldbury Pill and the church; to the right is West End, the Ship and the "Toot". Straight on is Featherbed Lane.

We climbed a stile by Featherbed Lane and found ourselves on the Warth, alongside Oldbury Pill. This is deep and muddy, and barges used to enter it at high water to discharge cargoes near Pill-house. The turf of the Warth is soft and springy, like that of downland, and I was intrigued by the manœuvres of a flock of small birds with long legs. They would run about among the grass above highwater mark, and then, for no obvious reason, all rise into the air suddenly and sweep in an undulating semicircle to the opposite bank, where they would tumble into the grass and start racing about in all directions until something else startled them, when they'd take the air again, as though tossed up by invisible hands, their silvery undersides flashing moment-arily in the sun. Meeting Fred Bennett, who lives in Pill-house and fishes the Kipe Weir at Curty Hole, near High Heron Rock, George asked him if they were dunlin or stint. He didn't know. They were always called "spear" locally, he said. We got talking about the salmon fishing, and he said: "Why don't you come out to Curty with me sometime? You'll have to bring waders, of course. But if you've never seen a weir of kipes on Severn, it'll be an experience for you." I promised that I would, and he set off for Salmon Lodge, where he has a workshop near the sea-wall. George, who had *not* promised to go out to "Curty", assured me that if I went I should certainly catch my death. George is not an "heroic" type.

It is a stiffish walk up the hill from Pullen's Green to the church of St Arilda. But the view from the churchyard is worth it. St Arilda's stands on a knoll, and from it you get a wonderful panor-ama of Vale and estuary. Aust Cliff can be seen between a couple of yew-trees to the south-west. So can the Severn's great sickle-shaped curve north-eastward, with the hills on its farther shore topped by the Forest of Dean, and the Vale of Berkeley in the foreground and to the north-east, concomitant with the estuary. From here it looks quite thickly wooded, and but sparsely in-habited; but that is the result of conspiracy on the part of orchards and hedgerow-elms. An unforgettable scene this, when sunshine and cloud and a hurrying wind dapple it with sunlight and cloud-shadows. It is one of the best places to get a general picture of the Vale. But not so pleasant when a south-westerly gale is blowing. Then you may be glad to escape into the church of St Arilda, content to listen to the sound of the wind buffeting its stout grey walls. A wonderful site for a church, it was (if there's any truth in Oldbury legend) chosen by a cow, or rather, by *two* cows, in somewhat peculiar circumstances. It seems that Oldbury people first tried to build their church on low-lying ground near

Shaw's Green, but what they built during the day was destroyed during the night. So they defied convention and consulted their local Wise Woman on the matter. She told them to yoke together two maiden heifers and let them wander at will. Wherever those two heifers should first stop, there must they build their church.

The heifers were yoked, and they wandered off. At the top of this hill, south of the village, they halted; and here the Oldbury people built their church. And if proof be needed to support the legend, the name of this hill is Cowhill, and there is a hamlet nearby named after it. A former rector of Oldbury used to claim that the present church occupies the site of a Roman temple to Jupiter, and that it may even have been used as a shrine before that, by the Druids. But it is doubtful if modern antiquaries would go so far on such slender evidence.

There's another legend about Oldbury's patron saint. St Arilda is said to have been a pious virgin, foully murdered at or near Kington by a tyrant called Muncius. Her well (all these saints had wells, the curative properties of which were locally famed) was somewhere at the back of what is now St Arilda Guest House on the Kington–Littleton Road. Just opposite, the road is flanked by a dark little copse, where I once spent two miserable hours which I don't suppose I shall ever forget. Because the day had begun well, I set out for Oldbury without hat or coat, but by the time I got to Kington it had begun to rain. It developed into a regular downpour, and I sheltered beneath these trees at the St Arilda cross-roads as the rain fell in sheets and a thunderstorm crackled and roared. I know one shouldn't stand under trees in a thunderstorm, but there didn't seem to be any alternative. At the time, though, I wasn't so much concerned about the storm as annoyed at my own stupidity. For right up to the time I was forced to take shelter, I'd been treasuring the notion of a quiet smoke. Even if there's a cloudburst, I told myself, I can find a bit of shelter and have a pipeful of Old Favourite; and this quiet smoke under the trees would have redeemed the storm and taken the edge off my failure to reach Oldbury. And then, when I'd found a dry spot under a horse-chestnut, I stuck a pipe between my teeth and searched for my tobacco pouch. Without success! Feverishly I turned my pockets inside-out. No

The "Basket" (top) and "Black Letter" (bottom) Bibles in Elberton church

use. I must have forgotten it. The world went black. My tree began to let in the rain. I began to realise that I was cold and miserable. Shortly afterwards a sneeze convinced me I'd caught a cold, and I was obscurely and bitterly glad. It wouldn't have been very difficult to cross that road and knock at the door of the Guest House, but I stayed where I was. What did it matter if I got wet, or was struck by lightning, in this hollow sham of a tobaccoless world! If only I could have had that smoke, the world would have retained its poetry: there would have been a serene pleasure in watching the sheeting rain, listening to the *drip-drip* of raindrops between the great explosions of thunder, seeing the landscape revealed as in a photograph by momentary flashes of lightning. I could have marched into the St Arilda Guest House and acted the jovial traveller even. But without tobacco I was nothing; like a bather who's lost his clothes.

In the end, I took advantage of a lull to "run between the drops". If I'd had to stay in the place much longer I should probably have seen the ghost of St Arilda.

Mr Thurston of Kington once told me there was a religious foundation of some kind near these cross-roads. A pond nearby is still called the "Stir", which suggests that the monks kept fish there. At least, that's what it suggests to Mr Thurston. To me it suggests something rather different and quite irrelevant. It was Mr Thurston—whose ancestors have lived at Kington from time out of mind, and provided Thornbury with many of its mayors—who showed me a very curious document. It is a deed, or agreement, dated 1742, legally drawn up, signed, sealed and witnessed, in which Oldbury church choir solemnly swear to attend every choir-practice on Thursdays "at seven o' the clock", with a fine of Two Pounds (and £2 was a great deal of money in those days) in case of default. Only exceptions to the rule were to be two fishermen, Edw. and Matt. Hunt, who would be excused "if they were obliged to be A'Cunning Putts in Severn". Mr Thurston told me that his ancestor, John Thurston (Gent), who extracted this promise from them, is reputed to have been a music-lover. Apparently the Oldbury choir's failure to practise had rendered their singing past bearing, and, as it happens, their Squire, John Thurston, was in a position to

7*

The Ship Inn, Alveston

enforce his wishes. This document is still kept, framed, in the drawing-room at Kington House.

That phrase "Cunning Putts" reminded me of Aaron Taylor. John and Aaron Taylor were perhaps the most famous of Oldbury's salmon fishermen. And their descendant, Miss Wilcox, who lives at Camp House on the "Toot", still has their old account-books going back to 1802. This record of catches and prices from 1802 to 1847 exhibits some remarkable ups and downs. Prices obtained for the salmon vary from as low as fivepence to as high as ten shillings per lb. Of equal interest and more amusement is a pamphlet printed about 1850 by Jane Brown, Printer, of Thornbury. It has an impressive title:

AARON TAYLOR'S SPEECH
to the
NOBLEMEN IN LONDON
about the
SALMON FISHING
and
His Scheme explained in all points

It seems that Aaron had been asked to present his opinion to a Commission which was enquiring into the salmon fishing. He did so, and was chagrined when they did not put his suggestions into practice. Twenty years later, Aaron told the Commission what he thought of it. His speech begins:

"Don't you mind about Eighteen or Twenty years back you had a Meeting in London to pass a Law for all the Kingdom here the fish much upon the decline in all the rivers through the Kingdom here, and that is the case now, the fish is much upon the decline in all the rivers throughout the Kingdom now, but you could not agree, upon time it came to nothing. Now is there a river in the Kingdom you can say you ever done a bit of good by the Laws you been passing here, in England, Scotland, or Wales?"

Aaron proceeds to give the Noblemen lessons in geography and natural history, wandering from Lapland to Sardinia and describing in detail the life and personal eccentricities of that aristocrat of fish, the Salmon. Sometimes he divagates from the main issue to deliver his opinion on other matters. As when he remarks, "If people do want Salt Salmon, let them buy Fresh Salmon *and salt it theirselves*." His speech is in ripest Gloucestershire. At times, indeed, in Double Glo'ster!

One wishes Aaron were still alive to give us his frank and vigorous opinion on the salmon fishing. I should like to hear him on the subject of river-pollution. . . . However, salmon fishing did not die with Aaron Taylor. Every day in season at low tide, Bob Knapp and George Morgan of Oldbury go forth with their lave-nets to fish from the Standings in Salmon (locally known as "Load") Pool, whilst Fred Bennett of Pill-house fishes Curtis Weir ("Curty"), between Oldbury and Sheperdine.

Bob Knapp lives alone in a cottage among the apple-trees in Chapel Road, and one day last autumn I dropped in for a yarn about the salmon fishing, with particular reference to the Standings in Salmon Pool. He brought out a pile of old parchments, written over in spindly copperplate, and old maps, one dated 1708, showing the scenery of and workings on the river-bed. As we talked and examined these old documents, the sound of wind and rain outside (I had narrowly escaped a thunderstorm) made his fireside, a pipe of tobacco and a glass of Oldbury cider all the more pleasant by contrast.

I was intrigued to know that, when he goes fishing alone at night, Bob Knapp always takes two watches with him. There's no great mystery about it. Indeed, the reason is obvious. If one of them stops, he'll still know the time.

"And why," I asked him, "should time be so important to you?"

Everyone who knows the estuary will know the answer to *that*. When you are dependent on Severn tide, time may be a matter of life or death!

The Standings in "Load" or Salmon Pool are unique. They were erected many centuries ago, and each one (there are now two, but in 1708 there were five) consists of three great blocks of stone, one on top of the other. Usually Bob fishes from one Standing, whilst George Morgan fishes from the other. But sometimes one or other of them will go out alone. And then, if it's after dark, he will take two watches.

Lave-net fishing here is quite different from that farther

upriver, say, on Lydney sands. On the firm sandbanks, lave-net fishermen sight the salmon from boats and pursue them on foot, trying to head them off. Here, in Salmon Pool, the lave-net fisherman waits on the top-step of the Standing, with his rock-staff resting against his shoulder, until a salmon is seen. Then he must mark its course and strike swiftly. It is a question of co-ordinating hand, eye and brain with speed and skill—the skill that's only acquired with long years of practice.

It would take too long to describe here the component parts and fine art of the lave-net. Anyway, it has been fully dealt with (except that he makes no mention of Oldbury Standings) by Brian Waters in his *Severn Tide*, where it is described as "a noble weapon of great antiquity, the last true hunting weapon used in Britain today". Although at first sight it looks unwieldy, and you wonder how a fisherman can use it with sufficient speed to catch a fish in rapid motion, it is amazing how swiftly and easily the fishermen can make their "lave".

Try and imagine yourself out there, on one of those Standings in Salmon Pool. It is night, and all around you lies the strange scenery of the riverbed at low water, under moon and stars. You are quite alone. Since you aren't able to see the fish in the dark-flowing water, you're standing, thigh-deep, on the second step of the Standing with your net held down in the water. So dark is it, that you won't know a salmon's in your net until you feel it strike. Then you must act swiftly, grounding your rock-staff and killing your salmon by striking it with the "knocker" on the head and between the eyes. It will then be left in a specially built rock-pool called the "Cupboard", until you leave for the shore. Having made a catch, you are on your toes. Time passes swiftly. So much so, that you aren't aware of its passing. Your watch has stopped, but you don't let that bother you, because you feel quite sure you haven't been out more than half an hour. And then, to your surprise and mortification, you realise that the level of the pool is rising—you can hear the surging noises of the incoming tide.

You make a dash for it. But you should have left before. During these first five or six minutes of flow, the level of the pool rises five or six feet. And Salmon Pool is a quarter of a mile out from shore. You fight and struggle for it, but you are too late. Just as you have caught your salmon, Severn has caught you. Its grey-brown waters close over you. The coroner's verdict, *if* you are ever found, will be "Death by misadventure. Found Drowned." And discussing you, other salmon fishermen will say, "He ought to 'a known better."

. . . That is why, when Bob Knapp or George Morgan of Oldbury go fishing alone at night, they carry two watches with them, in case one should stop. At the risk of repeating myself: Time can be a matter of life or death on Severn!

Bob Knapp isn't entirely dependent on watches. He gets a queer sort of premonition when it's time to leave, and nearly always his watches confirm its accuracy. Perhaps it is an instinctive warning. It may be that, in his subconscious mind, certain tiny movements of air and water are associated with this necessity to get away before flood-tide. Although this intuitive warning is right nine times out of ten, however, it would be dangerous to rely on it. You have to be right *ten* times out of ten to survive as a salmon fisherman on Severn.

"Still," I asked Bob Knapp, "there must have been times when you've had close shaves, in spite of all your precautions?"

"Oh, I dunno."

But when I persisted, he allowed that he'd once had a bit of a scare. Fortunately he wasn't alone. George Morgan and he had been out in the Pool when a thick fog came down. Fog is their worse enemy, and this was a real pea-souper. They were completely enveloped by it, as though, already, they were at the bottom of the sea. They knew they had time to get ashore, if—and it was a pretty big *if*—they could find their way. For although they knew Severn like the back of their hand, it had become impossible to see anything—every recognisable landmark was blotted out.

They started off, but as they plodded through mud and water, it became increasingly evident that they weren't approaching the bank. They were lost!

And then, miraculously, the fog lifted a fraction, and from the Tidenham shore, opposite, a navigation light winked. It was enough. They were able to get their bearings, and ten minutes later scrambled up the sea-wall—just in time.

Soon after Bob Knapp had told me this story, the boys and

girls began to arrive. For Bob keeps open house for the youth of Oldbury. His cottage is a sort of youth club, where lads and girls can come of an evening for a chat or a game or music on the radiogram. His notion is, that young folk between sixteen and twenty need somewhere to meet, apart from their own homes or pubs. He is a good and generous host, and enjoys their company, for he is still something of a boy at heart and not, therefore, unsympathetic to the Young Idea.

Going back to our walk of last August, from which we were diverted by these stories of church and salmon fishing: George and I got talking to a man in a battered felt hat, who was weeding the churchyard. He told us that the church of St Arilda had nearly been destroyed by fire in the 1890s. Only the fifteenth-century tower and the beautiful mediæval north porch survived. On his advice, we took the green lane opposite the church as a short-cut, and had no cause to regret it. A stony track, bordered by wild-flowers and between high hedges, it is certainly a short cut to Kington.* You might be in the seventeenth century here, for evidences of modern hustle and machinery are (or were, that day) completely absent. No telegraph wires (we spend most of our lives now separated from the sky by a network of wires), no cars, no people. Rabbits scuttered away before us. Small birds fluttered deeper into the hedges. George looked down a hole and stared straight into the bright yellow eyes and brown muzzle of a fox. It was a path into the past between herbaceous borders. There was self-heal, locally known as the carpenters' herb, with its violet-striped tongue and hood, pink-flushed restharrow, yellow meadow-pea, purple tufted vetch, sweet-scented marjoram, wild parsnip and fennel. One rabbit, more venturesome than the rest, sat up and looked at us, curiously, then hopped a short distance down the path and looked back. When he found we were still following, he lolloped on again, and again looked back. Had we carried a gun, or even a catapult, I fear he would have paid even more dearly for his curiosity than Adam and Eve did for theirs. As it was, this Brer Rabbit escaped. He had satisfied his curiosity regarding *homo sapiens*, had maintained his dignity throughout,

---

* Though coming this way you unfortunately miss the charming little hamlet of Cowhill.

and would probably return to the warren with the mien of a hero, lording it over the cowards who had vulgarly fled.

Where the lane returns to the Cowhill–Kington road, there's a farm, surrounded, as are so many of the Vale farms, by apple orchards. Its trees were loaded with little green apples, and I remember thinking that if they all developed into good-sized fruit, the branches would snap. A quarter of a mile on, to the left, another farmhouse looks across fields to the road. Its shape uncompromising, its windows square, its plaster flaking, so that it seems the slightest bit despondent and ashamed of itself. Yet there's something about it that makes you stop and stare. Had I been an artist, I would have painted it, I think. For although it was not—*is* not—beautiful, it has character and what Blooms-buryites call "significance". That farmhouse struck me as being peculiarly interesting, in a stolid, square-cut, self-consciously rather-the-worse-for-wear way. It looked at you, as though it had a story to tell. I told George this, and he said he'd never heard such nonsense in his life!

Soon we passed that dark little copse at the St Arilda cross-roads where I'd spent my tobacco-less vigil already described. Remembering the bitter feelings of that time, I took out the pipe of peace and charged it. Blue smoke-trails drifted behind us on the still evening air, all the way back to Thornbury.

One other memory of that walk remains. It is a picture, briefly glimpsed but vividly remembered, of an orchard at Kyneton Quarr. The orchard was a small one, above the level of the road, and surrounded by a low stone wall. Among the trees a playful young porker was chasing half-a-dozen ducks. He made little grunting rushes at them, whilst they fled from him cackling, waddling awkwardly on bandy legs. He trotted up and looked over the wall, grunted amiably at us, opened his mouth in a piggy grin, and then made another rush at the inoffensive ducks, who by now were in a state of high excitement and indignation.

CHAPTER V

HILL AND SHORE

BETWEEN Thornbury and Berkeley lies some of the most characteristic country of the Vale. Follow almost any of the minor roads from A.38 and you will discover it. Falfield and Stone have both, unfortunately, been gutted by the main road. Otherwise they would be pleasant enough, especially Stone, which has an inviting little Green, flanked by pleasant, though unremarkable, cottages. But no village can survive a trunk-road through the middle of it. Æsthetically and socially, the main road, with its unceasing flow of traffic, destroys the character and individuality of the place. Falfield and Stone have, in effect, been filleted: their backbones removed.

Does this metaphor seem mixed when, hitherto, I have mentioned A.38 as backbone of the Vale? Perhaps it is. But, as I see it, a village only remains strongly individual and independent so long as it is self-contained; so long as, coming into it, you can feel you have arrived somewhere. And that is what you cannot feel about Falfield or Stone. They are *termini* on the way to Gloucester or Bristol; places you pass through; events in a journey. Dominated by the ribbon of white which cuts right through them, their houses look out to the road which connects them to the cities, and substitutes a moving current of urban commercial life for any static and personal life of their own.

However, both to the east and west of A.38 there's plenty of country unspoilt. To the west, towards Severn, are Hill, Rockhampton and Sheperdine. To the east are Tytherington and Cromhall, Tortworth and Michaelwood. For the moment we are looking westward, so I propose we explore this country together, following the sea-wall path from Oldbury to Berkeley, and coming back via Whitcliff Park, Hill and Rockhampton. This is fine country for rambling, with a wide variety of scene in small compass. Yet I've never encountered other walkers here, and can only suppose that, apart from the walk along the sea-wall, which is famous, this country around Hill and Rockhampton is little known.

Back, then, to Oldbury-on-Severn for the first stage of our exploration. Climb the stile by Oldbury Pill, and you are on the sea-wall at once, in country that is a little like downland. It was here that I saw the flock of *spear*, and George asked Fred Bennett about them. And that reminds me. . . . Didn't I promise to go out to "Curty" with him one day? Well, then, this is a good time to go; because "Curty" is about a mile on the way to Sheperdine, opposite Salmon Lodge in the direction of High Heron Rock, and right in our way.

On a gusty day of intermittent sunshine and cloud, I sat on the sea-wall here, smoking a pipe and watching, with philosophic detachment, the evolutions of a ladybird on a sow-thistle. It was on the landward slope that I was sitting, not a stone's throw from Salmon Lodge—to which, in former times, the wives of Severn fishermen used to come to take and prepare the shrimps as they were brought in, alive and kicking, from the forewells (vor'eels) of the "fixed engines" offshore. The "fixed engines" at "Curty" are *kipes*, or—as they used to be called—*putts*.

On this, the landward side of the grass-covered sea-wall, grow sea-asters and restharrow. On the side facing Severn there are fewer flowers, and the sea-wall slopes down to mud which is in process of being colonised by cord-grass. This has already been mentioned in connection with the Warth between New Passage and Aust, where it is transforming many acres of mud into meadowland. Here, there is only a fringe of cord-grass. But it is spreading, and Fred Bennett is not exactly jubilant. This grass, which is tough and fibrous, can grow on saltings which are underwater twice a day and impregnated with salt. It forms clumps: spreads, unites, colonises. And its tough leaves collect more and more mud around them until it has built up a new shelf of land for itself, only awash at unusually high tides. Introduced to this part of Severn by a former squire of Hill, Jenner Fust, it has seriously damaged some of the basket fisheries, for a salmon's instinct will not allow it to swim over grass, probably because it is a danger-signal denoting that the salmon has left the main stream and is in flood-water.

There are few places so pleasant as the estuary on a fine day! A boisterous wind sets the trees a-roaring, and gratuitously combs and brushes and then disarranges one's hair, like a playful child. Sea-birds cry above the mud of the river, whilst swallows sweep along the hedges on this side of the sea-wall on their sickle-shaped wings. It is no place for people who like to be in a crowd. Yet, although it is lonely, there's plenty of activity here: plenty to see and hear.

Of the man I had come to see, however, there was no sign. Far out across the mud I could just distinguish a row of kipes, and even as I scanned them, a diminutive figure waved, and I waved back. Not that Mr Bennett is diminutive; he isn't. But on the river-bed, distances can be deceptive to a landsman. In general, things seen on or across the river are farther away than they look.

Mr Bennett made a movement as if beckoning me to come out to him. So I took off my shoes, slipped on waders, and climbed down to the mud—carefully, because I had no desire to begin this exploration by falling, head first, into Severn mud.

Through the cord-grass the going was good. Then I got into the soft, squelchy mud beyond, which grew deeper and more sticky at every step. When I put my foot down it seemed as if it would never touch anything solid, and when it did, it slithered. Not only that, either. When I tried to pull it up to make the next step, mud and waders only parted company with great reluctance. It was rather like wading in a sea of glue. Alarming at first, but you soon get used to it. When I came across Mr Bennett's footmarks, with the padmarks of his dog alongside, I followed them out to the first row of kipes, with their great mouths (five or six feet across) gaping up-river like a row of hungry pelicans.

Pointing out to me how the fishery took advantage of a little valley in the river-bed, here more undulating and curious than on the flat sandbanks, Fred Bennett proceeded to initiate me into some of the secrets of basket-fishing. These "fixed engines"—as they are legally termed—form the figure of a flat-bottomed V. The two slanting sides are formed by a basketwork fence called a leader, or hedge, and this checks the salmon when it tries to break out of the pool, heading it back into the mouths of the kipes, which close the pool and form the base of the figure. If the salmon elects to remain in the pool and refuses to enter a kipe, he is caught with a lave-net. Otherwise he will be found in the basket, his head in the forewell, his body in the butt.

On the subject of kipe-baskets, Mr Bennett pointed out that they resembled the Holy Trinity in that they were three-in-one and one-in-three. First, there's the mouth of the basket, called the *kipe*. Then the waist, or *butt*. And lastly, the easily detachable *forewell*, a bottle-shaped basket which is designed as a trap for small fish, eels and shrimps. The opening at the extremity of the forewell is stopped-up with kelp (seaweed), and even this "stopping" of the "vor'eel", Mr Bennett told me, calls for an expert. If it is not done properly the ebb will push it out, like a cork from a bottle, and the fish will escape.

Everything has its distinctive name, which may vary somewhat up- or down-river. For instance, the curved shoulder-basket which the fisherman wears to carry home his catch is known locally as a *welch*, whilst upriver it is called a *witcher*. Likewise the smaller openwork baskets which are used only for salmon-fishing (other fish pass through them) are here known as *putchers*, whilst in other parts of the river they are called *putcheon*.

The old fishermen who taught Fred Bennett in his youth had a language of their own, full of local terms and technicalities. "You see this what I'm doin' now?" he said. He was taking the kelp "stopping" from a forewell and tipping it up so that a shower of shrimps, eels and flatfish fell into his welch. "Well, the man who taught me as a boy always called this 'Cunning out the vor'eels'." At once I thought of that phrase in Mr Thurston's old document, wherein Edw. and Matt. Hunt were absolved from attending choir-practice if "they were obliged to be A'Cunning Putts in Severn".

Casually, he delved into the welch to pick out a couple of tiny sand-dabs, which were still flapping about among the shrimps, and tossed them over his shoulder. He also threw away a baby whiting, about two inches long, dead, with its mouth wide open, literally at its last gasp!

One of the kipes had caught a putcher, probably discarded by a basket-fisherman upriver. Mr Bennett pulled it out and threw it away. He obviously didn't think much of putchers. "There's nothing in them things," he said. "No skill at all. . . . Now *this* basket"—laying his hand affectionately on the side of a kipe he had woven himself from withy and hazel wands—"is *made*." I had to agree. The putcher does look simple and primitive alongside the magnificent trilogy of kipe-butt-forewell. And indeed the kipe is the most efficient method ever devised for fishing with "fixed engines". It will catch anything from a shrimp to a sturgeon, yet its history goes back thousands of years.

Bob Knapp has told me that he's found old kipes of great antiquity when the river-current has scoured out part of a bank in which they were buried. Black with age, they must have been centuries old, and Bob Knapp maintains that they were better made than any modern ones.

"Did you never keep one of them?" I asked.

He shook his head.

"They crumble away in a few hours. I suppose it's being exposed to the air, after being buried so long."

Both Fred Bennett and Bob Knapp complain that the catches have fallen off badly in the last five or six years. Like most fishermen they blame pollution and cord-grass. Pollution, because it poisons the fish before they can reach the spawning-beds in mid-Wales; cord-grass, because it colonises mud-flats and diverts the channel to the detriment of basket-weirs. Fred Bennett doubted if pollution could be entirely responsible for the decline, because "the degree of dilution in the estuary ought to make the waters safe". Bob Knapp thought pollution *must* be to blame, because the catch was best in the early months and subsequently fell off, which suggested to him that in the early months the volume of fresh-water coming down was sufficient to make pollution innocuous, whereas later in spring and summer when the volume of "fresh" decreased, pollution would be more apparent. Bob Knapp blames the city of Gloucester, which at present turns the whole of its sewage into the tidal reach of the river close to the town. This sewage can't get away to sea in a single tide. It goes backwards and forwards with the ebb and flow as far as Minsterworth, seven miles below Gloucester. Although Gloucester council have long intended to do something about this, it has not been done at the time of writing. Until it is, the catches of Severn salmon will go on decreasing.

That the salmon fishing has declined is very evident, for early this century the average salmon catch from the nets on Severn was 24,140 fish. In the 1920s it dropped to something like 17,000. In 1936 it was 15,000, but in 1940 it was down to 4,294, and each year it is getting less. Superfluous to add that this, in days of food shortage, is a scandalous state of affairs. To my mind it is symptomatic of the age we live in. Whilst we make large plans to conquer space, wipe out disease, exploit atomic power and the like, the elementary principles of life and sensible economy are ignored. There should be no question of building a Severn Barrage or any other large-scale public utility in the county until something has been done about the disgusting and unhealthy practice of using one of our greatest rivers as a sewage-ditch. Not that Gloucester is at all exceptional, of course. Many rivers fare worse than Severn. Some in the North and Midlands are poisoned with acids, discoloured by chemicals, and thick with sewage and refuse. One of our best and cheapest sources of food supply has been all but ruined by the irresponsible methods of crude disposal adopted by local authorities and factories. It is surely high time that some central authority was empowered to investigate all cases of river-pollution, with powers to insist on alternative methods of disposal in the case of untreated sewage and harmful dyes and chemicals. The ironical thing is, that our land has never been in greater need of natural fertilisers. All that sewage which is dumped into our rivers or sluiced into the sea ought to be going back into the soil of England. The old days of the earth-closet at the end of the back-garden are decried. It was unhygienic, objectionable, etc. But was it more unhygienic, objectionable, etc., to bury sewage in the garden where it would enrich and fertilise the soil, than to turn it into our rivers and streams, which are the veins and arteries of the countryside, where it destroys all the fish and plant-life, turns a beautiful waterway into a stinking sewer, and that when the land is crying out for organic manures? I do not see progress here, nor true economy. It is all too typical of the false values, silly prudery, and confusion between convenience and improvement that are a sign of the times.

Pollution (whether of air, water or food) is one of my pet abominations, and you must forgive my heat if you can. It is a subject on which I feel strongly. One of the few causes for which

I am prepared to mount a soap-box. One of my favourite didactic poems is Gordon Bottomley's *To Iron-Founders and Others*, which begins:

> When you destroy a blade of grass
> You poison England at her roots:
> Remember no man's foot can pass
> Where evermore no green life shoots.

And proceeds to point out that:

> Your worship is your furnaces,
> Which, like old idols, lost obscenes,
> Have molten bowels; your vision is
> Machines for making more machines.

But what am I saying? Where am I? I was out with Fred Bennett A'Cunning Putts at "Curty" before these bees began buzzing in my bonnet. And Mr Bennett, who isn't as young as he used to be, was admitting that he wasn't too keen on coming out to "Curty" at night.

"'Tis rather lonely out here at night," he said, with—to my mind—remarkable understatement. It was lonely enough in day-time out there, amid that strange country of mud-flats and rocks and sandbanks, ebbing pools and water-channels, above which the sea-birds wheeled and screamed. What it is like during the hours of darkness, I cannot conjecture, but lonely is surely an inadequate description. I asked Mr Bennett if it was at all danger-ous. Supposing, for instance, he slipped in the mud and twisted his ankle? "In that case," he said, "I should either try and crawl, which wouldn't be easy owing to the depth of mud; or I should drown. Years ago, when I was young, there were more fisheries, and they caught more fish, so that you'd usually see a couple of men going out to the kipe-weirs. Nowadays there's few who take up to it, and with the catches dropping off, I'm doubtful if the younger generation will take on the job. It's too much like hard work."

Calling his dog to heel, Mr Bennett led the way back through the mud. "Now, there!" he exclaimed. "When I was telling you what might happen out here if I was to slip down and couldn't get up, I forgot the dog. Yet that's why I bring him. He'd be a useful messenger, you see."

"He certainly would."

"Of course," Mr Bennett mused, "there's not much chance of my doing anything silly. I know the way as well as I know my own back-garden. I could find my way blindfold. And, as you've seen, the actual weir is as safe as houses."

"Yes," I said.

But I was thinking of a tragedy which I'd recently come across, and which may, for all I know, have occurred at this very weir. It happened about 1850, and it is told by Peter Peregrin (alias Thomas King, of Berkeley) in a booklet of *Sunday Afternoon Rambles*, reprinted from the *Berkeley Gazette* in 1898. One of these rambles was to Oldbury, where Thomas King had tea with a farmer who rented the fishery in question, and who told him the story of the tragedy. After explaining that there was very little time between the tides in which to make the journey out to the weir to collect the fish, this farmer said:

> "On a very dark winter's night a man in the employ of my father went down into the river [to collect the fish], when unfortunately he got caught and surrounded by the rising tide. When he saw his perilous situation, the poor fellow evidently made great efforts to save his life. He must have groped about in the dark until he found the highest part of the basket-weir, upon which he climbed, and cried and shouted for help. His calls for assistance were heard, but as they were not understood the ill-fated man had to stand there, on that dark and dismal night, for three or four hours, watching the fatal waters rise slowly but surely until they were above his head and his cries were hushed in death. On the morrow, his lifeless body was found entangled in a salmon basket, the weight of his body having broken in the basketwork."

I did not tell Mr Bennett this sad story, because I didn't want to depress him. And I only tell it here because several people have assured me that there is no real danger in walking out to a salmon weir and "Cunning Putts".

Soon Fred Bennett and I were sitting in his workshop behind Salmon Lodge, and he was showing me the implements he uses for basket-weaving. This is done during the winter months when there's no fishing. Every year some of the baskets have to be replaced, for wear and tear is rapid on the river-bed of Severn. Taking a bottle off the shelf, Mr Bennett asked me if I'd like a swig of cider. I said I would, and he handed me over the bottle, so that I could drink first. It was Oldbury cider, the Real Thing, with plenty of "heart" and "body" in it. Those who prefer their cider light and gaseous may not like it, but it's a good drink, even though, as a local wag assured me, "it rots your socks".

Crossing Newlands Gout and passing the footpath to Jobs-green Farm, you come to "the Windbound". Everybody calls it "the Windbound", but the actual name of this little pub is the New Inn, Sheperdine. It crouches under the sea-wall, with its bedroom windows so near to it that you could jump out of them on to the grassy bank. A curious place with a strange character is "the Windbound". It received its more familiar name in the days when sailing barges tied up there. The channel of Severn comes close inshore at Sheperdine, and it was convenient to tie up and have a drink. Sometimes, if the company was lively, the trow-men didn't stop at one or two. They kept on drinking till they couldn't stand up. And when they reached their destination—at Bristol, or Gloucester—they would explain away their late arrival by saying they'd been "windbound".

On the Warth, beyond the sea-wall, lies the hulk of the old barge *Onward*. At least, it did when I was there last; but Morris Bennett, landlord of the Windbound for forty-six years, was, even then, busy breaking it up for winter firing. So by the time this book is published, the *Onward* may be no more than a memory. That was a day in late January, and, although I have seen Sheper-dine in all kinds of weather, in summer, and autumn, and winter, on this day I saw it at its best. I had walked the four or five miles from Thornbury, through flat marshy country with high roads flanked by rhines along which reeds rattled in the wind and tiny wrens flittered like dead leaves, in the hope that I might find Mr Palmer, the Severn lightkeeper at home. Where two roads cross on these flat-lands, there are usually white wooden railings to prevent speeding car or homing toper from falling into a rhine. These are just the right height to sit on, and when I got home I discovered a white stripe across the seat of my trousers. Although my mission was fruitless, Mr Palmer having gone off rabbiting for the day, there was no cause for regret. It was good to sit on

Thornbury: Castle Street, from The Plain

the sea-wall, watching the miniature waves run up the mud and in among the cord-grass. Looking out over the river estuary to the enchanted country on the other side, I felt a little like Christian in *Pilgrim's Progress*, except that I hadn't braved any perils on the way and didn't particularly want to cross over. But that other shore, opposite, was like another world: a dream-world—insubstantial, timeless and lovely. It was nearly high water, and the rustling noise of the tide with that surge-and-sigh of encroaching wavelets brought a whisper of ocean to Sheperdine. I don't think I've ever known a day so perfect for colour—not in spring with all its bursting greens, not summer in full bloom, nor yet autumn tapestried in red and gold. The fields were emerald, and seemed to glow with a light of their own. To describe them as carpets would be to write them down, for no carpet ever looked so lustrous, soft and fine. Clumps of rushes and withered sedge cried out to be painted. Those tall reeds which carry plumes of bronze in autumn had turned a lovely silver-gold colour, and the sight of them, waving gently against a blue sky, flecked with lambswool cloud, was moving, even to one with no artistic pretensions. Trees stood out, naked and stark, in burnt sienna. But, best of all, I recall the sight of white gulls walking on chocolate-coloured mud, just beyond the frilled hem of the tide. Wavelets sparkled behind them, and beyond that again were the serene and unattainable meadows of the other side, with the wooded hilltops of the Forest on the horizon. The wind sighed; the gulls cried; the tide whispered; my heart sang that song by Ivor Gurney:

> *Severn's most fair today!*
> *See what a tide of blue*
> *She pours, and flecked alway*
> *With gold, see what a crew*
> *Of sea-gulls snowy white*
> *Float round her to delight*
> *Villagers, travellers.*

Sheperdine, or Shipperdine, as many of the local folk prefer, may have taken its name from the Danish ships which beached here in Anglo-Saxon times. Sometimes you see it spelt Shepherdine, and it has even been suggested that sheep were once kept here, and that this is the true basis of the name. But Miss Wilcox,

8   113

Salmon-fishing with a lave-net from Oldbury Standings

of Oldbury, dismisses this as an absurdity, for the land hereabouts, she told me, is too low-lying for sheep, and it was probably a good deal *more* marshy in olden times. There was anciently a chapel on the shore, the site of which is now occupied by Chapel Cottages, a group of sturdy stone-built cottages which lie out beyond the sea-wall, facing Severn. It may be that the four outside walls are the original walls of the chapel. Brian Waters evidently thinks so, for he traces the changes which have come to this building, first a chapel, then a farmhouse (Mrs Bennett, of the Windbound, remembers when the top floor was panelled in black oak, which was later taken out along with a fine oak staircase when it was converted), and now cottages.

Two or three hundred yards along the sea-wall is another house, painted white, alongside which are two navigation "lights". This house, too, lies beyond the protection of the sea-wall, out on the Warth. Aptly named "White House", it is the home of the Severn lightkeeper, Mr Palmer. The purpose of these and other lights is, of course, to aid navigation of the Severn at night. Each light has several different colours, and this helps the pilot to find the channel, which at Sheperdine runs close inshore.

When I passed this way on an overcast day between summer and autumn a year or two ago, I was lucky enough to come across Mr Palmer, leaning over his garden gate. He told me that he takes care of the lights down as far as Beachley and Aust, and once every week he goes down to the island of St Tecla's (or St Twrog's) off the Beachley peninsula, to attend to the light there.

He told me that the names used on the Ordnance Map for various parts of the river are not the names by which they are known to local folk. For instance, they don't speak of Pillhouse Rocks, but of the Inward Rocks, or, more familiarly, the Innards. The Slime Road of the map is better known as the Barnacle Channel. He went on to give me equivalents for each part of the river-channel and every group of rocks from Aust to Sharpness. Having lived beside her all his life (he was born beside Berkeley Pill), there isn't much Mr Palmer doesn't know about tidal Severn. I asked him if he didn't sometimes get flooded out of his house; if it wasn't tempting Providence to build beyond the sea-wall. But he assured me it was quite all right. "Sometimes a high tide will wash the front. It may even come into the garden," he said, but obviously he attached little importance to it, regarding it as the most natural thing in the world.

"Don't you ever feel lonely out here?" I asked, for his house stands quite alone except for the lights, with no road to it, only a footpath on top of the sea-wall, the silence unbroken except by the cries of sea-birds and lapping of the tide, and, at night, the syrens of ships going upriver to Sharpness Dock.

"Lonely?" he exclaimed. "Good Lord, no! Why should I be lonely? There's plenty to do and plenty to see here. And if I want company, there's always the Windbound."

I asked if he saw many wild-birds, and he told me that it was one of the advantages of living there. He had seen a few redshank go up that day, the first of the autumn migration. From his windows Mr Palmer sees dunlin and turnstones, oyster-catchers and cormorants, herons and wildfowl of all kinds feeding on the open grassland beside the river or on the saltings. He looks upon them as familiar friends.

Whilst we were talking, a few spots of rain fell.

"Ah, I see it's spitting a bit in the wind," he commented.

"That's bad," said I, "for I haven't a coat or hat."

"You won't need 'em!"

"How can you tell?"

"Well, you've only to look at they birds." He pointed to a couple of sea-gulls, flapping downriver. Even as he pointed, one of them suddenly twisted, banked, stalled and gave a little flutter before flying on. Then the other bird repeated the manœuvre. It was as though they were catching flies.

"That's always a sign o' fair weather," Mr Palmer assured me.

His prediction proved correct that day, for after "spitting in the wind" a bit, the drizzle stopped and it almost looked as if the sun might break through.

We went on to talk of river fishing. Mr Palmer helps Tommy Cornock with the Severn House weir, usually known as Hayward Rocks ("Ha'ard"), and has woven many a kipe. Before long we were comparing Then and Now. On Severnside, and where salmon fishing is concerned, the comparison is one-sided except in the matter of price per pound. When he was a boy, Mr Palmer told me, he used to help his father with the long-net off Berkeley Pill. They had then caught between 3 and 4 cwt. on a tide. I asked how much they might catch now with a long net, fishing the same area.

"We'd be lucky to get 28 lb., I reckon. You see, 'tisn't only the pollution coming downstream, there's all the burnt-oil from the ships going back and forth to Sharpness. It's inevitable with all the traffic there is on the river today."

It was with reluctance that I left Mr Palmer, for there were still many things I wanted to know. But I had planned to walk to Berkeley, and to have stayed yarning any longer would have imperilled my time-table. I didn't want to find myself wandering, at nightfall, somewhere near the mouth of Berkeley Pill. So I set off at a brisk pace for Hill Pill.

Crossing the bridge over the Pill, I met a man with a gun in one hand and a couple of dead rabbits in the other.

"Excuse me," he said. "Have you come along the sea-wall from Sheperdine?"

When I said I had, he murmured, "Dammit! Now it won't be any good going along there. You've probably scared every rabbit for miles."

With which flattering and friendly salutation, he passed gloomily on his way.

He hadn't gone two hundred yards before I heard him fire, and shots kept breaking the silence thereafter, so his pessimism was apparently unjustified.

Hill Pill was planned and made in 1750 by Sir Francis Fust of Hill Court. The same gentleman repaired Hill church, and his epitaph records these works without false modesty:

> To drain this parish from the daring flood,
> To model and repair this house of God
> Are paterns good I set to future time,
> Free profit yours, the cost and labour mine.

Perhaps it is no bad thing to remind the Present sometimes of the immeasurable debt it owes the Past.

Hill Pill is spanned by an impressive bridge. Before you reach it, you wonder what on earth it is. Then, as you get nearer, you speculate on the size of the creek it spans. This proves to be an anticlimax, for it is no more than a muddy ditch. Beside it, in a small field containing the ruins of an army hut, grows the Holy Thorn. It is not a very vigorous tree. Its trunk lies along the ground, with two spurs, like horns, carrying a meagre foliage. But its holiness is proved by the fact that it blooms at Christmas. There's a local legend that it grew from Joseph of Arimathea's staff when he landed and preached here at Hill. Readers may have heard a similar legend connected with the Holy Thorn at Glastonbury. I am not prepared to say that one is a ghost of the other, for I suppose that Joseph of Arimathea is just as likely to have come ashore at Hill as at Glastonbury, and I should be the last to discredit a good legend. Some writers suggest that the tree was more likely planted by a priest at Sheperdine to attract pilgrims, but that is surely to take a sceptical view, both of the Holy Thorn and of the mediæval priesthood.

There is no doubt that this thorn-tree does bloom at Christmas and is certainly very old. Moreover, attempts by Mr Palmer and others to propagate cuttings from it have never proved successful, and that, in itself, indicates an unnatural (even supernatural) origin! It was near Hills Flats that I came across four or five plants of that lovely wildflower the marsh-mallow. It is not a common flower in this part of the country, so it was with interest that I examined its pale pink chalice with the scarlet stamen. Marsh-mallow used to be considered a very good remedy for coughs, but it has been ousted by proprietary lozenges and peppermints now.

A bit farther on I began to notice increasing numbers of small waders on the salting beyond the sea-wall. Although I didn't have binoculars with me, I noted them down as dunlin, curlew, sandpiper and ringed plover; the latter a handsome, jaunty little bird with a bobbing action at once nervous and curious.

Above Hill, a tiny patch of woodland represents all that is left of the old Horwood Forest, which once stretched from Bristol to Berkeley. Sometimes it provides the Berkeley Hunt with a fox, but apart from that is of little interest or value. Hereabouts the sea-wall has been completely rebuilt. The original wall, which, like the one we've been following from New Passage, dated from the Middle Ages, was broken down in several places by the exceptionally high tides and south-westerly gales of 1945. Adjoining farmland was seriously flooded, and as this section of sea-wall had long been a weak spot, the council decided to build a wall which would effectively frustrate Severn tides. The new sea-wall is as different from the original as chalk is from cheese! It is far higher, thicker and stronger, with massive concrete buttresses, parapet and promenade. All the same, I prefer the old one, which is merely a ramp of earth, faced with grey stones on the river side, and overgrown with grass and wildflowers to landward. To the rambler there is the difference between walking along a pleasant barrow-like ramp of earth, on which you may find wildflowers and even mushrooms, and tramping along a concrete promenade which is as harsh to the feet as to the eyes. An engineer would see it differently, no doubt; but for my part I like the economy of the old builders who, without the aid of concrete mixers, cranes or excavators, made a wall which was both durable and beautiful because it fitted in with the scene. I may be unfair to the designer, but it seems to me that this new wall was designed to look well on paper, to be impressive. And that is a little ridiculous, since this is lonely unfrequented country, with no one to be impressed.

Severn House Farm stands in the lee of this new sea-wall, a little over halfway between Sheperdine and Berkeley Pill. A good-looking place in itself, it is horribly disfigured by two great cylinders perched halfway up the front wall, like stranded submarines. On enquiring about these of the farmer's wife, I was told that they held the farm's water-supply, which had to be pumped across a couple of fields. This good lady also told me about the breaching of the sea-wall by the storms of 1945. Flooding was so bad that but for the prompt action of the council the land near Severn might have deteriorated into salt-marsh. She thought that it would be a long day before the new sea-wall was breached, and I had to agree.

Near Severn House there are steps leading down to the muddy foreshore, and beyond that, about a hundred yards out in the bed of the river, is Hayward's Weir, fished by Tommy Cornock. At first I attributed the noise I could hear to an express-train, but when it persisted I looked for another cause and traced it to this salmon weir, which lies across the tail of a pool. Beyond the kipes is a shallow fall, and it was this which was making the noise which sounded exactly like a fast train. Away upriver lay the hulk of the *Rameses II*, which had run aground on Saniger Sands that summer. There she lay, as if about to turn into Sharpness dock—firmly and finally aground on those sands which are such a menace to Severn shipping. She had been only half a mile from Sharpness dock when, breaking away from the tugs which were towing her, she ran aground. The cargo of Russian maize was later salvaged from her hold, but the vessel, a steamer of nearly 5,000 tons, was a total loss.

It was a humid, overcast day, with the smoke from chimneys at Sharpness drifting lazily across the Severn in the direction of the doomed steamer. Smoke is of far greater significance in flat country. It is a signal, and to vessels steaming up the estuary it is often the first indication of a port. Newport, Cardiff, Swansea, Avonmouth, Lydney and Sharpness each flaunt their plume of smoke, like active volcanoes.

Above Severn House Farm I saw a heron fishing in a pool beside the sea-wall. It looked up at my approach, and then, laboriously, flapped away at a steadily increasing speed in the direction of Aylburton Warth. Before I'd gone half a mile, and when crossing a bridge over a small gout, I saw another heron, which had been pondering over the rivulet at the bottom of the gout, get up and beat away riverwards. Soon after that I came across a small enclosure in the corner of a field which contained stacks of putchers, butts and kipes, along with materials for making more. Unfortunately there was no one about whom I could ask, or I would have tried to contact the fisherman. In any event, the daylight was now fast waning, and I still had to get to Berkeley. The path had disappeared, so I turned right to avoid the mouth of Berkeley Pill, near a strange little building which would have puzzled me greatly had I not been told to look out for it by Mr Palmer. Somewhat resembling a miniature windmill without sails, it is called the Summerhouse. Isaac Taylor's map of 1777 shows it, and it seems likely that it was built about 1700. It was one of a pair. But the other summerhouse, on the opposite side of Berkeley Pill, has long disappeared. More gazebo than summerhouse, it is charmingly situated, with a splendid view of the river from its eminence.

Apparently this Summerhouse used to be a favourite place to picnic. It had one great natural advantage: the business of boiling a kettle being tremendously simplified by the fact that you could collect *real driftwood* for the fire. It was, of course, necessary to fix the day so that it would synchronise with an ebbing tide, and then one could cross the inshore belt of mud by stepping-stones to the hard red gravelly sand which led to Bull Rock. This is a comparatively flat expanse of red sandstone with rock pools populated by shrimps and small fish and sometimes a conger eel.

"Picnics at the Summerhouse," writes a local man, "were often part of a fishing expedition along the foreshore with a boat and net for the catching of soles and flatfish. This was a wholeheartedly mudlarking performance, particularly elaborated for the inexperienced. Dorney of Sheperdine, a real old-timer in the fishing business, was an expert at initiating the newcomer, and he thoroughly entered into the spirit of the thing after a mug or two of Sherry, which he allowed was the best cider he'd ever tasted. When the net came ashore for the shaking out of the fish, it was a good bet that the enthusiastic novice would be on the spot to pick up the fish. That was the moment for old Dorney's signal and his shout of 'Shuck um, SHUCK UM!' was followed by a shower of liquid mud and fish—a most pervasive mixture!"

Hamfield Farm, nearby, was the scene, in 1888, of a prize-fight which is still talked of in Berkeley. It began at the unearthly hour of five o'clock in the morning, and a carriage waited conveniently but inconspicuously at a strategic point for a quick getaway if the police arrived. I have heard it said that the fight was arranged by Lord Francis FitzHardinge, who was extremely keen on pugilism. Indeed, he was reckoned to be a fair exponent of fisticuffs himself, though he was small of stature. Nicknamed "the Giant", Lord Francis had the reputation of being a bit of a despot locally, but he was respected, too, by many of his dependants and tenants. Going back to the prize-fight, it is said that when, at last, the police arrived on the scene the pugilists had so punished each other that they could not be recognised at a few paces distant by reliable witnesses. My local informant comments: "It may be, of course, that the police were unfortunate in collecting only shortsighted spectators at the ringside."

Hamfield Farm is in the ancient manor of Ham, and John Smyth of Nibley says:

"This Manor of Hame (which I conceive to bee of it selfe without addition by patches at any time bought in or laid unto it, *the fairest of the wholl county of Glouc.*) was amongst many others granted by Kinge H. 2. in the first of his raigne to Robert the sonne of Hardinge and his heiress; by which deed also hee was, according to the manner of those ancient times, created a Baron and a peere of the Realme."

From Hamfield Farm I followed a track to a lane which presently brought me to the Mill. Here I turned sharp left, following a pathway past some cottages and beside the Little Avon, over-shadowed by trees. Although the "shades of night were falling fast" and I was hurrying to catch my bus from the Square at Berkeley, I couldn't help noticing that this would be rather a pleasant place to saunter, if one had the time. A boy and a girl whom I passed evidently thought so. They were so absorbed, so intent on each other, that I don't believe they were even conscious of my existence. Ah, well—

> *In delay there lies no plenty,*
> *Then come kiss me, sweet-and-twenty!*
> *Youth's a stuff will not endure.*

★　　★　　★　　★

Having explored Severn shore, we can turn to the inland countryside between Thornbury and Berkeley. This is one of the most interesting quarters of the Vale. Diverse in character, it cannot be described in general terms. So we'll catch the bus up to the Lower Stone turning on A.38, before setting out for Hill and Rockhampton. It is curious how, of many bus journeys, one will stand out in the memory whilst dozens of others fade into limbo. I suppose the reason is that on that one day, at that certain time, one was preternaturally aware of one's surroundings, "alert to the minutiæ of the scene", or "abnormally responsive to external stimuli", as one might say if one were one of the present-day booksy boys.

I remember travelling from Thornbury up to Hardwicke on a cold, bright day in winter, when some of the little orchards of Upper Moreton and Knap were so brightly illuminated by the winter sunshine, picked out in such perfect and delightful detail, that they looked almost too good to be true. The grass was so lush and green that you couldn't believe your eyes, and the slush of mud round the gates, the rosy piglets nuzzling into a complacent sow, the rainwater butts on which you could plainly see knots in the wood and splash-marks where the water had run over, looked as though they'd all been got ready for some immaculate artist who hadn't shown up yet. Little girls with bright scarves played in front of cottages in Falfield. A foal started up at the sound of our bus, and galloped round and round his field, kicking up his heels. On the ponds beside the road at Knap and Falfield I saw a pair of mallard as well as the usual coots and moorhens and a gaggle of domestic geese.

Falfield is in itself of little interest, though the surrounding countryside is worth exploring, and it will later be dealt with. But we are going on now to Stone, to make a journey to the interior, to discover what sort of country lies between Thornbury and Berkeley, A.38 and Severn. The by-road beside the black-and-white Crown had recently been resurfaced, and the gravel gleamed in the sun, turning the road into a ribbon of white which coiled between fields and farms. A modest road, too; for it carefully avoids all natural obstacles instead of charging straight into and through them as our trunk roads do, and as the Roman roads did. Every corner has its peculiar excitement; the thrill of finding out what's beyond it. And such roads have a pleasant habit of granting you tantalising glimpses and then, at last, rushing you into a village before you're properly aware of it. For my part, you can keep your Roman roads, if I can have an English lane; twisting, turning, doubling back on itself, maddeningly, tantalisingly beautiful.

However, I am anticipating. . . . I must go back to that bridge over the brook on the Lower Stone road, where I stopped to smoke a pipe and watch the rippling stream beneath. The water looked lifeless, despite the fact that there was plenty of movement and no sign of chemical pollution. But I noticed that the pebbles on the bottom were black with tar. One of the most frequent causes of pollution in the streams hereabouts is by tar-acids which have been washed from nearby roads by surface-water. Such streams are ruined, their water poisoned, because they are being used as convenient drains. Readers will know, by this time (if they have read continuously and aren't just *dipping*), that the pollution of air and water is one of the noisiest bees in my bonnet. I hope you will bear with me, even if you don't agree with me. River-pollution is one of my pet grouses. I don't know what I'd do without it, for a good grouse is as necessary to the heart of man (or woman) as a good scratch is to the heart of a dog. And just to demonstrate that I am not a mere gloom merchant, I will add that that bridge possessed a treasure which yielded me delight. It was a small patch of moss. Deep, dark green at the edges, it grew a lighter, brighter green and then, right in the centre, rich gold. The patch was as curious and exact in configuration as a work of Oriental art. Its surface resembled that of a very fine old velvet, artfully dyed and lighted, with an almost phosphorescent gleam to it, mellow and somewhat mysterious. I had never particularly noticed mosses before, though I'd often stopped to admire an old lichened stone-roof. To me, this little discovery, typical of its kind, represents one of the greatest pleasures of rambling: the discovery of minutiæ, something to stare at, meditate upon, identify oneself with—something which one's imagination can occupy and transform.

Lower Stone seemed to me a scattered, nondescript sort of place. There are one or two interesting cottages, but I was antagonised by the prevalence of chicken-farms. I must confess that I do not love the domestic fowl *en masse*. The sight of a chicken-farm has a depressing effect on me. The noise of fowls is, to me, sordid in the extreme. Indeed, the only time and place I see a fowl with pleasure is at mealtimes, when it is served up on a plate, roasted, with onion stuffing, roast potatoes and runner beans.

About a quarter or half a mile below Lower Stone, there's a turning on the right—up a lane. It is an unobtrusive turning. A narrow, stony way between an avenue of oaks (later elms). No signpost points this way, probably because it is not used by motor traffic and is therefore of no consequence to the sort of people who rush about "getting things done". Nevertheless, it is a charming lane, a lovely lane, worthy of celebration in a poem or painting. It reminded me of those lanes I see sometimes in my dreams. I am walking through familiar country, whose every feature is known to me. Suddenly I see a turning I'd never noticed before. It looks inviting. I turn into it . . . and that, of course, is the prelude to marvels! For it's soon apparent that it is more than a lane; it is a pathway, *the* pathway to Romance. At the end of it, I know, I shall find myself in a strange, new, beautiful land of wonder and fulfilment. Unfortunately I always wake up just before I get there, though sometimes I have known that this country was around the next turning, and have even caught vague glimpses of it through the trees. This lane from Lower Stone to Hill (and you couldn't wish for two more prosaic and practical names to grace a fantasy)—this lane, I say, revived the colour and promise of my dreams, whipping up excitement, delight, expectation and apprehension into the familiar potation. It was a day of sunshine, September sunshine : than which there is none more mellow and serene. My lane was floored with soft and gently-moving shadows. And I looked out, through a frame of trees, on to immaculate meadows, stage-lit by the sun, spotlighted and dramatic as though for the performance of a pastoral masque. Yet the fields were empty save for occasional groups of strangely picturesque cattle, which bore no resemblance to the common-or-garden cow. Surely no-one presumed to drive *these* lovely creatures off to smelly cow-houses, profaned *these* exquisite udders with grasping hand or impersonal milking-machine!

Rabbits lifted delicate noses and sniffed the air, waggled long ears and lolloped away with a flick of white rudders. But these were surely no *ordinary* rabbits; not rabbits which bred long families and could be shot with a gun! No, no. They were Brer-Rabbits, every one.

Wood-pigeons (we call them *quists*) flapped heavily and reluctantly out of trees, as I passed. Crows looked up and stared, forbodingly. And the lane itself was full of life and activity. Blackbirds fled raucously at my approach; a rabbit (alas! it had neither gold-watch nor white-waistcoat, but it *was* in a hurry) dashed across, only a few feet in front of me; a stoat gave me a crafty and stoat-like leer before disappearing into a rabbit-warren. I know all this is ordinary enough: the usual things one sees on any country walk. All the same, it wasn't ordinary. It had a mysterious, dreamlike quality. There was more than a suggestion of *Alice* and *The Wind in the Willows* about it.

Oh, you may laugh! But then, you've probably never been along that lane: never seen the September sun aslant those lush meadows, nor seen those dark-green woods which shroud the hill, nor felt the peculiar magic of that place. A mood? Yes, of course. But such a pleasant, memorable one that I doubt if I shall ever see that lane again. I'd be afraid to risk it. Next time it might not be the same. Might even prove to be only an ordinary stony track between trees, without any intrinsic magic at all. So I shall not be in a hurry to revisit my lane. Let it remain enchanted . . . if only for me.

Coming nearer to Hill, the trees came to an end and sunlight poured in. Yet it did not dissipate the magic. Golden fields of wheat had succeeded the green, with haycocks piled ready for gathering and stacking, and one field of oats was a rippling lake of silver. Small wooded hills rose and fell to the right. One of these, I knew, contained a moat. I had noticed it on my Ordnance Map before starting and had wondered what it was doing (or had done) there in the middle of a wood. No mention of a house. Just a square of blue with the word "Moat". I had half-promised myself I would climb that hill and search through that wood till I found it, but it would have meant leaving my lane, and having once left it, I might perhaps never find it again. So I allowed the moat in the woods to remain inviolate, keeping its secret (if it had one) and its silence to itself.

Very soon my lane brought me to Hill, where doves were crooning, rooks were arguing (or maybe preaching: it was a Sunday), but of human beings there was neither sight nor sound. A pond beside the road was attracting a crowd of swallows—some fifty or sixty of them—racing around and over it, diving, dipping, weaving in and out, drinking on the wing before coming to rest on the steep roof of a nearby farmhouse or the topmost bough of a dead apple-tree. They clung to those two perches, as though afraid they would fall, awkwardly, for swallows cannot perch with any ease. Their claws seem to come straight from their bodies, legless. Birds of flight, they become awkward and clumsy when they alight, like ducks on dry land.

Hill church was a spire against the tree-clad hill. It stands

near Hill Court, small, mainly of the Early English period.
Special features are the old benches with their Tudor linenfold
carving, and a canopied manorial pew resting on slender pillars.
South of the chancel is the mortuary chapel of the local big family,
the Fusts of Hill Court, built in 1700 by the third baronet. Two
fragments of sculpture on the sill of one of the chancel windows
represent (1) a clenched hand, and (2) a heart pierced by three
nails. Is there a mystery here? Miss Dorothy Sayers might well
have introduced these "devices" into that excellent story *The Nine
Tailors*. The nailed heart is not very mysterious, in fact. It was
the punning signature of Abbot Nailheart, a fifteenth-century
Abbot of St Augustine's, Bristol (now Bristol Cathedral). How
did it come to be at Hill? Well, that, too, is easily explained.
This little church was the property of the rich and powerful
Abbey before the dissolution of the monasteries by Henry VIII.

In 1816, the year after Waterloo, Hill was the scene of a tragedy.
The previous year had been a bad one for farmers. To make
matters worse, local landowners had been overbearing and unsympathetic. As a result, some of the smaller yeoman farmers had
begun to poach, almost as a matter of principle. For their poaching
killed two birds with one stone: it provided them with much-
needed meat, and that at the expense of the hated land barons.
Resolving to teach them a lesson, a few of the landed gentry set
spring-guns. A trip-wire was connected with the trigger of a
blunderbuss which discharged at anyone tripping over the wire.
Late in 1815, a Tortworth farmer called Thomas Till had been
killed by a spring-gun on Lord Ducie's estate, and this naturally
came before a coroner's court. Now, it had been ruled that spring-
guns were illegal, and that anyone killed by such a contrivance
had been murdered; the hand which set the trap being the hand
of the murderer. But the coroner's jury which assembled for the
inquest on Till was partial. Tenants themselves, they feared the
consequences of indicting a powerful landowner or even seeming
to uphold a trespass, which was regarded with horror in those days
of extensive game-preservation and land-worship. They brought
in a noncommittal verdict of "Found killed by a spring-gun".

Resentment against the landowners increased. At first smoul-
dering, it flamed into violence when a party of young men, most
of them sons of respectable farmers, laid plans for a raid. There

was little secrecy about their intentions. They had notified Miss Fust of Hill Court that they intended to pay her estate a visit, and that her gamekeepers had better keep out of their way. Miss Fust, presumably, felt that discretion was the better part of valour, for the poachers met no opposition at Hill Court and shot some of her pheasants before going on to Catgrove on the nearby Berkeley estates.

They had blacked their faces so that they'd be able to distinguish friend from foe and, at the same time, avoid recognition by keepers. Most of them carried guns. At Catgrove, it seems, they were expected, for they were met by a party of keepers only too eager for a scrap, but unarmed, probably by order. When he saw them, the head gamekeeper called out to them to fight like men and use no guns. To which their leader, John Allen, replied: "Never fear. We're not cowards."

Unfortunately, in the fight which followed, one of the poachers' guns did go off. The other poachers, thinking that it had been fired by a keeper, panicked and started firing. One keeper was killed and six others wounded. The firing brought more keepers on the scene, and the poachers, now utterly disorganised and frightened, beat a hurried retreat.

At the subsequent trial it was deposed that, after the firing, one of the poachers had exclaimed: "Now Tom Till's debt is paid!" Which seemed to establish that the raid had been planned as a retributive measure.

Anyway, the next move was the landlords'.

Colonel Berkeley organised a large force and himself went to arrest Allen. When they knocked at his door, Allen at once came out and surrendered. But Colonel Berkeley, who seems to have been a lout as well as a rake, acted in character. Displeased at Allen's gentlemanly bearing, he twice struck him to the ground with a cudgel. When Allen's servant attempted to remonstrate, the gallant colonel struck him down too. After which he so terrified the poor fellow, who had accompanied Allen on the raid, that he betrayed the whole party to save his neck. At the next assizes, eleven of the "marauders" were brought up and every one of them was sentenced to death. Two were actually hung (Allen and a John Penny), and the others were transported for life.

As for Lord Ducie, who, in a sense, began it all—he was not even mentioned. Such was English justice in the early nineteenth century.

At a cross-roads near the school-house I hesitated, wondering whether to turn right (north) for Whitcliff Park and Berkeley, go straight on (west) to Nupdown and Sheperdine, or turn left (south) to Rockhampton and Thornbury. I decided on the latter.

All the way my road was bordered by a rhine. Covered over with pondweed it moved sluggishly and bore a rich crop of rushes and sedge, with here and there the flower of a bur-reed. Although I often heard a moorhen's burbling warning-note, I didn't see one. Nor did I actually see any water-voles. But the frequent *plops*, like stones falling from the bank, suggested that there were plenty there. It was, of course, only circumstantial evidence. But it was pretty conclusive, as—to quote Thoreau— "when you find a trout in the milk".

Some of the ground alongside the road here was marshy, and on this, catmint flourished. Reeds, too. Especially a variety of sedge-grass which one finds in all the rhines hereabout, which grows to five or six feet, is jointed and tough, with a magnificent bronze-coloured plume. Not so attractive were the thousands of daddy-long-legs trailing their long legs, like abandoned stilts, over the low-lying ground. They made a rustling noise which got on my nerves. The truth is, I don't much care for these creatures. There is something ludicrous and repulsive about them. Or per-haps my attitude is the result of a childhood fixation, for as a child I slept alone in a queer-shaped room, all nooks and corners, lit only by one large window in daytime, or an ancient oil-lamp at night. The slightest draught from the window would set my lamp flickering, and then all sorts of weird shadows would jump about the room. And even when the lamp didn't flicker, the room would be haunted by these stilt-legged creatures, who had lurked in corners by day, to emerge after the lamp was lit, dancing up and down and round the walls, frantically, in a futile effort to escape. Their shadows, magnified, capered and fidgeted round and up and down, and I, who had always a morbid fear of such things, would pull the bedclothes over my head and try

A weir of putts on the bed of Severn between Oldbury and Sheperdine

not to think of them. Even when the light was out, I would still hear them, beating their wings against window or walls. Had I been braver I could have got up and killed them or put them out of the window. Instead, I lay listening, wondering where they were, hating and fearing them, yet suffering with them their frustration at finding no escape. (Whilst I was jotting down that note about crane-flies, two tiny beetles, of different species, alighted on the page of my notebook and showed the utmost curiosity in what I was writing. Both of them were clad in shining armour, brightly coloured, with a metallic sheen to it. And when they had seen all they wanted to see, they launched themselves on the air in search of further adventures.)

Although it was only the second day of September, autumn had already begun to reveal itself by the number of fruits in the hedgerows. Purple sloes, with a beautiful misty bloom on them; spikes of scarlet arum berries; green and red berries of bryony, nightshade, and wayfaring-tree. Green and red, too, were the blackberries, as yet unripe.

So far as most guides to the county are concerned, Rockhampton is a forgotten place, right off the map. It is certainly a little remote, but to my mind it is a charming little place, with its village-green surrounded by a rhine and its church hiding coyly up a side-turning. After eating my sandwiches and drinking cold tea beside the rhine, I looked around for someone to talk to, but there was no one to be seen. One old man had watched my approach from a cottage garden, only to retreat indoors before I came within hailing-distance. A little farther on, a group of children ran away and hid as though I were a policeman. Or maybe their mothers, influenced by a recent series of child-murders, had warned them against speaking to strange men. Most of the villagers were probably in church, or in a free-gospel mission-hut not far away, which displayed an alarming number of advertisements, asking "What Shall I Do To Be Saved?"—proclaiming "The Day is at Hand!"—asserting that "God is Love".

Neither Hill nor Rockhampton possesses an inn. I find this a little disturbing, for although I am not a regular or a large-capacity drinker, I hold that there are times and places when a pint goes down very sweet, and when the absence of it is felt to be a deprivation. Had George been with me, he would have put in

9*

a lusty *Hear, hear!* Curiously, the population of Rockhampton has varied little since Domesday Book, and there is a local legend that every time a new house is built here, an old one falls down. I notice that four council houses have recently been built near the church, so there may be some trepidation among those who occupy the older houses. A word of praise for these council-houses. They are grouped round a hummocky green outside the church, and they are most attractive. It is so seldom that one can look at a council-house and not shiver, that one ought to make a song about it when an enlightened council builds houses which "fit in". In company with the little church, they make a delightful group which, for once in a way, disproves Shakespeare's maxim that "Youth and old age cannot live together."

One of the oldest tombs in Rockhampton churchyard is to the memory of Mabel Mallett, who died in 1663. Her inscription begins:

> *Stand reader still*
> *And be Amazed Awhile*
> *Here lies an Israelite*
> *In whom was no guile.*

This good lady left twelve shillings a year to the poor of the parish.

CHAPTER VI

WOOD AND FARM

EAST of Thornbury the land rises to a ridge and falls away again in the direction of Rangeworthy, Tytherington and Cromhall. North of Cromhall the country is more broken, with many woods and streams and what was once parkland. This Iron Acton–Rangeworthy–Cromhall road used to be a busy one. You can still see the old toll-houses, and the one at Bagstone, the sign-board of which has been very neatly repainted by the boys at Tytherington school, revives memories of the weird and wonderful vehicles that used to travel this way.

BAGSTONE GATE

	s.	d.
TOLLS payable at this TURNPIKE		
For every Horse Mule Ass or other Beast drawing any Chaise Marine Coach Except Stage Coaches Landau Berlin Barouche	0	4
Sociable Chariot Calash Hearse Break Chaise Curricle Phaeton Gig Chair or Taxed Cart or any Cart not drawn by more than one Horse or two Oxen .	0	5
For every Horse or other Beast drawing any Stage Coach Licensed to Carry not more than 9 passengers	0	6
more than 9 and not exceeding 16 .	0	7
more than 16 . .	0	8
For every emty Carriage with 4 wheels affixed to any other Carriage	1	0
For every Horse Mule Ass or other beast not drawing .	0	1
For every drove of Oxen or other neat cattle per score .	0	10
For every drove of Calves Swine Hogs Sheep or Lambs per score	0	5

And so in proportion for any greater or less number.

By Order of the Trustees

April 14th 1837 OSBORNE DAUNCEY *Clerk*

Modern Rangeworthy is a straggling place, in unexciting country. But Rangeworthy Court is supposed to occupy the site of a manor which belonged to Hugh de Audley in Edward II's time. This was the man who married the widow of the King's favourite, Piers Gaveston, after her husband had been executed by the barons. The little church lies along a lane. Its north and south porches are Norman, and there is a grotesque of hideous aspect on the west wall—a man with bulging eyes and protruding teeth. I have often wondered about these strange manifestations of organised religion. Many of the gargoyles and wood-carvings of repellent features are blamed on the Gothic spirit, or on the sculptor's imagination "running away with him". But it would not surprise me if it went much deeper than that: if it was discovered that there were psychological parallels between these grotesques of our English village churches and those monstrous stone figures on Easter Island, those carvings on Indian totem-poles, and in eastern temples. It would be dangerous to speculate without any precise knowledge of the function of the grotesque element in religions, but that it is part of all religions, at any rate in their earlier, more superstitious phases, cannot be doubted.

Tytherington has a railway station, and a very pleasant little station it is. Unfortunately, passenger trains no longer run on this line, so that Tytherington is not very easily accessible. The village is dominated by the quarries. Ever since Squire Hardwicke —remarkable man!—started a quarry here, Tytherington stone has been well known. (Much of it was used for constructional work at Avonmouth Docks and Blagdon Reservoir.) It was Squire Hardwicke, too, who founded and encouraged the famous Tytherington Prize Band. Village wit is expressed in the names of local football teams. Their senior team is called "Tytherington Rocks"; the juniors are "the Pebbles". Dominating the village to the west is what remains of a Roman or pre-Roman camp. Locally known as Castle Camp, quarrying has unfortunately eaten into one side, and I have been told by quarry workers that they have often come across skeletons and coins in the past, here and at Tytherington hill. Mr Curtis, who worked in the quarry all his life, told me there were many such finds at one time, but "nobody took much notice in they days". Now eighty-four and retired from the quarry, Bill Curtis can boast that he went to work before ever he went to school. He was ten years old when the school was built in Tytherington, and he had then been working in the quarry with his father for nearly a year. Mr Curtis can also boast that he's never slept a night outside of Tytherington. As a young man he played cricket for Thornbury with Squire Hardwicke, his boss, and E. M. Grace. He told me that Squire was a good boss, but not very "free" (*i.e.* lavish).

In any conversation with the oldsters of Tytherington there will inevitably be much talk of Squire Hardwicke, and of that other great man, George Boyt, pork butcher and founder of the Baptist chapel. Arthur Boyt, his descendant, was just getting ready to go to chapel when I called on him, but he met me with a cheery smile and invited me in. His grandfather was one of those excellent old preachers who were not only good Christians but fine orators, and, occasionally, wits. Arthur told me that his grandfather was highly respected locally, and could be a formidable opponent. If he had a notion he hadn't seen some villager in chapel, he would make a point of stopping him next day and ask him what he thought of the sermon. His sermons were remarkable for their homely analogies. For instance he used to say that some men, like pigs, never bothered to look up until they were on their backs.

George Boyt did not love parsons. In his day they were all too often university men who regarded the church as a profession, and used their pulpit for expounding the rightness of the existing order. Like many free-churchmen he had cause to resent the power and prestige of the rector who has been foisted on them by the squire; but, unlike most of his contemporaries, he could turn the situation into a joke. He would tell the story of a stranger coming into a certain village (he wouldn't say where), to find a funeral in progress. Enquiring of bystanders whose funeral it was, the man is told it's old parson's. Curious about the cause of death, he asks: "Any complaints?" ... "No, no, sir," echo the guileless locals. "*We'm* all satisfied!"

It was Richard Leakey, the schoolmaster of Tytherington, who told me the story of the feud between a Tytherington squire and a parson, which culminated in the great Duckpond controversy. This is how it happened. . . .

The living of Tytherington was in the gift of the lord of the manor. Sometime during the mid-nineteenth century, a squire had it in mind to present the living to a young nephew of his. But, as it happened, whilst the nephew was still up at Oxford, the incumbent died and it was necessary to appoint a successor. So the squire entered into a temporary agreement with a Rev. Moncrieff Roberson, who was to remain rector until such time as the nephew had taken orders, and then vacate it in his favour. This Moncrieff Roberson was not, it seems, a humble man. Nevertheless, when the squire knocked down the wall which divided his house from the rectory, and rebuilt it closer to the latter, Roberson did not object. At the same time, the Squire enclosed the village duckpond, which was on rectory land, filled it in, and turned it into a garden. Roberson held his tongue, but he had seen and he would remember.

Now, the specific nephew named in the agreement between squire and parson died. Whereupon the squire brought forward *another* nephew and suggested he be substituted. This was Roberson's chance. He dug his heels in, and refused to budge from the agreement as it stood. He would admit no one's claim to the living but that specified in the document. Squire grew heated, threatened and insisted. Parson was adamant in his refusal. The result was a furious quarrel, which finally exploded when the squire, who seems to have been a somewhat impulsive gentleman, found that Roberson, quite within his rights, had locked the door of a short cut through which the squire's cattle were daily driven. Incensed, he smashed down the door, and drove his cattle over rectory land in such a manner as to cause damage. This, so far as the Rev. Moncrieff Roberson was concerned, was the last straw! He sued the squire, and the squire brought a counter-claim. Roberson won the day. Squire had to pay for damages, and restore the duckpond; and in a fit of disgust he sold all rights in the living and refused to attend or support the church. And that, Mr Leakey told me, was why Tytherington had no church school, for Roberson, in his turn, undertook no more than he had to. It was not until 1878 that the village acquired a National School —the school to which Bill Curtis came, at ten years of age, after working in the quarries.

Mention must be made of the small brass, dated 1755, which is to be found in the church here. It is to Richard Bromwich, and shows an hourglass, a sickle, the wings of Time, a skull and four cross bones. Less grisly is the sixteenth-century one-handed clock, which dates from a happy time when minutes were of no account, for it only tells the hours. For years the works of this clock lay, rusty and forgotten, in a corner of the belfry. Then, round about 1945 or 1946, when the bells were being restored, Mr Leakey discovered them and asked the advice of several local horologists. They confirmed that this was the original church clock—an interesting and almost unique survival. It was reassembled and erected, and ever since then has worked perfectly. Mr Leakey took me up the church tower to see it working. My reactions were of little value, for I am no horologist, but as we stood there, silent in the gloom of the belfry, watching the primitive machinery of that venerable old time-keeper, I had a sudden nightmare vision of Time, eating away at life like a death-watch beetle in a beam, which made me suggest departure. Mr Leakey might not have understood my hysteria. He looks upon that clock with the modest pride and absorption of an enthusiast. But I do not envy him his job of climbing up the dark and dirty stairway in the tower each week, to stand, amid the silence of centuries, and hear only the regular, insidious *tick . . . tick . . . tick!* of Time as measured by Tytherington's sixteenth-century clock.

Mrs Leakey, who teaches mathematics and botany, told me that there's great interest in wildflowers among the village children. Every summer a big feature is made of collecting and identifying flowers. I asked if rare species ever turned up. "Not really *rare* plants. But we've found bee-hemp-nettle, and the butterfly, pyramidal and bee orchids." She told me that one of their pupils had found a large patch of henbane growing in a field, and the farmer was warned accordingly. Which proves, if you like, the value of teaching botany.

Not far away is Fiddler's Green, where live the Pullen family, who have farmed here since the seventeenth century. The name Fiddler's Green had its origin in a triangular patch of ground which used to lie at the three cross-roads. Mr Pullen remembers when it was a favourite resort of the German bands which were once so familiar to English countryfolk. Sitting beside Farmer Pullen's modern heating-stove, we talked of farming. Or rather, Mr Pullen talked . . . I listened. He has always been one for keeping up with the times, and on the subject of mechanisation in farming, he told me: "It isn't a luxury, it's a necessity. Because it's quite impossible to get enough labour to farm the old way. In any case, with wages at their present level, farmers can't afford to employ much labour."

Mr Pullen thought that one of the finest things went out of farming when the farmworker's pride in his skill and his farm was replaced by distrust, independence and the minimum wage. Before that time, a farm was a truly co-operative affair, and farmworkers assumed responsibility for their separate part of the farm work. In his father's day, the carters wouldn't think of taking out their horses on a morning with dirty brasses, not even if it was "raining mud". And it was a case of fitting the horses to the men, for a good carter or ploughman wouldn't work behind a bad horse; they'd rather leave. Those old workers often had great dignity and pride in themselves. Woe betide the farmer who went off and bought a new horse (or sold an old one) without consulting his head carter, and taking him along to the sale. If he did so, the carter would regard it as a breach of confidence, and might well leave.

One of Mr Pullen's ancestors rode off to the Monmouth Rebellion from Fiddler's Green, with his fortune, in spade guineas, on his horse's martingale. I hope he came back, and was lucky enough to avoid Judge Jeffreys! Another of his forbears, on his mother's side, who took part in that same rebellion, was Colonel Wade, sometimes called "Traitor" Wade because he was believed to have betrayed his brother officers to James II. But you mustn't call Colonel Wade a traitor in front of Mr Pullen, for he knows the facts. It is true that Wade gave the names of some of his fellows, but not until they were safely dead. Confined to the Tower, as he was, many have claimed that he couldn't possibly have known if they were dead or alive. That was where they were wrong. In actual fact, Colonel Wade knew as much about happenings outside as his jailers did, for he'd discovered a means of communication. Every week he was allowed to send his washing to an old washerwoman in Bristol. And every week he concealed notes in the pleats of his garments. So did his laundry-woman when returning them. So that, when he knew the other officers had been hung, he made a show of giving them away, and

was fortunate enough to be released. That is Wade's story, as the
family tell it; and Mr Pullen is very sure of its truth. W. W. F.
Pullen, our Mr Pullen's brother, was a notable cricketer, who
played with "W.G."

When H.M. Commissioners of Prisons took over Tortworth
Court for an experimental prison, the move wasn't exactly
popular with countryfolk who had known and respected the Earl
of Ducie. And there were some who didn't much like the idea
of allowing prisoners such a measure of liberty. As a matter of fact,
in a period of ten days, soon after its establishment, eight men
escaped, and a parish councillor accused the Home Office of
"gambling with the safety of the people". That was six years ago.
In each of the last two years, only one man has tried to escape
from Leyhill, though it is not difficult to do so. Today it has
something like an international reputation, and it must surely be
admitted, even by those who at first opposed the idea, that Leyhill has notably succeeded in its work of reclamation instead of
recrimination.

The Governor of Leyhill, Mr Henderson, told me: "The emphasis here is on training rather than punishment. Men are led to
appreciate, perhaps for the first time in their lives the responsibilities of living in society as well as the advantages. And we try
to ensure that, on their release, men get a fair chance of making
good." What sort of men come to Leyhill? Usually they are first
offenders with long-term sentences, who have been considered
worth rehabilitating. Their crimes range from housebreaking,
forgery and fraud to high treason, manslaughter and murder.
They work a 44-hour week at shoemaking, carpentry, tailoring,
printing, farming and gardening; and the clothing and footwear
shops alone produced goods worth more than £33,000 for
Government contracts during 1950–51. Some prisoners work on
local farms, some assist in road-making and -mending for the
local council. They have dormitories instead of cells, and, after
four years, their own rooms. They swim and play cricket, football and putting (golf)—not only among themselves, but against
outside teams. They are allowed to form their own committees,
and even have their own magazine—*New Dawn*—which sometimes has hard-hitting "leaders" on prison-reform. A cinema and

a theatre are provided for their entertainment. Both Mr and Mrs Leakey take evening classes, which are apparently very successful.

In addition, each man has his own bit of garden. Leyhill Amateur Dramatic Society produces four plays a year, and there's also a Leyhill Theatre Orchestra and a Leyhill Military Band. I was glad to learn that there is a "Third Programme Room", where serious-minded prisoners can listen in comfort and in easy chairs.

I asked Mrs Leakey how she liked teaching at Leyhill, and her answer surprised me. "My work at Leyhill," she said, "is a tonic. I meet with unfailing consideration there, real courtesy, and the fulfilment of every teacher's dearest wish—namely, people who genuinely want to learn." Her husband makes a hobby of welfare work among newly discharged men, helping them to find jobs and make a new life for themselves. Some of them come out to see Mr and Mrs Leakey on week-ends, and when I have been there to tea, I have been introduced to their "old friends" who have made good and still visit them.

So violent a break with the past has, of course, disturbed the fabric of local life. Old men who remember "old" Lord Ducie do not take kindly to the ancestral home being turned into a model prison, though the survivors of the Poaching Affray at Hill (already mentioned) might regard it as belated justice. I remember talking about the old Lord Ducie with an elderly cottager at Brickmarsh, near Whitfield. He was stooping about among some fowls in a little orchard, and came to the hedge for a chat with great willingness. He told me that the "old" Lord had preferred a coach-and-pair to a car. He had apparently tried an automobile, but didn't like it, finding it uncomfortable and undignified. He also had qualms about its mechanism, fearing that it might blow up (this was presumably in the early days of motoring). Anyway, the Earl returned to his carriage-and-pair, and used to derive great satisfaction from driving around his own estate (the roads being cluttered up with the new-fangled and noisy motors.) He lived to be near on ninety. I have only the old man's word for all this, of course, but he looked a truthful sort.

It was this same old fellow at Brickmarsh who told me how to tell what kind of animal has killed a fowl by the way it's killed and eaten. Badgers, he told me, will eat the fowl's back, whilst foxes bite their heads off, and stoats nip them in the neck. He said he'd seen a stoat trundling an egg along the ground with its nose. More than that, he'd seen a stoat roll a dead rabbit down a hill and into a ditch—giving it little tosses with its nose. Having kept fowls at Brickmarsh for a great many years, he has been much persecuted by foxes, stoats and badgers, particularly by the first two. But he obviously regards the stoat with greatest respect. "Foxes is crafty," he said, with sly emphasis "but stoats is *clever*." He wasn't a friend of the prison-without-bars. It was alien, foreign, something forced upon them by "they up in London". His respect for they up in London was considerably less than he was willing to accord his domestic enemy the stoat.

Between Falfield and Cromhall is Priest Wood, where local people sometimes go nutting. The name of this wood, coupled with a nearby farm called Abbot-side, suggests a monastic site, and the old man at Brickmarsh told me that he'd heard it said there used to be a priory here. Opposite Priest Wood is a hill, topped with a ruin which adds a romantic touch to the scene. I asked an exceptionally pretty girl, who happened to be passing, if she knew anything about it. She blushed, and I realised that, as usual, I had been tactless, for the place might well be a notorious rendezvous for the amorous. All that she could tell me was that her father, who had farmed here all his life, called it the Keeper's Look-Out, and said that it was used for observation purposes by the keepers on Lord Ducie's estates. But for as long as she could remember, it had been a ruin.

The scenery around Tortworth is perhaps as good as any in Gloucestershire. Though it is not on a grand scale, it is varied and interesting, well wooded, with a sleek and comfortable air about it which makes it peculiarly English. Tortworth church stands well, and is, indeed, one of the most fascinating churches in the county. Its fifteenth-century tower is especially beautiful in that rolling, peaceful countryside, with its elegant open parapet, eight pinnacles, carved buttresses and grotesques. Within the tower is a mediæval bell with a tiny Crusader's ship engraved upon it.

The church stands back from the road, across a green around which a few old and interesting houses squat. It is a quiet place, somnolent and "withdrawn" in summer, when the sound of a cuckoo and the monotonous burbling of wood-pigeons are all that disturb the silence. Within the church, the fine canopied tomb of Thomas Throckmorton is strikingly beautiful. His coat-of-arms is painted on the canopy, and the helmet and gauntlets he may have worn lie on the tomb. Nearby is another Throckmorton, also Thomas, whose effigy in marble depicts him in the armour of Shakespeare's day, decorated in red and gold. Above him are the figures of Age and Youth; helmet-and-sword as symbols of war, axe-and-spade symbolising peaceful cultivation; whilst a black eagle lies at his feet, possibly symbolising falconry. The other great local family, the Ducies, also have a vault here. It has an intricately carved top and a wooden canopy. Behind the church, at the end of a churchyard in which cowslips grow thick among the graves, is an elaborate shelter, or retreat, erected to the memory of the Countess Julia, by Earl Ducie.

Like Tytherington, Tortworth has had its feuds between parson and squire. In the eighteenth century one of Tortworth's parsons seems to have aroused a great deal of enmity by his method of collecting tithes. He insisted on being paid in kind, claiming all the milk every tenth day. Two farmers, Cullimore and Limbrick, considered he was only entitled to every tenth *milking*, whether morning or evening. The argument was a fierce one, and it eventually came before the House of Lords, when the vicar produced yield tables in his defence, whilst the farmers pleaded that calves being fattened for the butcher must be considered. Moreover, the farmers complained that parson didn't collect his milk, and they couldn't spare their buckets. Parson protested that they added more than a mile to his journeys by deliberately blocking the roads. He also said that they put rennet into his milk, and that Farmer Cullimore had told his milkmaids that they needn't rise early or strip the cows on the "devil's day." The parson won the day, but the farmers' costs were paid by Lord Ducie, and it may be that this was the Lord Ducie who had his vineyard destroyed rather than give the rector a tenth of his grape-crop as tithe.

Older even than the church is Tortworth Chestnut, one of the most remarkable trees in the country, famous enough to be specially mentioned on the Ordnance Map. Nobody knows how old it is, though a plaque on the railing which surrounds this

Spanish chestnut declares that it was "supposed to be six hundred years old" in 1800. The tablet bears a verse, which was composed by someone who may have meant well but was certainly no poet.

May Man Still Guard Thy Venerable Form
From the Rude Blasts and the Tempestuous Storm,
Still mayest thou Flourish through Succeeding time
And Last, Long Last, the Wonder of the Clime.

Nowadays it is a really fantastic growth, ruinous and broken. Yet it still puts forth in the spring and continues to cover its twisted limbs and shattered trunk with a fresh-green foliage. John Evelyn knew this tree, and said it was known as the Great Chestnut in the time of King Stephen. There is a tradition that King John, whilst hunting nearby, held a council under it.

Before the Throckmortons' time, Tortworth was the property of the Veels. Near neighbours to the Berkeleys, the two families seem to have been friendly over a period of 250 years. Together they made pilgrimages to the Holy Land. Together they fought against the French. And together they raided the deer in Painswick Park. All this ended when the feud sprang up between Lord Berkeley and Viscount Lisle. Living halfway between these two contentious lords, Robert Veel was not in an enviable position. Forced to take sides, he threw in his lot with Lord Lisle, and attempted to capture Berkeley Castle by bribing the gatekeeper. His scheme failed because the gatekeeper was honest. And the outcome of it was the battle of Nibley Green.

Tortworth and Michaelwood are divided by the little Damery valley, with its narrow floor of meadow and steep wooded hillside. The prospect from the top of Damery hill is indeed a fine one, and at the foot of the hill, on the daffodil bank, used to be the woodman's cottage occupied by Jack Stinchcombe, "a fine figure of a man with a grand head and shoulders, and the carriage of a guardsman. To see Jack swing an axe was a sight to remember", I was told. "His crony, Jim Bye, who lived at Wick, was a different type: of shorter stature, but of incredible strength and skill. He was, moreover, a natural humorist whose quiet wit made his world as pleasant as it is beautiful."

Michaelwood Chase occupied an area upwards of a 1,000 acres

in the Middle Ages, and being situated at some distance from Berkeley Castle, policed by only one ranger and two keepers, it was not surprising that stags were frequently poached. In 1580 Sir Thomas Throckmorton himself was accused of organising a gang of deer-stealers to raid Michaelwood, but this may have been part of a scheme to stir up trouble between the Berkeleys and the Earls of Warwick and Leicester. However, there do appear to have been organised raids on the Chase by men of fairly substantial position, who seem to have used deer-nets and dogs. Round about 1598 a party of ten poachers were surprised by the ranger, who was fortunately able to call upon an equal number of "good men with staves". A fight ensued, as a result of which several men were injured and one of the deer-stealers killed.

Michaelwood is now a mere shadow of itself, and when I was there last, extensive felling was in progress. The fine oaks of the Chase will soon be gone, and future plantations of fir will not remind us of the glory that was Michaelwood, with its great oaks and slender birches, its holly thickets and glades. A local worthy has written:

> "At any time of the year Michaelwood has some attraction peculiar to the season. A misty fog in the afternoon of a white frost used to enthral me with its eerie unreality, and this seemed to similarly affect the wild things of the woodland who set aside their lack of confidence. A cock pheasant would strut across the ride and rabbits unconcernedly hop along from one patch of cover to another, whilst wood pigeons came homeward to the oak branches overhead."

Strontia,* I am told, has been dug in the Furze Ground, and marle from the extensive excavations near the Mule Street approach to Michaelwood and at a place a little farther north called The Pits. The Manor of Alkington has long been celebrated for its marl, and Maurice, Lord Berkeley, was using it in 1256.

Mention has already been made of the battle of Nibley Green. This, the last private battle to take place on English soil, occurred on the morning of March 20th, 1471, when the Lord Lisle's forces met those of Lord Berkeley in open combat. Earlier that year, the

---

* Sulphate of strontium, a rare mineral which is mined in quantity nearby at Yate. In fact, 95 per cent of the world output of strontia comes from Yate.

young Lord Lisle had tried to bribe the porter of Berkeley Castle. But the man was honest and refused, so the impetuous Lisle sent Lord Berkeley a message challenging him to a battle on Nibley Green, under the Cotswolds. The challenge was accepted, and, on the night of March 19th, Berkeley's army of 500, including men from Bristol and the Forest of Dean, camped in Michael-wood Chase. Accounts of the battle vary. Some say that it took place on Nibley Green, as arranged, and some that Berkeley's archers ambushed the Lisle army on the outskirts of Michaelwood. There is a local legend that, on the night of March 19th, you may still see Berkeley's men walking or riding through Michaelwood. I have not tested the legend, however, for although Michaelwood is not extensive now, it is still large enough and lonely enough to be unpleasant at night, and I have no desire to encounter Black Will or James Hiatte in one of those shadowy and forsaken rides.

Apparently the casualties of the battle numbered about 150 when Lord Lisle fell, mortally wounded. At once his men turned and fled in the direction of Wotton-under-Edge, where they hoped to gain refuge in Lisle House. Before they had time to make the house secure, however, Berkeley's men had come up with them—they were wiped out, the house was looted and sacked, after which, one supposes, the Berkeley troops returned to the Castle to celebrate their victory. Had the times been more settled, there is little doubt that Berkeley would have been reprimanded by the King. But it all happened during the Wars of the Roses, when the country was in a state of turmoil and no one except those implicated were much interested in the private quarrels of the houses of Berkeley and Lisle. One curious thing about the affair was the disappearance of Lord Lisle's body. Whether Lord Berkeley had it buried in a common grave with the rest of his troops is not known. It has been suggested that some of Lisle's men carried his body away with them to Painswick, and it is certainly a possibility, for there is an altar tomb of about that date in Painswick church which bears no name or identification.

Mule Street is the name of a lane leading from Woodford to Michaelwood. Whether "mule" is derived from "marl" I cannot say. There does not *appear* to be any connection with mules as a form of transport, unless they were used to carry iron ore from Berkeley Pill to the furnaces in Michaelwood in and after 1610, when a commercial optimist called Thomas Hackett bought an interest in the Chase, using the timber for conversion into charcoal, with which to smelt iron ore from the Forest of Dean. The venture was not successful, and he sold his interest to Sir William Throckmorton, who was equally unsuccessful. Mule Street certainly had one connection with transport, for it was the headquarters, in fairly recent times, of a retail business in Cromhall lime, carried on by the Allens and Hazels. Their convoy of two or three spring carts, each with a wicker bushel measure hanging beneath, and accompanied by a couple of lurcher dogs, used to be a usual sight on the local roads, and I understand that that picturesque old lady Mrs Allen was the moving spirit and chief financier of this concern.

Above Damery Quarry is an earthwork, known locally as the Old Castle. The situation and surroundings suggest that it was the home of a hunting or pastoral people who appreciated a quiet life and did not wish to be unduly obvious. In the valley below this camp the Little Avon runs lively: as carefree and talkative as a mountain stream! How pleasant in springtime to idle on the bridge here, listening to the swirling sound of the water-music! The song of the river at Damery is rhythmic, sonorous, bell-like —in a liquid rather than a percussive sense, as though the bell were underwater. The tiny island which, above the bridge, divides the stream, is fringed with kingcups which grow with their feet in the water, their lovely golden cups swayed by the current. A large patch of garlic scents the air beside the road, and in the woodland, covering the steep hillside, bluebells, primroses and windflowers grow in wild profusion. I shouldn't be surprised if the colony of adder's-tongue spearwort, now extinct outside Gloucestershire, but known to be somewhere "between Yate and Wotton-under-Edge", was somewhere hereabout; though I have never found it myself, and doubt if I should have recognised it if I had.

A mile or so down this lovely little Damery valley (a vale within the Vale) is Middlemill, a pleasant spot, where the stream is bridged near the ruins of an old water-mill. Not far away, the Little Avon is joined by Oldbrook, which has its source in Tortworth Lake, straggles over to Falfield, round Heneage Court, and past Oldbrook Farm before its confluence with the Little

Avon. Heneage Court is an unpretentious country house of the better sort. You come to it along a pleasant lane from the Falfield road, and (in the words of a writer in *Country Life*) it is "happily placed on a gentle rise amid meadows, under the lee of its own little wood, Skey's Copse . . . making the most of its luck in the possession of quietly beautiful views of valley and rounded hill. . . ." Heneage is a long, low, pleasant old house, kindly and unpretentious, with no conscious architectural adornment, and without "heraldic or other suggestion of distinguished or assertive possession". Its general effect and character suggest an Elizabethan origin, though it seems to have been rebuilt during or before the Civil War, the usual thrifty use being made of serviceable parts of the older structure, especially its timber-work. The walls are of local stone but plastered or roughcast, with scarcely any dressed stone or freestone in the fabric. Little is known of the early history of this house or its owners, except that, on the attainder of the Duke of Buckingham, Henry VIII granted it to a Thomas Henneage. This may have been the (Sir) Thomas Henneage who was a courtier in Queen Elizabeth's day. They almost certainly had some connection, for this Sir Thomas married Anne Poyntz, daughter of Sir Nicholas Poyntz, of Iron Acton, nearby. However, the Henneages do not seem to have remained long in possession, for in 1649 the house was sold by Richard Allen, a fuller of Bath, to Thomas Skey. Having acquired the place, the Skeys seemed reluctant to let it go. It was held by successive Skeys, father and son, for the next century and a half, and their connection with the locality is perpetuated to this day by the small wood near the house called Skey's Copse. It was not until the Skeys died out in the male line that Heneage Court changed hands. But when, in 1810, Jane Skey, last heiress of the line, married Peter Scobell of Penzance, she went to Penzance to live and Heneage was let out as a farm. Not unnaturally, this change of tenancy meant a change of treatment, and neglect and rough usage began to have their effect. When, in 1912, it was purchased by that well-known Bristolian, Russell Thomas, Heneage Court was dilapidated and unprepossessing. All praise, then, to Mr Thomas for taking such trouble over its repair and enlargement. The architect in charge, Edward Warren, made his alterations fit the old fabric so that its original style and character should not be

Berkeley church: West Front

impaired. He had it entirely re-roofed with stone slates from Stonesfield, restored the fine old panelling of parlour and dining-room, and installed an early eighteenth-century chimneypiece, which had been taken from a house at Bristol, in the drawing-room.

In the stable-yard is the circular stone basin of an old cider-mill. It is dated 1707, and bears the initials W.S. Many such troughs are still to be found, often overgrown by nettles, in and about the Vale. I know of another at Kington. Needless to say, none are now in use.

We seem to have strayed from the Little Avon, which, approaching Berkeley, flows through Stone and becomes the Matford Brook. At least, that is what the Little Avon used to be called hereabout, taking the name from Matford Mead, of which it was the boundary. John Smyth, steward and historian of the Berkeleys, says that in his day Matford Mead was "a spacious plaine and fertile meadow of an 100 acres or more". If this were so, it must have occupied the whole of the alluvial area from the main road at Stone to the original junction of the Matford and Doverte brooks. It was apparently divided into a number of areas, which the owners had the right of mowing, and the "lattermath" was grazed in common. John Smyth is not very complimentary about the management of this common pasture: "The inhabitants wherein pretend their ill custome, viz. hand over hand, pell mell, on Lammas-day, to thrust in all manner of their Cattell, whether they have any ground therein or not; whereby the herbage, to the small benefit of anyone, is, in one weeke or sooner, eaten up and consumed. . . ." He also mentions that Matford is the "trayninge place of the disciplined or trayned soldiers of the Villages thereabouts, within the tithinge of Alkington". It is no longer used for military exercises, but it *is* used for the Berkeley Hunt Point-to-Point, and this wonderful expanse of level turf makes an admirable racing course. The rising ground at the southern end of the Mead forms a natural grand-stand which, besides commanding a view of almost the whole of the racecourse, gives a distant perspective of the Castle, standing on its knoll above the flat water-meadows and backed by trees.

Brown's Mill, farther downstream, no longer stands. And it is not easy to discover who Brown was, or when he lived there.

This might mean searching back through centuries, for such associations between man and place are tenacious, as, for instance, Butler's Grove at Breadstone. Thomas Butler, after whom it was named, owned the Grove in Henry VIII's time. Pollard willows surround a quiet pool at Brown's Mill, and it is good to lean over the parapet of the bridge and smoke a contemplative pipe whilst cows stand up to their hocks to drink in the pool below.

An amusing story is told of Castle Meadow, the last of the flat, wide water-meadows immediately adjacent to the Castle. Part of it lies under the Castle walls, and is therefore within observation from the windows, so that a former Steward of the Berkeleys was surprised to come across Old Jim pitching hay minus his trousers.

"Jim, Jim!" he apostrophised. "You can't work in front of the Castle without any trousers on. Not in front of the Castle, Jim! Whatever made you leave 'em off?"

"Well, zur," said Jim, "we tapped a vresh cask o' zider this marnin. An' you do know what vresh zider be, main zurchin. It've bin servin' I out crool, an' I've took me trousis down so often I thought 'twould save time, like, if I lef' 'em off altogether . . . just until the zider have 'a done workin' me."

Normally, any scheme for saving time would have recommended itself to the Steward, but there were exceptions, and this was one of them. "Not in front of the Castle, Jim," he said, reprovingly. "You must remember where you are."

And so we come to Berkeley.

Chapter VII

BERKELEY

BERKELEY CASTLE stands upon a natural shelf of red sandstone. Even before the coming of the Normans, there was a castle of sorts here, and before that a stockaded fort. But it was ideally situated for baronial occupation under the feudal system, and that was when Berkeley was at its zenith. In those days the castle occupied the southern extremity of what was, to all intents, an island almost completely surrounded by fresh- and salt-water marshes. Even today the low ground to the east is subject to flooding, and wild geese and duck are sometimes to be seen hereabout in winter.

The "island" of Berkeley is about 200 acres in extent, and it has an altitude of 63 feet, which makes it safe from even the worst flooding. The "island" could be self-sufficient, for it formerly had its own mill and even a mineral spring, and there were great forests of oak nearby to provide building materials and fuel. It also had access to the sea, whilst the two-and-a-quarter miles of winding, muddy creek which was (and is) Berkeley Pill made surprise invasion from the sea impossible.

It was a wonderful strategic position, commanding the Bristol–Gloucester road and at the narrowest part of the Vale, where a spur of Cotswold (Stinchcombe Hill) is only four or five miles from Severn. It also commands the narrows of the Severn between Lydney and Sharpness. The Castle is not aggressively military. It stands above Castle Meadow, framed by trees, not at all grandiloquent or assertive, perhaps a little too modest and snug. It fits so perfectly into its background that you begin by being rather disappointed with it. But its beauty is not to be apprehended at a glance, or in all kinds of conditions. V. Sackville-West has described the walls as being the colour of old brocade, and a well-known local personality has told me that their fascination lies in their apparent power to absorb light. Those two comments describe it far better than I can.

148

In the old days the Castle was defended on the north and west by a deep moat, isolating it from the town. Since 1587, however, the entrance has been over a permanent bridge which presumably replaced drawbridge and portcullis. Passing through the portal you enter a triangular courtyard, of which the outer gatehouse forms the apex, with the inner gatehouse and keep as base. The great breach in the west wall was made by Colonel Rainsborough in 1645, and it was enlarged on Cromwell's orders before the Castle was restored to the Berkeleys in 1648. Passing through the double archway of the inner gate with its portcullis grooves, the Greater Courtyard is reached. To the left is the Norman keep built by Robert FitzHarding; to the right are the staterooms and other apartments; in front are the fourteenth-century chapel and Great Hall (a magnificent affair, 61 feet long), the butteries and the kitchen.

The eighth and last Earl, who died in 1944, took pleasure in enriching and beautifying the Castle, and I have heard that he used most of the proceeds (nearly two million pounds) from the sale of his Berkeley Square property, to bring the internal fittings and arrangements up to date and to preserve the fabric of the building. This makes it all the more sad that the Castle should now be shut up and forsaken, its gates bolted and barred, silent and empty except for caretakers. Not only that, but visitors are strictly excluded from the Castle precincts, so that Berkeley town has not only lost the advantage of a resident great family, but, possessing one of the most remarkable private homes in England, is not in a position to offer the interested visitor more than a sight of the walls from Castle Meadow.

After the Castle, and except for its splendid church, Berkeley town is disappointing. In fact, it isn't really a town at all but a large village. True, it has a cinema and a fair number of pubs. But it lacks the animation that a town, even a small country town, ought to have. You get the impression that if it wasn't for the buses—the Bristol to Gloucester bus leaves the main road to visit Berkeley, when passengers can slip over to James's Café for an ice-cream or a cup of tea—Berkeley would fall asleep. Maybe things would have been different if the canal from Gloucester had come down to Berkeley Pill instead of joining the Severn a few miles upstream at Sharpness. That was the original intention of the canal company. But funds ran short, and they simply made for the nearest part of Severn. And Sharpness, which was merely a landmark, became a port, whilst Berkeley men drifted away to the towns where there was better chance of employment.

The trouble is that Berkeley town depended on three sources for its income and employment: from the manufacture of clothing (with Cotswold wool); from Berkeley Castle and estate; and from farming. Writing in his *Itinerary*, 400 years ago, Leland comments: "The towne of Berkeley is no great thynge, but it standyth well, and in a very good soyle. It hathe very much occupied, and yet somewhat dothe, clothinge." Then the bottom dropped out of the woollen and clothing industries, and Berkeley depended on the Lords of Berkeley and local farming. In course of time it became the centre of cheese-making, the famous Double Gloucesters—or, as they were sometimes called, Double Berkeleys—being marketed in the town. Many elderly people of Berkeley still remember the cheese-market in the old Market House, where the Recreation Rooms (pseudo-Georgian, the gift of the late Baron Fitzhardinge) now stand.

Now that Double Gloucesters are no longer made and the castle stands empty and the clothing trade is not even a memory, Berkeley gradually dwindles in importance. One thing it still has—a very good soil. And that will always be a source of revenue. But it is the buses that bring life to Berkeley. Without them I fear it would become comatose, for it seems to possess very little life of its own.

Two of the most gruesome legends I know come from Berkeley. First, there's the story of the Witch of Berkeley, that old woman who gave her soul to Beëlzebub and repented too late. You may read of it in the Latin of Matthew of Westminster or in the Nuremberg Chronicle, but the original authority seems to have been William of Malmesbury, who declared that he was told it by a man who had seen the happening with his own eyes.

It seems that there lived at Berkeley, in the ninth century, a notorious Witch. When she was sitting at her dinner one day, a chough (some say a raven) appeared, and began chattering at her. She went as pale as a corpse, and she said: "This day is the plough come to its last furrow." Whereupon she sent for her son, who was a priest, and her daughter, who was a nun, and implored them to pray for her. She also gave instructions to her children for her disposal after she was dead. They were to sew her body into a stag's skin, put it into a stone coffin with bolts of iron, which was to be further bound round with three great chains. It must then be placed upright in church, watched night and day for three days and nights, and then buried, with prayers and masses for her soul. By taking these precautions, there was a possibility they might prevent her being carried off by the foul fiend.

After she was dead, her children did just as their mother had told them; but on its first night in church, demons contrived to break one of the chains round her coffin. On the following night, they broke another chain. On the third night, a demon of terrible aspect entered the church, and, in spite of all, snapped the third chain as though it were cotton and commanded the body of the Witch to rise. Slowly the corpse rose up and followed him from the church. Outside, a black horse was waiting. The demon sprang on to it, swept the Witch up behind him, and galloped into the darkness. As she found herself being carried off to Hell, the Witch uttered shrieks of such intense anguish that they were heard four miles off.

This terrifying story has been told in verse by Robert Southey, who never could resist a tale which was both superstitious and moral. There are some nice Gothic touches in Southey's version, as, for instance, when his Witch confesses:

> I have 'nointed myself with infants' fat,
> The fiends have been my slaves,
> From sleeping babes I have suck'd the breath,
> And, breaking by charms the sleep of death,
> I have call'd the dead from their graves.

And when the climax is reached . . .

> Then in He came with eyes of flame,
> The Devil to fetch the dead,
> And all the church with his presence glow'd
> Like a fiery furnace red.

It is not good poetry, but I imagine it went down well in village reading-rooms and church halls in the old days. No doubt some of the young ladies felt quite faint. But it would take more than that to frighten them now!

The second legend concerns the Berkeley Toad, which you may see carved in stone on the capital of a pillar in the lovely nave of Berkeley's mediæval church. The representation shows a hideous toad, clutching two frightened human heads. This was the toad which the Berkeley's were supposed to have kept in their dungeon, feeding it on the bodies of prisoners until it grew to a monstrous size. If I may be allowed to venture an opinion, I suspect this tale was concocted by Berkeley mothers of long ago, who, in an effort to frighten naughty children into obedience, used the toad as a device. "If you don't do as you're told, the Berkeley Toad'll get you!"

From many visits to Berkeley, two remain in my memory with peculiar vividness. One of them was in company with George, on a blazing summer's day, the hottest day of a heat-wave. In Castle Meadow the boys and girls of Berkeley were disporting themselves in the Little Avon. We watched them for a while, George mourning the fact that he hadn't brought a bathing costume. Brilliant insects and dusky-brown butterflies droned and flickered above the grasses of the meadow. The air was warm and sweet-scented, and the banks of the Castle Moat were a tangle of willow-herb, meadowsweet, purple-loosestrife and cow-parsley. Above and beyond the meadow, Berkeley Castle (which can look grim and forboding, or insubstantial as a vision, according to the mood of the weather) was a castle of romance. This was the Castle's brighter face, revealing it as the home of chivalry from which brave knights set forth for crusades or for court. On such a day you felt that Castle Meadow must have been the perfect setting for joust or tourney, with gay pavilions, pennons flying, a great banquet, and (because this is, after all, romance)—a stranger knight, in black armour on a coal-black charger, who refused to lift his visor or announce his name. . . . ("Obviously Ivanhoe," says George, with cynical relish.)

The other visit was on an overcast, changeable day last autumn, when, having discovered that I was writing a book about the Vale of Berkeley, Frank Rogers offered to introduce me to some of his old friends in Berkeley town. Frank was born at the White Hart, Berkeley, over eighty years ago. He spent his youth and young manhood there, and he still goes back to pay his friends a visit once or twice each year. I was glad to go with him, for I thought it would be a worthwhile experience to see Berkeley through the eyes of someone else—someone with memories of the place as it was seventy and more years ago.

Our first call, I remember, was on another octogenarian, Frank Hancock, the undertaker—a gruff, genial man with a prodigious memory. Mr Hancock it was who told me about the prize-fight down by Hamfield Farm, and the whale which was washed up on the mud at Littleton in the 1880's. He said the town was livelier when he was young. Not only was the Castle a centre of activity, but the town had its cheese-market once a month, a cattle market (now removed to Berkeley Road Station), and a weekly produce market. All these have gone. Together these two octogenarians yarned about old times when, on voting-days, you could have as much free beer as you could hold. When recruiting-sergeants, with flashy uniforms, big talk about a man's life, and offer of the Queen's shilling, were occasional visitors. When barges were bow-hauled up Berkeley Pill, to discharge their cargoes of coal and stone at the Stock. And when holiday breaks (wagonettes), from Bristol, attracted all the urchins of Berkeley, because the merrymakers had a pleasant habit of throwing pennies into the mud of the roads to see the children scrambling for them.

On our way down to the church we met another of Frank's acquaintances, Joe King. Mr King's father, Thomas King, was one of the best-known Berkeley personalities of half-a-century ago, in great demand as a preacher, and jocularly called "the Bishop of Berkeley" by Lord Fitzhardinge. Many amusing stories are told of Thomas King, who was a rare wit. Meeting him on his way back from preaching a sermon at a chapel in some neighbouring village, Lord Fitzhardinge winked at his steward, and said, in a somewhat facetious tone: "Well, Bishop; and what was the text today?"

"The text, sir?" says Thomas King, with deceptive simplicity.

" 'I went forth to seek my father's asses—and lo! I have found two of them.' "

Mrs Cook, a daughter of Thomas King, very kindly sent me a copy of a little book he wrote under the pseudonym of "Peter Peregrin", printed in 1898. It is a selection of Sunday evening rambles from Berkeley, each to some place of interest at which "Peter Peregrin" found a church, listened to a sermon, and reported upon it. One of these peregrinations was to the Independent Chapel at Newport, "which is supposed to be the oldest Dissenting place of worship anywhere in the neighbourhood of Berkeley. The date inscribed on the front of the chapel shows that it was first built in 1710 . . . so that a house for religious worship stood here when George Whitfield preached on Stinchcombe Hill."

This is not the place to quote largely from Thomas King's booklet, though it contains much that is out-of-the-way and peculiar to the Berkeley country. In any case, Frank Rogers is very anxious to show me the church and Jenner's Hut. . . .

St Mary's parish church is outstandingly fine; and strange, too, since its tower is disconnected from it, at the other end of the churchyard. Its oldest feature, apart from a Roman tile,* is the Norman doorway on the south side. But its greatest beauty is undoubtedly the delightful thirteenth-century west front. Here are still traces of damage done in 1645, during the Civil War, when the church was used by the Parliamentary forces in storming the castle. More disturbing are the traces of that insidious enemy of our churches, the death-watch beetle. Indoors this church is unusually bright with colour, with painted walls and a stone rood-screen of red, blue and gold. This interior used to be brighter still, for the arcades were formerly gilded and there was a Doom painting over the chancel arch. On an enormous alabaster tomb lie the effigies of Thomas, Lord Berkeley, and his lady. This was the lord who received as prisoner Edward II. He is dressed in armour, his head resting on his helmet, his feet upon a lion, whilst his wife rests her feet upon a hound. All around this tomb, as though to protect the effigies (or prevent them rolling off) are tiny battlements carved in the alabaster.

* Discovered, with the bases of two Roman columns, during restoration work on the church in 1856.

John Trevisa, friend of Wycliffe and translator of the Bible, is buried here. Caxton mentions his English Bible, but no copy of it is extant and little or nothing is known of it, though it may have had some influence in his own day. He died at Berkeley Castle in 1412.

In the chancel rests Berkeley's most famous son. He was not a member of the Berkeley family, but a son of the rector and himself a local doctor. His name was Edward Jenner, and he was the discoverer of inoculation as a cure for small-pox. Jenner was a remarkable person—a great man, and also a happy one. He never exploited his discovery commercially, as he might easily have done, and seemed to prefer obscurity to fame, Berkeley to London, locality to Society. He loved the Vale, and never deserted it. Even as a boy, he knew the cries of every bird and could name all the wildflowers that grew by the roadside. He wrote poetry, too, some of it not at all bad. His early poem, *Berkeley Fair*, begins:

> 'Twas Berkeley Fair, and Nature's smile
> Spread joy around for many a mile.
> The rosy milkmaid quits her pail,
> The thresher now puts by his flail;
> His fleecy charge and hazel crook
> By the rude shepherd are forsook;
> The woodman, too, the day to keep;
> Leaves Echo undisturbed in sleep;
> Labour is o'er—his rugged chain
> Lies resting on the grassy plain.

He began his studies under Dr Daniel Ludlow, a surgeon of Chipping Sodbury, and it was in those early days that he heard something which was to have a great influence on the health of all the world. A dairymaid told him she would never get small-pox because she had had cow-pox. On enquiry he found that it was an old country belief that people who'd once had cow-pox (which was what is nowadays called an "occupational" disease) never got small-pox. Now, whilst cow-pox is insignificant, small-pox was in those days a terrible scourge. Other doctors thought the saying was, like so many country superstitions, just an old wives' tale. But Jenner knew that there was nearly always a grain of truth in these old sayings, for did they not embody the folk-experience of the ages? Anyway, long after he had gone to London to study under the famous John Hunter, he was still investigating the connection between cow-pox and small-pox.

In 1780, when he was back in Berkeley, to which he'd returned to set up in practice, he made a discovery. He discovered that there were really two different forms of cow-pox. Only one of them acted as a defence against small-pox. He went on investigating, experimenting, probing to the heart of the matter. Eventually, in 1796, he took a bold step. He inoculated a small boy by the name of James Phipps with cow-pox vesicles. Six weeks later he inoculated the same boy with small-pox germs. It was a dangerous thing to do. If the experiment had failed, Jenner would have had a rough time of it, and his colleagues were not slow in criticising his conduct. But the experiment succeeded. James Phipps became part of medical history, and the doctor's colleagues turned from criticism to adulation. Before long doctors were advocating vaccination for almost every disease that flesh is heir to . . . very much against the advice of Jenner, who was more careful than most, and never hasty in reaching conclusions.

If Jenner had chosen to keep his cure a secret, he might have made a fortune. But he gave it to the world. His fame spread. But at home, in England, he was the centre of controversy and envy, and after he had struggled to get funds for a National Vaccine Institution, his rivals took advantage of his absence from London to squeeze him out of his directorship. Napoleon Bonaparte so greatly honoured him that, when Jenner interceded on behalf of English prisoners in France, the Emperor exclaimed: "Ah! we can refuse nothing to that name!" and released them.

When Jenner interceded on behalf of French prisoners in England, however, he learnt the truth of the old proverb about a prophet never being honoured in his own country. The British authorities found it quite easy to refuse "that name".

Back in Berkeley, Jenner was far from idle. He had his practice as a G.P. He was devoted to the study of natural history and

geology, and he built the first balloon ever seen in Gloucestershire. When Gilbert White of Selborne was pulling down an old
cottage to search its thatch for hibernating swallows, and wondering if there was anything in the belief that they spent the winter
in the mud at the bottom of ponds, Jenner was making notes on
"The Migration of Birds". Not only that: a study of Jenner's
notebooks shows him to have been on the brink of discovering
the theory of evolution. He wrote:

> "The student of geology scarcely passes the threshold of his
> inquiry before he finds himself in a bewildered country. The
> Mosaic account of the Deluge on one side, and the order in
> which he finds the mineral cabinets arranged by the hand of
> nature, on the other."

James Phipps, the boy whom Jenner experimented on, contracted tuberculosis and Jenner built him a house, which still
stands, and helped him plant a garden. Frank Rogers told me
that when he was a boy he knew James Phipps. I must have
looked sceptical, for he said: "That's a fact. He lived to be about
a hundred, and when I knew him he was very old, and I was very
young. But I can say I've seen the first man ever to be inoculated
against small-pox."

Jenner's Hut is just inside the rectory wall, bordering the
churchyard, and it is certainly worth preserving. From outside,
it looks more like a witch's hovel than the laboratory of a great
doctor. When Frank and I saw it, the hut was not in very good
repair. The windows were empty of glass, the thatched roof
disintegrating, the interior bare and rather pathetic in its neglect.
It is a pity some organisation cannot make itself responsible for
Jenner's Hut, for it is a curious and intriguing relic of a great
man who was also a loyal Gloucestrian.

The churchyard contains some remarkable tombs, and a splendid crop of epitaphs. One is reputed to have been written by
Dean Swift, who was Chaplain to Charles, Earl of Berkeley.
The subject of it, Dicky Pearce, was a household jester. I have been
told that he was the last of the household "fools", and that he was
killed at the Castle during a drunken brawl, when he was kicked
to death. That is only hearsay. I can offer no documentary proof

and it is quite possible that this story may be a malicious invention. The epitaph reads:

> Here lies the Earl of Suffolk's fool,
>   Men call'd him Dicky Pearce:
> His folly serv'd to make folks laugh,
>   When wit and mirth were scarce.
>
> Poor Dick, alas! is dead and gone:
>   What signifies to cry?
> Dickys enough are still to come
>   To laugh at by and by.

(Buried June 18, 1728, Aged 63 years.)

The other well-known epitaph is to another Pierce, who must have been a great man in a small way:

> Here lyeth Thomas Pierce, whom no man taught,
> Yet he in iron, brass and silver wrought;
> He jacks and clocks and watches (with art) made
> And mended too when others' work did fade.
> Of Berkeley five times mayor this artist was,
> And yet this Mayor, this artist, was but grass;
> When his own watch was down on the last day,
> He that made watches had not made a key
> To wind it up; but useless it must lie
> Until he rise again, no more to die.

(1665)

To a virtuous woman:

> Here lies a Woman by all the good esteem'd,
> Because they proved her really what she seem'd;
> If thou would'st die as highly priz'd as she,
> Add to thy virtue true sincerity.

And this sad and revealing epitaph to one of life's invalids:

> Pain was my portion,
> Physick was my food,
> Groans was my devotion,
> Drugs did me no good;

Christ was my physician,
He knew which was best,
To ease me of my pain,
And take my soul to rest.

Finally, a verse of real poetic merit in the Shakespearian mode:

Farewell, vain world, I've known enough of thee,
And now am careless what thou say'st of me;
Thy smiles I court not, nor thy frowns do fear,
My cares are past, my head lies quiet here;
What faults you've seen in me take care to shun,
And look at home, enough there to be done!

These reminders of mortality had a curious effect on Frank and me. It made us feel peckish. So he took me back to the Market Square, to have tea with his old friend Walter Shore. Mr Shore is a well-known Berkeley figure, in appearance rather like a Flemish burgher of the eighteenth century. Frank Rogers and he were friends as boys, and they are friends still. They sat side by side in the choir of Berkeley church, and on one occasion, Frank Rogers reminisced, when *he* had been fooling about in service, a blow aimed at his head by the choirmaster missed him and hit Walter Shore. Chuckling, Frank asked him if he remembered it. "No," smiled Mr Shore, "I haven't got your amazing memory, Frank."

Mr Shore's shop in the Square is dated 1660. He began life as a shop assistant, and worked his way up. Frank Rogers, on the other hand, came into a thousand pounds (and that was a lot of money in those days!) on his twenty-first birthday. One friend worked his way up, whilst the other (so Frank assured me, with philosophic humour) worked *his* way down. I asked him how much of that £1,000 he still had. He laughed, and—"Not a ha'penny of it!" he said.

According to the Official Guide to Berkeley, Wanswell Court is a pleasant walk across the fields. No doubt it is, if you know the way! I didn't; and after wandering round in a half-circle, ended up in a recreation ground. Thereafter I followed the road to Berkeley Station (a pleasing Victorian relic, which still has an occasional train to occupy it, and to prevent grass overgrowing the track), where I again took to the fields.

Keeping to the right of Tintock Wood, I crossed a bridge over a stream and shortly afterwards was "electrocuted" by an electric fence. This delightful evidence of progressive farming was treated to a flow of invective which was completely wasted on it, before I came into the little lane which leads to the front of Wanswell Court. This used to be reached by two drawbridges, which have now been replaced by stone bridges over the moat. It is an extremely old house, rich in interest for the antiquary. In 1256 Philip de Leicester obtained a licence from the Abbot of Bristol to erect a chapel within the manor. In the fifteenth century the estate came, by way of marriage, into the hands of a Bristol burgess, John Thorpe, and this family continued to occupy it for ten generations and nearly three centuries. It was either John or his son who built the oldest portion of the existing house.

One of these Thorpes was apparently governor of Berkeley Castle or held some other official position there, for Thorpe's Tower still exists. It was not until the eighteenth century that the Thorpes relinquished Wanswell, when it was sold to the ancestor of a family of antiquaries, Daniel Lysons. In 1818 his great-great-grandson, also a Daniel, sold it to Colonel Berkeley, who has already been mentioned in connection with the poaching affray at Hill. It is still part of the Berkeley estate, though it is now a farm and has begun to look its age. When I was there, the west side of the house, which is a gabled Elizabethan addition and is often photographed, was somewhat marred by a large pile of gravel and some empty oil-drums which detracted from the beauty of the house and its surroundings. From a farm building came the hum of electric milking-machinery, and a car stood near the pile of gravel.

It was in a field nearby that Sir Maurice Berkeley was once discomfited. The story was told me by Mr P. G. Davies, who in his turn was told it by his wife. Mrs Davies' father farmed Wanswell Court Farm up to about seventy-two years ago, and her mother was the daughter of John Cary of Ham Green Farm, Berkeley, and the licensee of the Berkeley Arms Hotel. Her sister married John Ayris, who was huntsman to the Berkeley Hunt. Anyway, the story goes that Sir Maurice was cub-hunting

Tites Point, between Sharpness and Purton

one day, and had drawn several coverts without success, when the hunt came to a field of beans near Wanswell.

"You'd better draw those beans," Sir Maurice instructed the huntsman.

"I shouldn't put the hounds in there, sir. They beans is dead ripe," said the huntsman, and he was backed up by the farmer who was standing nearby.

"Oh, they won't do any harm," Sir Maurice said airily, more interested in sport than good husbandry.

Into the field went the hounds, killed seven cubs, and made a frightful mess of the crop. Seeing that the damage was considerable, Sir Maurice rode up to the farmer, who was still standing by, and said: "Afraid the hounds have made rather a mess of your beans."

"Yes, they have knocked 'em about a bit. But they bain't *my* beans, Sir Maurice."

"No? Whose are they, then?"

"Yours, sir. I sold them to your steward this morning."

Gatehouse of Frocester Court

CHAPTER VIII

SHARPNESS AND THE NEW GROUNDS

WANSWELL leads on to Sharpness, a curious corner of the Vale, with much of interest but little of antiquity. Sharpness is effectively divided by the railway-line into two separate communities, Newtown and Dock-town. Newtown does not arouse our curiosity; it is one of those suburbs which might be on the outskirts of any town, anywhere. But Sharpness proper, across the railway-lines and a couple of intervening fields, is a rather likeable jumble of docks, fields and streets. Ranks of red-brick houses huddle round the granaries and derricks, almost in the shadow of masts and funnels of steamers from Russia, Germany and elsewhere. On week-ends, when the port is quiet, you can wander along the wharves without meeting more than an occasional seaman or a mother showing her infant the big ships. Here you'll find fowls happily foraging between the railway-lines, and swans (by the dozen) standing on the grassy shore beyond the wharves, unhappily trying to clean the thick black oil from their feathers. Here, too, I saw gulls, asleep, head under wing, on a petrol installation.

Sharpness is unusual because it is a dock in the country, not surrounded, as so many docks are, by the factories of a town. There are green fields just beyond the warehouses, and the air is country air, scented and sweet. The harbour is a fine sight. Not nearly so large as the Royal Edward Dock at Avonmouth, it is compact and can be the better comprehended by the casual visitor, who appreciates the homely atmosphere and the modest proportions of the vessels being discharged. Most of the ships which come to Sharpness are in the 5,000–7,000 tons class. And in addition to ships which bring traffic from foreign or coastwise ports to Sharpness, a large number of small motor craft and lighters use the canal which connects Sharpness and Gloucester and short-cuts the tortuous and difficult Severn. The imports at Sharpness are chiefly oil and spirits (385,624 tons in 1950), grain and flour (55,941 tons), oilseeds and nuts (13,190), foodstuffs (10,231), and timber (4,188). In 1950, 52 foreign and 3,193 coastwise vessels arrived at Sharpness docks. In the same year, 369,947 vessels (chiefly lighters and small motor craft) passed through the canal. The latter operate between Bristol Channel ports and Gloucester, Worcester and Stourport on the Severn. A large volume of oil traffic is carried upriver in this way by special tank-craft, the largest capacity of which is 400 tons. Regular tonnages of foodstuffs, metals, timber and grain, etc., are carried through to waterheads at Worcester and Stourport for distribution in the Midlands. Under normal circumstances ships of 1,000 tons can navigate the canal to Gloucester. But with present conditions of silting the maximum tonnage is 500.

Most of the Sharpness trade depends on the canal. It is usually called the Berkeley–Gloucester because, when it was begun, the intention was to effect a junction with Severn at Berkeley. But the company met with many difficulties. Engineers proved incompetent. Landowners were difficult. Materials were bought and then found unsuitable. And there was further trouble with estimates and contractors. The original plan was for a canal $17\frac{3}{4}$ miles long, 70 feet broad at water-level and 18 feet deep. Its estimated cost was £120,000 and the authorised capital of the company was fixed at £140,000. Work began at Gloucester in 1794, and some idea of the difficulties that the company had to meet may be gathered from the fact that, by 1797, when the whole of the company's capital had been exhausted, the cutting had got no farther south than Hardwicke, $5\frac{1}{2}$ miles below Gloucester. In desperation the committee suggested the original plan should be modified. Instead the canal might link up with the Stroudwater at Saul, which would connect Thames and Severn. Or, alternatively, the canal could join Severn at Hock Crib on the New Grounds. The shareholders were not enthusiastic, and *for the next twenty years* the committee wavered between a number of possible junctions before they finally chose Sharpness Point. It was a government subsidy that made completion of the canal possible. There was, at that time (1817), a great deal of unemployment, and special commissioners were able to authorise loans to new projects offering employment to unskilled labour. Thomas Telford was inspector for these commissioners, and it was he who pronounced the undertaking "a good risk". But even now the company's troubles weren't over. By the time they had made their junction with the Stroudwater at Saul, all their subsidy had gone, and once again began a feverish search for funds to continue the work. After an interval, the government's commissioners again came to the rescue, and the canal was opened in 1827, "two Boats, Band and Colour" carrying the committee to perform the ceremony. At the time of its completion, the canal was the greatest in Britain, taking ships of anything up to 1,000 tons burthen.

For many years the company were in financial difficulties, chiefly because of the interest on their borrowings. In fact it wasn't until 1847 that they were free from persistent attempts to sell them up, and not until 1871 that they were able to call their title-deeds their own. I do not know when the swing-bridges were made and the bridge-keepers' lodges built, but they certainly don't suggest financial extremities. The bridges are neatly-painted, black and white; and the lodges, built in the Grecian style, are delightful to look at, whatever they may be like to live in.

As I have not explored Sharpness Point I am not able to confirm that the golden samphire, which grew there in 1864, still flourishes. Sharpness Point would seem, according to the Gloucestershire *Flora*, to be an exciting place botanically, for the spreading bellflower, bogbean and herb-Paris have all been reported from there.

The Severn Bridge, above Sharpness, is 4,162 feet long and took four years to construct. It looks attractive from a distance, and affords the traveller by rail to Lydney or Severnbridge one of the finest views in the county. I shall never forget the first time I crossed it, on a clear, fine day in July, seeing the great tidal estuary below at high tide, and, on the canal running parallel with it, a gaily-painted "narrow boat" going up to Gloucester. Sea-gulls drifted below the carriage-window, and a coaster sounded its syren as it entered Sharpness Dock. Unfortunately, the bridge is not equal to heavy traffic, and is crossed only by the railway to Lydney from Berkeley Road, so that comparatively few travellers get this remarkable view of Severn.

There are two Purtons, one on each side of the river. But whilst our Purton is a village, the other, on the far side of Severn, is only a hamlet. Strangely enough, they seem to have no parochial connection. Purton is a real riverside village. Indeed, it owes its cricket-ground to the river, which deposited it conveniently near to the Berkeley Arms. To score a six on this ground you have either to knock the ball into the river or hit walnut-tree or pub. If you break one of the windows of the pub you not only don't have to pay the cost, but the landlord will stand you a bottle of whisky. The walnut-tree is a fine one, about fifty years old. According to local report, it made scarcely any growth during its first ten or fifteen years, until someone suggested that it was "rind-bound" and the bark of the tree was slit from top to bottom in eight or ten places. After that there was no stopping it, and its girth is now so great that you can scarcely get your arms round it.

Not far from the walnut-tree, four and a half steps lead down to the cricket field. These are all that are left of the *twenty-two* steps that used to go down to Purton Passage, all the others having been covered over by the building-up of this New Ground. However, the river is not so beneficent as it might appear in the matter, since it has eroded a large part of the old Purton race-course, where Purton Races used to be run. For the most part, though, Severn has been a good friend to Purton men. According to Brian Waters, in his book *Severn Tide*, eighty men left Purton village daily, in the heyday of salmon fishing, to fish in Severn. It was remunerative in those days, and explains why, although they lived in the Berkeley country, much of which was owned by the Lords of Berkeley, Purton men were able to maintain their independence and own their own homes. Today few men, from Purton or anywhere else on Severn, are able to maintain themselves with a lave-net alone, though "there are still a few casuals who wander out over the sands with a lave-net on their shoulder; in the same way that a farmer potters about with a gun when he has an evening to spare". Most of the older men feel that both they and the river have had their best days.

Purton Passage was once a famous crossing, but it was bought out by the Great Western Railway in the hope, one supposes, that people would thereby be forced to cross the Severn Bridge by train. The road which led to the Passage was grassed over, and a gate put across it to keep the cattle in and vehicles out. This right-of-way would have lapsed but for the efforts of one man. Old George Cooke kept it open for more than sixty years, by driving his pony and cart through once a year. One day in each year he harnessed his pony to his cart, drove up to the gate and demanded of the farmer that he should open it; he then requested him to open the second gate, for there are two gates between Tites Point and the slipway. On reaching the river bank, old George drove home and unharnessed his pony. Brian Waters goes on to make a point which is so excellent in itself and so perfectly expressed that I cannot do better than quote him:

"It takes a steadfast and far-seeing mind to carry out such a simple and lonely ceremony for over sixty years; but actions like this give real meaning to law and constitution. If there had been one man of old George Cooke's character in every English village throughout the last three hundred years, the face of England would be unrecognisable to us as we know it today."

Unfortunately such men are few, and they are now, in these days of standardisation and compulsory schooling, almost extinct. My own grandfather Lewis was such a one, liking to spend what little spare time he had asserting local rights-of-way. But the rest of the world looks upon them as cranks; and, indeed, those footpaths which do still exist are so little used that it's difficult to find them, and so badly neglected in the matter of stiles and gates that it is next to impossible to follow them when found. I remember a story about such a character (a woman in this case) in the southern part of the Vale, whose neighbour tried to discourage people from following a right-of-way through his garden. He did succeed in discouraging everyone except Mrs Yeoman. She alone regularly climbed the overgrown stile and made her way steadfastly through the middle of his potato patch and among his sprouting broccoli, following the line of the ancient footpath. He tried all sorts of expedients, but still she kept on, partly because the path was a short-cut for her, but chiefly as a matter of principle. Exasperated, the man eventually knocked out the rungs of the stile in the hope that she, being old and frail, would find it impossible to negotiate. As it happened, he hadn't told his wife what he'd done, and that very evening, after dark, she took this same short-cut, mounted the stile, and, surprised by the absence of rungs, lost her balance and fell to the ground. One of her legs was broken, and it was a crestfallen husband who came out, in answer to her cries, to carry her home. Old Mrs Yeoman, of course, considered that this was a heavenly judgment upon him, and a token of encouragement from the Almighty. She continued to use the path until she could walk no more, and when, at last, she lost the use of her legs, it was her great grief that she would no longer be able to assert her right-of-way. No one followed in her footsteps, and that particular footpath has long been lost. Other neighbours took the line of least resistance. Faced by a tyranny, most of us, I'm afraid, give up our privileges too easily, mutter something like, "Anything for a quiet life!", and try to quiet our consciences by telling ourselves it's not worth making a fuss over.

It *is* worth making a fuss over, and George Cooke and Mrs Yeoman were right to take the attitude they did. They fought for freedom and for their individual rights but, alas! the majority of us are too apathetic, too timid, too cowardly or downright lazy to "put ourselves out".

A mile or so from Purton, in the direction of Berkeley, is Halmore where, until his death recently, lived a well-known member of the Berkeley Hunt, Hastings Neale of Halmore Farm. Old readers of the *Dursley Gazette* and *Horse and Hound* will be familiar with the initials W.N.H. below which, for many years, his excellent hunting articles appeared. Unfortunately I never met him. I had always meant to, and when at last I wrote, in December 1951, it was to learn that, after seventy-two years hunting with the Berkeley *without a break*, he had had an accident in the hunting field a fortnight before and was laid up, or, to quote his own metaphor, had been forced to close the stable door. From his bed he wrote to tell me that he had "put many memories of places and personalities into cold storage—memories pregnant with the trials, tragedies and triumphs of the Chase". He regretted that he was not young enough to help me more actively, but asked me to come and see him, when we could talk about local places and people, hunting and the Berkeley family, "their history, frivolities and leadership in field sports." Perhaps he knew what lay ahead, for in this same letter he wrote: "I now have a little leisure in which to turn the pages of a delightful past. And, looking down the long trail, am content to follow in the footsteps of all those good fellows who have gone before." In point of fact, Hastings Neale never (to adopt his own metaphor) unbolted the stable door again. He died that same spring, before I had a chance to meet him, and I shall always regret the conjunction of circumstances, illness and laziness (on my part) which kept us apart.

Hastings Neale was a sort of Jorrocks of the Vale. Not a hunting man myself, I could never read his hunting column without being infected with some of his enthusiasm. His literary style was inclined, at times, to be idiosyncratic; but it was none the worse for that. Here is a quotation from an old clipping of W.N.H.'s column which I discovered the other day. It is not Hastings Neale at his best, but it does give an idea of his quality.

"On Saturday last, Capt. Berkeley voted for the Vale again; always a popular choice. A fox was soon roused at Hill village —an outlier, one of a litter that we disturbed there a month ago. It was fast followed up the Vale, but on the main road he was turned, and a turned fox creates commotion among hounds and extra work for huntsman. But the prospect of a fast hunt got pinched in the bud. And when the line of this lucky fox was carried into Churchill Wood his responsibilities seemed to have been shifted onto at least one confederate. . . . During the day a companion queried of me: 'Did you see my horse fall in that gateway?' 'No,' I replied, 'but it reminds me that it will be sixty-two years ago come next February that the hot-headed horse I was riding killed himself in that very same gateway.' And in the years between I have never witnessed so gruesome a victim of the hunting field. Those who saw that accident, or its outcome, including the late Joseph King of Newpark Farm who got there with his gun, have now, with one exception, all passed on to the Happier Hunting Grounds."

All too soon Hastings Neale was destined to join them. I hope that his new Hunting Grounds yield good sport, and that there's not too much "wire" to distress this good old sportsman.

As a descriptive title, "The New Grounds" is rather misleading, since this land was very similar, though in an immature condition, in 1600. Before that, part at least of the silt was on the other side of the river. For long the area was described in two sections. The drier and more stabilised land was known as Warth, and that part of it which was liable to be more volatile, to come and go with the set of the tides, was known as Dumbles. The name Dumbles or Dumballs has persisted for 300 years, and is still in use, as members of the Severn Wildfowl Trust will know, for the Dumbles is the favourite feeding-ground of the wild geese. Before 1550 the Dumbles and part of the New Grounds was a tidal area in course of formation, intersected by subsidiary channels and partially clothed with coarse grasses. At that time there was a large body of silt continually in motion, but its movement was arrested when, a large part of it coming to rest on the Slimbridge shore, the Berkeleys proceeded to impound it to form the New Grounds. How this mass of material accumulated cannot be clearly defined, but it seems probable that it came into being partly by the liquefying of the Lias formation on the Slimbridge side and washings of Old Red Sandstone and Red Marl from the Forest foreshore. There is no doubt that foreign admixtures of silt from other parts of the river combine with the local material to form a composition of extraordinary fertility.

Naturally, the building of banks and breakwaters, together with internal drainage, fencing and the planting of shelter belts, cost the Berkeleys a great deal of money. In 1846, for instance, Lord Fitzhardinge contracted to pay Joseph Trotter a sum of £742 10s. for executing a bank of 38,000 cubic yards. Within living memory the sailing trows *Lavender* and *Industry* brought stones for this purpose from the quarries at Chepstow. These trows carried a cargo of forty to fifty tons of block stone, and were manned by a crew of three. I am told (and I pass it on for the interest of seamen, who have a passionate curiosity for details of a vessel's destiny) that the *Industry* was wrecked at last, whilst *Lavender* ended her days, ignominiously, as a freshwater canal barge.

The surface of these New Grounds is about 26 feet above sea-level, but 3 feet *below* the level of high tides, whilst the sea-wall is 5 feet 6 inches *above* high tide. Since the opening of the

Berkeley–Gloucester canal in 1827, it has become an artificial boundary to the east, so that we may assume that the New Grounds, as now constituted, extend from canal to Severn, and from Frampton Pill in the north to Royal Drift in the south: about 1,320 acres. Of this, the Dumbles constitute only about 210 acres, which are very exposed to south-westerly winds coming up the Bristol Channel. In 1886–7, when the Fishery Board made an investigation, they found that the wind blew south-westerly for 225 days in the year, there were spells when the wind blew north-easterly in the early part of the year and in autumn, and the average annual rainfall was (and is) 30 inches.

When, in the sixteenth century, there was an alteration in the course of the river-channel, which brought a large accretion of silt to Slimbridge Warth, landowners and farmers at Awre on the other side of the river felt their misfortune very keenly. For Severn had taken this silt from *their* Warth, which they found to be rapidly diminishing. And when it was discovered that Lord Berkeley and his steward, John Smyth, were taking action to ensure that the land stayed on their side, Awre folk were naturally annoyed. For if Smyth proved successful, it meant that the Warth would become permanent, and could never return to Awre. Their only hope was in legal action. If Severn was proven to be a Royal river, Lord Berkeley could be prevented from tampering with it, and then (they reasoned) there was a fair chance they might get their Warth land back again, when Severn next changed its course. A Commission of Enquiry was appointed, and they—meeting at Newnham—discovered that a part of the river had been wrongfully enclosed. As a result, the Attorney-General to Charles I "exhibited an Information of Intrusion against George, Lord Berkeley, Elizabeth Longe, widowe, John Smyth, and John Dryver, his tenant".

It was our old friend, John Smyth of Nibley, steward and historian of the Berkeleys, who had been instrumental in getting Lord Berkeley to reclaim and protect the New Grounds. And one can understand Smyth's feelings about this injunction, the more so when one remembers that the Commission had refused to hear the Berkeley case, declining to admit any of the evidence which Smyth had, with great labour, prepared. But John Arundel and Sir Sackville Crowe were not to get it all their own way.

There were numerous law-suits, claims and counter-claims, of which Smyth says:

> "Divers great and tedious suites have been contynued from the Seaventh yeare of King James to this daye; which have produced Commissions of Surveys out of the Exchequer and Court of Wardes with perticular maps, two decrees in Chancery, five decrees in the Court of Wardes, Trialls at Lawe both in Kingsbench and Common pleas, Inditements in the Country, and bills for ryotts and other misdemeanours in the Star Chamber. The bookes and breviatts whereof are *elephantini libri*, a wholl porter's burden; wherein I have longe had my unprofitable part. The further narration whereof (through the great expence thereby occasioned) I take noe comforte longer to contynue."

The Berkeley case, when it came up for hearing, opened thus:

> "This river of Severne is capable of private property. Soe, de facto, the said river, the soile, sands, shore, Channell and rockes to the middle of the streame or channell, have byn in all ages (as for 500 yeares and more wee shall proove *by more than* 1,000 *peeces of Evidence*) possessed, held, and enjoyed, by the Lords of the Great Manor of Berkeley."

Some idea of Smyth's industry in collecting his evidence can be gained by the fact that it could scarcely be contained in "2 trunkes and 3 baggs". It was not, perhaps, surprising that the Barons of the Court decided not to examine all the evidence, but to take it as read. They agreed that the Berkeley title to the land was in order, and the case, so far as Arundel, Crowe and Awre were concerned, fell to the ground. Far from being pleased, John Smyth seems to have been extremely vexed that he was not allowed to fire his 1,000 peeces of Evidence at the enemy. The Court's sudden decision took the wind out of his sails, prevented him from delivering his splendid Invective Speech against Sir Sackville Crowe, and left him with 2 trunkes and 3 baggs full of Evidence to carry back to the Muniment Room of Berkeley Castle.

That was not the last squabble about this particular land. A later one resulted in the Slimbridge Inclosure Act of 1801. And the last one was in 1908, *the Lord Fitzhardinge v. Purcell*. Lewis Purcell was a local man, a great sportsman and a first-class shot, who enjoyed nothing better than a trip down the river in his boat, with a shot at the wild geese from the sandbanks. This led to one or two minor disagreements, but nothing serious would have occurred but for an unfortunate combination of circumstances.

One winter's day when Lord Fitzhardinge and his friends were goosing on the New Grounds, Lewis Purcell was idling downriver in his boat. Now, Lord Fitzhardinge and his friends hadn't been having much luck. In fact, they had had a poor day; and when a couple of geese which Purcell had shot at from his boat fell on the foreshore not far from the proprietorial party, it was —so far as Lord Fitzhardinge was concerned—the limit! And then, when Purcell had the audacity to come ashore, in order to retrieve *his* geese, Lord Fitzhardinge challenged him. Purcell took little or no notice, and there was a legal application for an injunction. Once more the 1,000 peeces of Evidence travelled up to London, and, after a hearing of five days and the examination of twenty-four witnesses and some hundreds of the documents, Mr Justice Parker confirmed the Berkeley's ownership of the foreshore, and granted an injunction.

There is a reference to the great productivity of Slimbridge land in Fuller's *Worthies of England*, wherein the author reports that so great is the "fruitfulness of the land nigh Slimbridge, that in springtime, let it (the grass) be bit to the roots, a wand laid along therein overnight will be covered with new-grown grasse by next morning". On being told this, James I replied that he knew a field in Scotland where, if a horse was turned into it on a Sunday, it would be in vain to look for it next day. But that story seems to be equivocal; a reflection on the honesty of certain Scotsmen.

Slimbridge church-tower is a famous local landmark. In the flat and comparatively little-wooded country of this part of the Vale, it is a conspicuous object. And if it attracts visitors they will not be disappointed, for Slimbridge church is of great beauty. The greater part of it is thirteenth-century: the parapet on the nave, the unusual south doorway with its elegant foliage-pattern, the splendid nave arches and the arch and vault of the tower. One of the capitals near the south door has been described as one of the six best things in Gloucestershire churches. It is doubtful if any better example of stone-carving of that period could be found in England. The interior is even more impressive than the outside, with its two arcades and angels making music and praying in the roof, whilst the chancel is fourteenth-century, and so is the tower with its open parapet and elaborate niches. Here is one of the few lead fonts in England. Though when I say "few", I actually mean thirty-eight, of which nine are in Gloucestershire. This particular font was made in 1664.

Near the church is the vicarage, which stands on a site of some antiquity, for its garden is ringed by a moat. It is, in fact, the site of the old Slymbridge Manor, at which an Earl of Berkeley slept on his way to fight at Bannockburn. On the other side of the road is the site of an old priory, but this apart, the village of Slimbridge has little of interest architecturally. Red-brick of a not especially attractive kind is the order, and the style is chiefly Victorian. An entry in the parish register for January 25th, 1643, proclaims of one Giles Parker that he "was murthered in his owne house, and no crowner sate on him".

Beyond the village of Slimbridge with its red-brick cottages, church and moated vicarage, the road winds round to Shepherd's Patch. This is a curious spot, as distinctive as its name, where a swing-bridge crosses the canal and there are usually boats tied up and barges passing through. I don't know why, but Patch Bridge is quite exciting. There is a quickening of interest, a feeling of expectation, when you see it for the first time. You recognise it as a "place", with its own character and moods. Moreover, it is the sort of place at which things might be expected to happen. I am sorry I cannot be more explicit, but Shepherd's Patch is a place you must *see* to understand.

From the bridge-head you get a good view of the New Grounds: a level expanse of grazing land, much of which was ploughed for the first time during the recent war. A farm road runs, very straight and direct, to the centre of the New Grounds, where there are three cottages, once occupied by shepherds, but now the property of the Severn Wildfowl Trust.

It is not known when the wild geese first began coming to the New Grounds, but they have certainly done so for centuries. They begin to arrive in September, and leave in March. Their numbers vary from year to year, and from day to day, during the migration south. There may be anything between 2,000 and 6,000 geese on the New Grounds during the winter, and they spend most of their time on the Dumbles. Whitefronts (*Anser albifrons*) are the chief visitors.

"Goosing" used to be the traditional sport on the New Grounds. It is *not* another name for wildfowling, having all the ritual of a partridge drive or of shooting grouse from butts. One writer calls it "a truly regal sport, for which it would be difficult to imagine country more perfectly suited". Goosing was distinctly tinged with feudalism, however, and would not absorb modern innovations. The Hon. Grantley Berkeley, that sporting buck who was also a novelist, apparently regarded the sport with unbecoming levity. Perhaps his substitution of something more modern and lethal for the orthodox "weapon" was not too popular at Berkeley. Writing in 1854, he has this to say concerning goosing in his day:

> "The geese, if properly taken as they come towards the shooter and almost directly over the gun, when killed fall behind the gunners in the mud. Generally one or two of the guests are seen with bloody noses, and holding their right arms in hideous positions, as if their shoulders were out; it being settled by the Leader that old single-barrelled, overgrown muskets, with bell mouths, five feet eight in the barrel, and hammers that carry a flag-stone for flint, with pans the size of soup-tureens and stocks so short that a man's nose rests on his thumb when he takes aim and presses the trigger, ARE the only things that men shall kill geese with. One or two wounded men are always seen in a dilapidated state.
>
> "'Master So-and-so,' asks a sly old keeper, 'what be the matter with you?'
>
> "'Oh,' replies the guest, with a suppressed groan, 'my shoulder's out.'
>
> "'No 'teant,' says the keeper. 'They do all zay so, as do shoot wi' her, but I never knowed none on 'em but got well by dinner time.'"

The alluvial flats and saltings of the New Grounds provide very nearly perfect wildfowl country. Anciently the wild geese and duck were protected by the Lords of Berkeley for sporting purposes. Since 1946, however, the Severn Wildfowl Trust has succeeded in establishing here the most extensive collection of wildfowl in the world. There are about 920 "residents", some of which are full-winged, of 130 different species and sub-species. Swans, geese and duck of every conceivable shape and coloration live in natural surroundings a life of comparative freedom. Most of them are quite friendly and amiable. All of them look amazingly healthy, active and happy. The noise they kick up in Big and Rushy Pens when there is food in the offing ranges from a thin, high whistle to a basso-profundo *quark*! To the left of the entrance-gate, Big Pen contains a large open pool and many decoy-side pens. Beyond it are two smaller enclosures with a linked system of ponds most attractively laid out. Swimming on these ponds and waddling about the grassland are Greater Snow Geese, Greylags, Blue Snows, Barhead and Bean Geese, Emperors and Whitefronts; Whistling, Whooper and Black Swans; and more ducks than I can possibly enumerate.

In front of the entrance is the smaller Orchard Pen, and beyond it a spinney with a decoy pool of about an acre. This used to be known as the New Decoy, for it was made as a substitute for the Old Decoy at Purton, which, it was thought, might be spoilt by the proximity of the Berkeley–Gloucester canal. In point of fact, the Old Decoy was not seriously affected by the canal, and, with its delightful woodland, the Old Decoy has retained its interest for the duck in winter and nightingales in spring. However, the New Decoy is also attractive and very successful. Visitors to the enclosures have a unique opportunity for spying on it, for on the edge of the spinney which surrounds the decoy pool there is a hut on stilts, or gazebo, from which you get a splendid view of wildfowl on the pool. These may be either "residents" or, in season, "visitors", which are decoyed for ringing. Species which regularly visit this decoy are Mallard, Wigeon, Teal, Pintail, Shoveler, Garganey, Gadwall, Pochard and Tufted Duck.

Leading out of the decoy pool, one at each corner, are four wired-in lanes (or "pipes", as they are called), down which the duck are enticed, so that they can be captured for ringing. Various methods are used to entice duck into the pipes. The most effective of these has been the use of a specially trained dog and o fermented grain (very plentiful in the autumn of 1950). Record catches were achieved in 1950–1 by feeding spoiled wheat into the pipes of the decoy. But the use of a dog as decoy exploits a weakness of ducks—their mixture of curiosity, bravado and exhibitionism. Observing the dog to enter one of the pipes, they follow it. Then, when they are safely inside the pipe, a member of the staff (who's been watching the manœuvre from behind a screen) shows himself to these duck already in the pipe, and as he is between them and the entrance, they retreat still farther into it, where they can be captured and ringed. It is noticeable that different species react differently. For instance, Teal, Mallard and Gadwall are easily attracted, whilst Pintails and Shovelers are either not so curious or not so brave. Ducks will, of course, follow all sorts of creatures for one reason or another. Here at the New Grounds they have been observed to pursue water-vole, grass-snake, sparrow-hawk, and (rather half-heartedly) a heron.

Rushy Pen is to the right of the entrance-gate, a large and most attractive enclosure containing open ponds fringed with rushes. Many of the ducks and geese fly about quite freely, and it is exhilarating to see a trio of wildfowl come flying in, to surface with a splash, breasting the water like racing seaplanes. Upkeep of the enclosures, conservation and rearing are only a part of the Trust's work. It is also responsible for the feeding-grounds on the Dumbles, on which, in winter, there may be as many as 3,000 geese feeding. In 1940 four pillboxes were built on the sea-wall overlooking the Dumbles. It was subsequently discovered that these made fine observation posts for watching the wildfowl, and they have now been supplemented by specially made observation huts, so contrived that, wherever the geese happen to be feeding, they can be observed at fairly close range. Beyond the Dumbles are the estuarial mudflats and sandbanks, on which swans, geese, duck and various waders roost. About the river-estuary here-abouts, Peter Scott, who is Honorary Director of the Trust, says: "It is a sort of oasis for cross-country migrants, and a number of interesting birds, such as Spoonbill, Night Heron, Bewick's Swan, Scoter, Goosander, Black-tailed Godwit, Curlew Sand-piper, Little Stint, Great and Arctic Skua, Black Tern, Snowy Owl, Peregrine and Hobby, have been seen in recent years."

Most famous member of the Trust is Her Majesty Queen

Stroudwater Canal, near Saul

Elizabeth II, who is also its Patron, and has visited Slimbridge several times. Just recently she came across from Badminton to see how the five Trumpeter Swans which were presented to her when she was in Canada were getting on in their new home. As the Trumpeters were found to be basking in the sunshine on the far side of Big Pen, Mrs Scott and Nicola (Peter Scott's daughter) had to go across and drive them in the direction of the Royal party. At the same time, Her Majesty saw the famous Hawaian *Ne-ne* geese, of which little more than thirty were, until recently, existent. Two hens and a cock are being kept here in the hope that, with careful and sympathetic treatment, the species may be propagated. The last news I had was encouraging. Both of the female *Ne-nes* had nested, and there was a possibility that the eggs of one, at least, were fertile. They were being incubated by bantam foster-mothers.*

We are privileged to possess such a fine conservation centre in Gloucestershire, not only because such ventures are always good and of scientific value, but because you can go there whenever you please and see ducks. It is not easy to say *why* ducks and geese have such a curious attraction, are so intriguing to watch. But it *has* been said, and by a Gloucestershire poet—

> *From troubles of the world*
> *I turn to ducks . . .*

After which F. W. Harvey goes on to pin-point the eccentricities of the species, and to remark on the diverting and recuperative effects on humans of *watching* ducks. It is true. Ducks are—like, in a lesser way, pigs—a solace to the worried or city-wearied brain. And I know of no better escape, in this age of anxiety, than to go to Slimbridge, where from troubles of this world you can turn, for an hour or two, to ducks.

---

* No less than nine goslings were raised from those eggs—a notable achievement, as *The Times* remarked. In view of the fact that *Ne-nes* else-where are faring badly, the success of this project may well save this particular species from extinction.

Wheatenhurst church

CHAPTER IX

CAM, FROME AND STROUDWATER

ELEVEN miles below Gloucester, the main Gloucester–Bristol road is met by the Dursley–Cam road at the roadside hamlet of Cambridge (Bridge-over-the-Cam), a mile or so short of the Slimbridge crossroads. Like Slimbridge, it is a red-brick place, standing above low-lying water-meadows through which wander the Cam and the Stroudwater canal. These meadows are frequently flooded and are, indeed, flooded at the time of writing (in May).

Cambridge used to be a "stage" in coaching days, when the hamlet would have had one eye at least on passing trade. According to a history of Slimbridge published in the last century, there is a field at Cambridge called Little Cheston which was the site of an ancient building. Coins of the period of Constantine suggest that it may have been a Roman sub-station or a villa, "probably used for depasturing their cattle", whatever that may mean. The fact that it lies almost in a straight line between Aust and Cirencester is mentioned as being of a very special significance.

The main road (A.38) has been considerably widened hereabouts to take the increased (and increasing) motor traffic. It is useless to moan about such "improvements". They are necessary, and that is that. But they further isolate motorists and other users of the road from the countryside, which the double-strip trunk-road does *not* adorn. It is all right for those who simply want to get from Bristol to Gloucester in a hurry. For those ramblers, cyclists, poets and philosophers who believe that the Journey is of greater importance than the Destination, it is disastrous, and they would do well to choose another route.

Between Slimbridge-street and Coaley, the Cam has been canalised, and you can follow it to its junction with the Berkeley–Gloucester canal along a road which presently becomes a lane and eventually crosses a swing-bridge to the New Grounds. The Old Canal, as it's called, is no longer in use. Nowadays you may even come across wild duck and heron on it, though in the last century it was used for carrying the coal and iron to Coaley Ironworks. In those days the ironworks of George Murry Cooper & Co. was famous for its edge-tools. Here were made the trenching tools for the Crimean War; but the ironworks, like the canal, is closed, beaten by mass-production methods which can produce tools and implements cheaply. The fact that their products were superior in quality mattered little. In the competition between quality and cheapness, the winner, in our age, is cheapness. Most Coaley people now work in the cloth-mills of Cam or at Listers' in Dursley. I am told that it is one of them that pollutes the river at Cam. It certainly *is* polluted, and there does not seem to be any other more likely source.

Coaley village is a surprise. Its name suggests a coal-mining hamlet: one long double-row of brick tenements in a country soiled by pit-heads and eruptions of slag. But Coaley is nothing of the kind. Eighty years ago a guide-book of Gloucestershire described it as a "picturesque village", and apart from a new housing-site, it is little changed. Situated under the Cotswold escarpment, it belongs to Cotswold and Vale alike, and I imagine fine summer days make Coaley Peak as inviting as winter makes it forbidding. South of the village the whale-backed Cam Long Down* rears against the sky. Unlike the Cotswolds, this outlier,

---

* There is a legendary reason for Cam Long Down being where it is. Apparently, the Devil, having a dislike of Gloucestershire (perhaps on account of the great number of churches there), decided he would tip the Cotswolds into Severn. So up he went to the hills above Dursley with a wheelbarrow and a spade. Filling his barrow, he began pushing it down into the Vale, but the day was hot and the load was heavy and he soon grew tired. At length he sat down to rest, when along came an old cobbler with some shoes round his neck. He was carrying them home to mend, for the soles were worn through, but the Devil looked at them suspiciously and asked him how much farther it was to Severn. Now, this cobbler was no fool, and seeing a monstrous black fiend about 250 feet high with a gigantic barrow full of Cotswold earth, he straightway guessed the Devil's purpose and decided to frustrate him. "How far is it to Severn?" he repeated. "Well, see for yourself, sir! I've just come from there, and have worn out one pair of shoes on the way." Saying which, he pointed to the shoes he was carrying home to be repaired. This so convinced the Devil that he gave up his plan there and then, tipped out his barrow-load of Cotswold, and went home in a huff. The barrow-load became Cam Long Down.

which was in prehistoric times the home of pit-dwellers, is quite bare of trees. It has no hanging-woods. Instead, its stiff slopes are clothed with bracken, through which, from afar, you can see a green path winding its way to the top. The tableland on the summit, however, is free of bracken, which gives it the appearance of a shaven crown, like a monk's head. Mr Norton, well known locally as a naturalist, told me that the reason why Cam Long Down wears no bracken on its crown is that it is capped with limestone. He also told me of a vineyard which used to be cultivated on the south slope of the hill, the grapes from which were sent to Woodmancote Priory.

Beyond Cam Long Down to the south-west is the great spur of Stinchcombe, which juts out into the Vale opposite Berkeley. To the south-east of Coaley is Hetty Pegler's Tump, with its camp and its famous longbarrow. To the west, Coaley Peak also has its ancient burial-chambers, and seen from the fields around Coaley village, it really *is* a peak. The Cotswold scarp here is almost mountainous . . . to those who haven't extensive standards of comparison! Looking north, we see Nympsfield longbarrow, then the Stroud Gap—a fault in the limestone formation, in which lies the town of Stroud—and then, above it to the north-east, Maiden Hill above Stonehouse, and Haresfield Beacon above Standish.

Like Stinchcombe, Frocester, Leonard Stanley and Standish, Coaley looks up to the hills. And Silver Street, which represents the ancient village of Coaley, lies considerably nearer Cotswold than does the present village, which has of late been drawn by that powerful magnet, the Gloucester–Bristol road. When I ventured to point out the unsuitability of the name Coaley to Mr Norton, he told me that the name of the village used to be Cowley, but that it was altered to Coaley in the last century by the postal authorities. Apparently they already had a Cowley somewhere else in the county, and feared confusion.

Coaley church is modern, apart from the fourteenth-century pinnacled and embattled tower, for the old church was burned down. It is still worth going inside, if only to see a very fine brass which has been in the chancel here for three centuries. It is of Daniel Stayn, in a cloak and ruff, Mrs Stayn in a long dress and veil, and their three children, all kneeling. At the end of the churchyard is a gate and a field-path, and, following this path, I came to Mr and Mrs Norton's cottage, which was once (they told me) a cloth-mill. It makes a charming picture, but lacks convenience and is very inaccessible. Not that this worries Douglas Norton, for he has always enjoyed walking and rarely uses a bus. Few footpaths hereabouts are unknown to him. Although he is seventy-seven, he still walks to Stroud to do his shopping and to Slimbridge for a day's fishing. Mrs Norton, however, is more concerned at being what my father would certainly call "off the beaten track". No road passes their home, and the path across the fields from Coaley church deters tradesmen from serving them with coal, milk or newspapers. Betworthy Cottage, where the Nortons live, has a crutch roof, with extraordinarily thick outside walls and beams of chestnut. Their well provides "the second purest water in Coaley", and Mr Norton told me that apples do well on the Coaley lias. Coaley cider used to have a great reputation among local tipplers. Bramleys seem to be most popular for dessert, though Mr Norton, who doesn't care for them, has planted several other varieties. There were until lately two cider-mills at Coaley: one of them an old-fashioned hand-screw stone-mill; the other a modern electric steel-mill. The latter, at Silver Street Farm, is still thriving. But the stone-mill has gone.

Douglas Norton took me across the fields to see a badger's sett in the shady corner of a field. He often comes here at dusk to smoke a pipe (tobacco home-grown in his own garden) and watch the badgers, who are used to him, and don't seem to mind him smoking. "But if I move suddenly, or light a match—they're gone!" He chuckled. "It's always amusing to see them come out, snuffling and peering like little bears. Then, if they're startled, they retreat backwards. It's surprising how fast they can go in reverse." He pointed out to me two Tudor farmhouses. One of them, Field Farm, is still well preserved. The other, Trinley House, has been re-roofed with asbestos tiles, in place of the original stone slates. It is not a change for the better. Other historic houses nearby are Garter Court and Frocester Court, the latter a Tudor house in which Queen Elizabeth reputedly slept.

Behind Betworthy Cottage is a little stream called Back Brook.

It is a tributary of the larger Wicksters Brook which finds its way into the canalised Cam, near Slimbridge-street. Nowadays Back Brook carries no fish, except, perhaps, a few bull-heads and minnows. Yet Mr. Norton remembers the time when, although it's no more than knee-deep and he and I easily jumped it, the brook was an excellent coarse-fishing stream. It wasn't pollution in this case, but a very severe drought during one of the summers between the wars, when Back Brook was almost dried up. All the larger fish were killed, and they have never reappeared.

Douglas Norton, who used to be a river-bailiff, has been a keen angler all his life. But he assured me that he'd rather fish an interesting stream and catch nothing than fish some miserable canal and get a good catch. "It isn't only the catching of fish which matters, though of course that's the reason why you're there. There are other diversions which are enjoyable without being productive. A cautious family of wildfowl: an exploratory water-vole: an otter or a kingfisher: swallows drinking on the wing—these sights are common to fishermen, part of the pleasure of the day, and just as enjoyable as catching fish."

"They don't eat so well!" cut in Mrs Norton—the voice of practical commonsense.

I am not myself an angler, but I enjoy listening to Douglas Norton. Like Izaak Walton, he does not only go angling for fish. He told me that our rivers of the Vale used to provide fine coarse-fishing, though they are heavily polluted now. The Cam receives pollution at Dursley and Cam, the Frome and the Stroudwater canal are polluted at Nailsworth and Stroud; though they contrive to purify themselves somewhat before they reach the Berkeley-Gloucester canal, which provides the best coarse-fishing in the region. Anglers come from Bristol, Gloucester and even the Midlands to fish this canal. I asked Mr Norton what, in his opinion, was the best part of it. "For catching fish, I should say Hardwicke. But it's not a favourite haunt of mine." I was later to learn why.

No walk with him could be boring, for Douglas Norton of Coaley is a naturalist of the old type, whose knowledge is based on what he has seen rather than what he has read. Nature is his book, and he reads stories in it that you or I might miss. Every movement, every snatch of birdsong has its meaning, and he knows his own country with an intimacy denied to most. He stops to show me the line of an ancient trackway, remembers that this is on a butterfly migration route, and points to where the Bassett hounds from Eastington "found" a few months ago. He has the patience, long sight and unappeasable curiosity of those who

> Find tongues in trees, books in the running brooks,
> Sermons in stones, and good in everything.

Although he enjoys following, Mr Norton is more naturalist than huntsman. I wonder if he was present at a meet of the Berkeley at Coaley in autumn 1951, when they first drew at Ashmead, but the "lots of people" who were on the scene had to

"contain their ardour until we arrived at Leslie Smith's kale crop at Moorend. At the brush of a big fox the pack put on pace and the field were soon strung out in a gallop that led by Gossington and over the L.M.S." [the nationalisation of railways meant nothing to Hastings Neale], "dangerously close to an express train. Then the hounds re-crossed the track by Tumpy Green, the band of music going by Billow Farm to pass Ben Gough's covert. Frank Jones, the local tenant, viewed the hard-hunted fox and hallooed, and Harry Scott had hounds on the scene in a matter of minutes. . . . It was then just a race for Redwood. Just touching the corner of that wood, the pack then made for the moors and looked to be coursing their quarry, when the crafty varmint got to ground on the banks of Gilgall Brook. Although the run lasted only thirty minutes, it was a good gallop, and they who took a wrong turn could never catch up with the leaders again."

The quotation is from one of Hastings Neale's contributions to the *Gazette*, and gives a good impression of the breakneck spirit of the hunt. Unfortunately "W.N.H." never attempted anything of book-length, his explanation being that he was "too aware of his educational shortcomings", which was rot! The truth was, he was too busy farming and hunting to love writing in quite the same way. He simply hadn't the time for it.

Between Coaley and Frocester is an abandoned church. It is Frocester parish church, but because it is a mile from the rest of the village nobody comes here, and it has been allowed to fall into ruin. It is fifteenth-century, and though it now stands alone it was once surrounded by houses. The houses were half-timbered and thatched, as were so many old houses in the upper Vale, and they were laid waste by a great fire in Tudor times, after which the village moved farther away from Wicksters Brook, which had then a tendency to flood. Consequently the church, being the only building of stone, alone survived, to experience neglect when villagers no longer felt inclined for a mile-long walk to and from service.

A curious story is told of this old church. It seems that the bell-ringers of Coaley once planned to steal its solitary bell, and, going there one night after dark, they unhitched it and carried it halfway down the stairs of the tower to a landing, where they left it to go down into the churchyard for a rest and a smoke. When they returned to the landing to bring it down the last flight, however, they were astonished to discover a little old lady sitting on top of it. Now, they had seen no one enter the church, so that it puzzled them how she had contrived to get in without being observed. Anyway, they asked her if she would be kind enough to get off it, so that they could carry it away, but the old lady took no notice. Assuming that she must be deaf, they started shouting at her. Still she took no notice, so they took hold of the bell, resolved to carry it and her together, for she looked very frail and light. Yet try as they would, they could not budge that bell an inch. They struggled and sweated to no purpose before it began to dawn on them that there must be something queer about this old lady—in fact, that she was not of this world at all. No sooner did the thought occur to them, than they left the bell, turned and ran down the stairs and across the fields to Coaley as fast as their legs would take them.

Oddly enough, there is a local tradition that, when the bell was being cast, the lady who was giving it to the church threw her jewellery into the bell-metal. So it has been assumed that, to prevent her gift being stolen, it was this lady's spirit which returned to Frocester and sat a-top the bell. It is certainly a fact that the bell was once found on a landing halfway down the stair after someone had apparently tried to steal it. And it is also a fact that George and I stood on that landing, and George (who

knew nothing of the story) remarked: "I say, there isn't half a
rummy sort of feeling about this place!"

Frocester Court has already been mentioned as one of the countless places where Queen Elizabeth slept. She did really sleep here,
on her way to Berkeley Castle, for the parish registers record her
stay. Originally a college belonging to Gloucester Abbey,
Frocester Court was rebuilt in 1554 by Sir George Huntley. It is a
lovely house, with gables and mullioned windows in the Cotswold style, and a gatehouse which is more truly of the Vale.
Adjoining the Court is a barn which has been called the greatest
tithe barn in England. It was built by the Abbot, John de Gamage
(1284–1306), and is a good example of mediæval commercial
building. It is 184 feet long, 30 feet wide and 36 feet to the roof-
ridge. Outside, it is roofed with Cotswold stone-slates, covered
with moss and lichen, and pierced by a tiny dormer window.
The two large porches are high and wide enough to receive the
largest of wagonloads. Inside, it is as impressive as a church. Vast
oak beams divide it into twelve bays, each of which will take a
large rick. The roof must be a tremendous weight, yet these
great oak beams, aided by vast buttresses, have held it true for
seven centuries.

Leonard Stanley, or Stanley St Leonard, as it used to be called,
has several things worth seeing. It is situated right under the
Cotswold escarpment, and traces of its ancient Priory (founded
by Roger de Berkeley between 1121 and 1129) can still be seen,
though they have been incorporated into the fabric of farm
buildings. Here is a half-timbered farmhouse of the Tudor period,
vaulted cellars which probably belonged to the monks, an old
fishpond, and a Roman earthwork said to have been built as a
refuge from Irish raiders. At a corner of the village green stands
the church, much of which is the original Norman church of
the priory, modified by fifteenth-century alterations when the
monks of the priory gave up their nave to the parish. It has a
Norman doorway whose fluted capitals support a zigzag arch
framed by dragons. Above it, in a niche, a crude Norman
sculpture depicts three figures which are supposed to represent
the Trinity with the Book of Life across their knees. The west
doorway is also Norman, but it has been much "restored", which
is another way of saying it has been severely damaged. Inside it

is impressive, both in length and height. The nave, in particular, has a fourteenth-century wagon-roof, with open timbering. Norman vaulting of the chancel was removed in the fourteenth century, but the shafts are still there, with two capitals showing the Nativity and Mary Magdalene wiping Christ's feet. Also in the chancel, over a great Norman aumbry, is a curious piece of sculpture depicting the Fall. Adam and Eve are beasts with human faces. Eve grasps the serpent's tail and offers Adam, sitting on its head, a bite from her apple. Here, too, are patchy remains of fourteenth-century wall-painting, two piscinas of the same date, a fifteenth-century rood stairway, a twelfth-century coffin-lid, and two more Norman doorways, now blocked, which once led to the cloisters. Outside, in the churchyard, are the old village stocks and a lychgate with a stone roof of four gables, sheltered by a venerable yew.

Leonard Stanley must be our farthest point west, for here we are dangerously near Cotswold, with Sandfords Knoll and Wood-chester Park due south, and Doverow Hill, above Stonehouse, to the north. Through the Stroud Gap comes the Frome and the Stroudwater canal, taking us, through Cress Green, to Eastington, where the Stroud Valley broadens into the Vale of Berkeley. A few centuries ago it was a little township of weavers who "wore uneasily the yoke of the Cliffords of Frampton". Within living memory there were textile workers numbering about half the population, and they were extreme radicals with a strong Chartist tradition. Since the eighteenth century, its population has declined, and Eastington is now a "dormitory" village. Buses take workers to Stroud and Cam, Dursley (Listers') and Frampton (Cad-burys'). "Agriculture," I was told, "is mostly a family affair hereabout. Farms are small, and two of my neighbours run their farms with only the help of their daughters."

The Hoopers were, until this century, a very influential local family. They occupied Eastington House, "a handsome and spacious mansion in the Elizabethan style", and they owned three cloth-mills, where my informant remembered having seen old women turning spinning-wheels in his boyhood. One of these has been demolished, one is now occupied by a grain-drying and seed-corn business, and the other packs cereals. Eastington has never had a squirearchy, only rich people who came and went without leaving much to mark their passing. The nearest to a squirearchy was the advent of the Stephens family, who did hang on for three or four generations, only to fade away after the Royalist Stephens turned Roundhead shortly before the execution of Charles I.

One of the outstanding personalities of recent times is Alfred Keys, magistrate and councillor, of Alkerton House, who told me that his great-grandfather came from Minchinhampton, about 1830. He was a cider-maker, beer-retailer, farmer, brewer and baker; and he always carried a sword-stick because he lived in terror of mad dogs. He was succeeded, in due course, by his son Alfred, who concentrated on farming (as his son and grandson have done), though he did specialise in teazle-growing for the local cloth-mills. The Keys family remained cider-makers until 1939, when Alfred Keys was forced to close down, beaten by factory cider—by the combination of big business and public apathy. I asked Mr Keys to tell me something about the cider-making, and he said that his great-grandfather, Charles Keys, made his cider by the age-old millstone-and-trough horse track. On the twenty-first birthday of his son Alfred (our Mr Keys' grandfather), he gave him a new-type mill with steel cutters and two revolving stones, as made by Workmans of Slimbridge. The motive power was provided by two men taking a handle each side, and very hard work it was, with the apples dropped one by one through a hole in the floor above by a boy. About 1890 Mr Keys' father modified the mill for horse-power, and in 1919 Mr Keys himself fitted a 5-h.p. oil-engine. This cider-mill gave good service for eighty-eight years, until the cider-making was finally discontinued, yet when it was first installed the older men on the farm said it was flimsy and wouldn't last. And from their point of view they were right, because the older stone-mill, which they had known, was capable of lasting centuries, and indeed, Mr Keys tells me that the stone trough is still intact, and the millstones, now in his rockery, could easily be put back in place. These old stone cider-mills are all but indestructible. I have seen them at Kington and Falfield as well as Eastington, and have been told that, until recently, one was still in use at Slimbridge.

All four generations of Keys' made cider, privately and for sale.

At first, most of it was made from apples supplied by particular farmers for those farmers' own workers during hay and corn harvest, when enormous quantities were drunk. Later, Mr Keys' grandfather supplied nearly all his cider to inns and public houses, and in 1920 Mr Keys was supplying about six of these, buying up orchards as well as growing apples himself. But one by one these "free" houses were acquired by brewers, and "tied". All the breweries did not, at first, "tie" their houses to cider factories, but Stroud Brewery, the last to do so, followed the line of other breweries in 1932, and this meant the end of many small cider-makers. There were other problems, too. It was a cold and dirty job; not dirty in the usual sense, but because one's hands were "as black as a coal" after a week of it, and persisted black for a week or two after one had finished. In 1938 Mr. Keys made his last hogshead. He had hoped, in 1939, to instal new machinery, but the war came and the call was for food. So he concentrated on farming rather than making cider, and he has not made it since. It is his opinion that the taste for farmhouse cider has gone. None but a few old countrymen drink it now. And he is pessimistic about the future of factory-made cider. In the Victoria, at Eastington, he told me, where the Keys' used to deliver 30 gallons a week for many years, they don't sell that amount of cider now in months!

Naturally I was keen to hear Mr Keys' impressions of farming in the old style, as practised at Eastington. He remembers allotment-holders, who spent their spare time growing winter corn and vegetables, using the breast-plough, which he said was "the heaviest job man ever did". Occasionally corn was dibbed, three grains to a hole, and beans were always dibbed, even on large farms. The allotment-holders' corn was either threshed by themselves with a "nile" (local name for flail), or taken to one of the local millers at Fromebridge, Framilode or Cam, who would take a part of the corn as payment. Mr Keys can still point out one or two outbuildings which were built as threshing-floors, and were in use throughout the winters of seventy years ago. The small crops of the allotment-holders were cut with a sickle at the rate of a quarter-acre a day. Corn was cut just below the ear to facilitate threshing and the straw would be later scythed in the dew of early morning.

The first horse-mower was introduced locally about 1890 by "young" Tom Nicholls, who died, in his nineties, in 1943. But the mowing-machine didn't displace the scythe on the broad acres of grass until the first war. Scythemen were better and cheaper than machines until wages rose above the 1913 level of 4d. per hour. At that time, this was higher wages than the factories paid. Their workers were paid 12s. a week. "In 1904, my father built a brick cowshed. The bricklayer charged 5d. per hour, his labourer 1d." Mr Keys regrets the passing of that fine old institution the Harvest Supper, and he told me:

"My memory is full of the racy talk of the fields in my youth. . . . It is poor work today by comparison, for tractor-drivers are much alone and anyhow you can't talk and laugh for the noise of the brutes. An outstanding event of my youth was the burning in effigy, after a procession round the parish, of a parson whose interest in horse-racing and other things gave offence. His lady-friend's effigy was also burned. That was about 1901. . . . Scores of odd personalities lived nearby when I was young. There was Charlie Powell, who used to scythe two acres of grass a day where one acre was most men's maximum. There was Bill Carey, a 12-shillings-a-week clothworker who was also a champion skater and a cricketer. I remember when he opened the innings on Frampton Green and carried his bat through a long afternoon, without scoring a single run. Many half-pints were wagered on him. Not pints, for it was really not much different from his usual form. Then there was "Foreman" Burford, assistant over-seer—he was a ballad-maker, who celebrated births, marriages, deaths, cricket matches, concerts and so on in parodies of the popular songs. And the parish sang them, too. In fact he was instrumental in an officious night-watchman being literally sung out of the parish. The tune was so catchy, and the words so scurrilous, that it nearly drove the victim mad. The night-watch-man's descendants still visit Eastington from the Midlands, but we are too polite nowadays to mention the song.

"Old Jim Bloodworth was a deep student of the Bible, and, I regret to say, slightly cracked. In youth he prayed to the Lord for a Voice, and his prayer was answered. When the drink was in him, he became a Prophet and preached his message in a voice which would have drowned a modern electric amplifier. I have heard every word, including asides to hecklers, half a mile away on a still night. Mostly he took a hint from the police, and pronounced the benediction as he turned for home. On the one occasion when he was arrested, he emulated Samson, so that it took four policemen to get him to the station. And they would not have succeeded, even then, not with 'a wagon and four horses', if he hadn't been weak after influenza."

Outstanding character of that period was Billy Goodrich, who for half a century lived alone in an old shepherd's or gamekeeper's cottage in the fields, half a mile from road or neighbour, which he called the Wilderness. Billy was the son of a cottage girl, though his father was reputed to be one of the county gentry. It was a subject Billy never mentioned, but it was noticeable someone saw to it that he had at least the bare essentials of life without necessity for work. He might sometimes take a temporary job as gamekeeper or bird-minder. Or he might travel from farm to farm with his ferrets, clearing out the rats. But most of the time he just stayed at home in his cottage, like a lesser squire, his pigs and hens around him, pets rather than stock. Pigs trailed after Billy like dogs on his rare strolls through the village, and they would answer to their names. One pig, Knowledge, used to dodge in and out at his heels on his shopping expeditions to Gloucester. Finally it grew so big that railway officials could no longer wink at the smuggling of it into the railway carriage, all too ineffectively camouflaged beneath a meal sack. Shortly afterwards, Billy and the Midland Railway (as it then was) fell out, because in a full compartment of returning shoppers his performing rats escaped, and, hiding among the passengers' legs, defied recapture.

Billy was nearly always at home to visitors, who were usually made welcome, though only a favoured few were offered a drink of cider. Standing right outside "class" himself, he was punctilious about observing class-distinctions: squire, parson, farmer, shopkeeper, blacksmith, etc., down to the labourer—who was as welcome as the others, but was never offered a drink until he had performed some small task. Being annoyed at the too-frequent visits of a gang of young fellows who came only to pull his leg, Billy invited them to dinner and served up rabbit pie. When they sat back at last, happily replete, he showed them the pelt of the cat whose carcase had provided their "rabbit". He never called anyone by their right names, but coined nicknames for them. So apt were they that some of them still cling to their descendants. "Afternoon Willie", for instance, was always behind with his cultivations; "Cuffs and Collars" was a ladies' man; "Poor Pity" was full of self-pity, drank himself out of his farm, and sank to labourer's status.

"How much of Billy was genuine and how much an act put on for our benefit," says Mr Keys, "I could never guess. He especially liked talking to educated people, asking them questions and treating them to his own reflections. His comments on men and things were keen, profound and at the same time childish, so that you never *quite* knew whether you were listening to Diogenes or Simple Simon. His visitors were almost exclusively male. He mistrusted women, and those who occasionally called were not made welcome. He had a mania for collecting things. His cottage contained dozens, maybe hundreds, of walking-sticks; and empty match-boxes by the thousand. Upstairs, where no one else ever went in his lifetime, the room was stacked from floor to ceiling with neatly folded empty sacks. There was just a lane from door to bed, and from bed to window. When he died at last, a few years before the war, his secret died with him, for he never told what, I am sure, he might have done. He sleeps in Frocester churchyard, where a stone (which cost money, though Billy left none) says of him that he was 'A good and faithful servant'."

It is worth lingering over the Keys family, because they typify the old Vale yeomanry. Independent, obstinate, observant, self-reliant, they went their way and faced their destinies unflinchingly. Charles Keys the Elder is a good example. Living in the middle of the last century, he was brisk, energetic and hard-headed: drawing his bread from his own oven, testing the gravity of his beer with a float, supervising his men in field or barn, serving behind his bar, weighing up tea from the chest or lard from the tub, breaking sugar loaves into lumps; in later years sitting back in his bar-parlour, solemnly pulling at his churchwarden pipe; for smoking was a serious matter then, never associated with the hurry and bustle of work. "I like to think of him," his great-grandson says, "commending Shakespeare to his children in the week, but sternly ordering it back to the shelf on Sundays in favour of the

Bible, *Pilgrim's Progress*, Foxe's *Book of Martyrs* or Young's *Night Thoughts*."

His son Alfred was delicate and studious. The old family doctor, with a tactlessness which may not have been so stupid as it sounds, told him he probably wouldn't live to manhood. But the Keys are an obstinate family, and soon Alfred, taking up a bakery business, began to push a bread truck round the parish. He made a little money, reared a big family, retired at fifty to become a councillor and later J.P., and until he was over ninety continued to sit on the bench, where—as an old policeman solemnly assured his grandson—he did "surprisingly little harm".

Another brother, Aaron, walked off to London to seek his fortune, and returned, many years later, in the guise of a doctor, with a large and lucrative practice. He did very well, too, until a patient died on his hands, when it was discovered that he was not on the register. He was summoned to trial for manslaughter, but was not able to appear as he had just left on a holiday and nobody knew his address. Needless to add, Aaron never returned from that holiday. Where he went and what he did remains a mystery, though the family always supposed him to have gone to Australia.

There was apparently a Roman villa at or near Eastington, for tesseræ are sometimes turned up by the plough, as, in one particular field, were quantities of flint implements and nodules of what looked like smelted iron ore. Ox "chawms" (*i.e.* shoes) and wide horsehoes of very early date are turned up in the "green" lanes of an old ploughland here. Modern methods of cultivation are obliterating the S-shaped, high backed ox-ridges.

Until the Thames-and-Severn canal was closed to barge traffic in 1893, after being allowed to fall into disrepair by the Great Western Railway Co., the smaller Stroudwater canal formed an integral part of the national system of waterways. The Stroudwater was about seven and a half miles long, possessed thirteen locks, with a minimum width of 16 feet and a depth over the lock sills varying from 5 feet to 6 feet. After the Thames-and-Severn canal was abandoned, the Stroudwater was still used for a time, transporting Forest of Dean coal to the gasworks, bringing roadstone from Chepstow and sand for iron-founding to fac-

The Garden House, Frampton Court

tories at Stroud. But it is now badly silted, and will soon be past help.* All the way from Stroud to Framilode, the Frome keeps it company, wriggling where the canal keeps straight on. There is something odd and fascinating about two watercourses in the same valley, if you can call this gentle undulation a valley. Even from the main road, the sight of the Frome and the Stroudwater is exciting, and promises better fishing than it can, in fact, provide, both streams being polluted by the factories of Stroud.

Near Frampton-on-Severn are several gravel-pits which resemble lakes and add to the interest of this part of the Vale. It was here that excavators, removing the top-soil prior to quarrying, uncovered the evidences of Bronze-Age earthworks described in the first chapter. Quarrying is not, however, the chief industry of Frampton, for Cadbury's have a condensed-milk factory on the banks of the Berkeley–Gloucester canal which employs nearly 200 workers. It was built here because of the large milk production of the surrounding countryside, and it is con-nected—by water—with the factory at Birmingham. Another feature which decided its placing was that the lack of railways in this vicinity prevented large towns competing for the milk supply before the war. And that's quite enough about the economy of Frampton. . . .

In most people's eyes, Frampton-on-Severn is the loveliest village of the Vale, and I have heard it described as the loveliest in Gloucestershire. It is certainly beautifully placed, fringing the delightful Rosamund's Green, which, with its 22 acres, must surely be one of the finest village greens in England. Moreover there are individual houses and cottages which are as good examples of timber-and-thatch as you will find in a day's walk, provided you walk south or east. There is a splendid farm, timbered, with a stone roof, gables, and tall chimneys, which was reputedly the birthplace of Fair Rosamund, Henry II's mistress, of which more later. Frampton Court, however, which also faces the Green, is Georgian, and out of character with the rest of the village. But I must be truthful. Although there are some lovely things here, Frampton also possesses some quite hideous

* Whether the Stroudwater will ever be put into working order again depends, of course, on the industrialists of Stroud.

13*   193

Manor Farm, Frampton-on-Severn

houses: as bad examples of unimaginative, red-brick Victoriana
as you'll find in Gloucestershire. Oddly enough, it is not difficult
to accept them and fit them in, if one's broadminded enough to
enjoy a little comic relief. Anyway, the loveliness of the Elizabethan farms and cottages and their grouping around the Green
cannot be destroyed by a few monstrosities, or even by the terrifying number of advertisements which surround the village shop.
There are three ponds on the Green, fringed by rushes, where
the water-crowfoot blossoms luxuriantly, and flotillas of domestic
duck add point and animation to what would otherwise be merely
a charming setting.

I came to Frampton on a day in mid-May, a lovely time of
year. It was 80 degrees in the shade, the sky was cloudless, the
Green was golden with buttercups. Sheep lay and panted beneath
the chestnuts. A cricket match was in progress, for it was
Saturday, and the white-clad cricketers performing their ritual-
istic movements were perfectly in keeping with the scene. As I
sat beneath one of the horse-chestnuts, with my tongue hanging
out, waiting for the pub to open, I divided my attention between
the cricket and the ladies. For it seemed to me that Frampton
still possessed a high proportion of fair maids, most of whom were
mounted on bicycles.

Rosamund's Green was once a marsh, and Frampton folk have
to thank Richard Clutterbuck, who built Frampton Court, for
turning their marsh into a pleasaunce. Knowing village folk
pretty well, I doubt if they did thank him. They probably mut-
tered something about it being very well as it was!

About Henry's Fair Rosamund there are many legends. Dryden
says her name was actually *Jane* Clifford:

> *Jane Clifford was her name, as books aver,*
> *Fair Rosamund was but her "nom de guerre".*

Apparently she was a girl of much vivacity and wit, who liked
to wear "garments of transparent linen, called *Nebulae*", took
great delight in viewing the wild animals in Woodstock Park,
and was much followed by young men of fashion "to obtain a
sight of her". Drayton claims that Rosamund was seduced by
Henry with the connivance of her governess, though even then
he would not have succeeded had he not given her (as a reward

for her assistance, one presumes) a reliquary for her private chapel, on which "were finely represented the sports of men and animals". This story, surely, would have delighted Flaubert or Maupassant, to whom the unconscious irony would have been irresistible.

Rosamund had two children by the King, and he lived in open and notorious adultery with her, not caring "a rush" for the opinion of his queen or his neighbour kings. It was said in her own day that Rosamund was so fair that the blood could be seen to flow through her veins. About her death there are many and conflicting stories. One is that she was poisoned by the Queen, who was desperately jealous. But since there can be no exact corroboration, I incline to the other story: that she retired to a nunnery, partly from remorse, but mainly because she had no real love for Henry, who was much older than she, and whose passion became disagreeable to her.

The legends do not end with her death. One ancient chronicler writes:

> "It befel that she died and was buried whyle the King was absent; and whanne he cam agen for grette love that he had to hyr, he wold see her body in the grave; and whaine the grave was opened, there sate an horrible tode upon her breste, bytwene her teetys, and a foul adder begirte her body about the middle; and she stank so, that the King and non other might stand to see that horrible sight. . . ."

It is not a happy ending to this romance, and it may not be a true one, but at least it holds a moral—for puritans.

The Cliffords have been the principal family of Frampton since the twelfth century, and Major and Mrs Peter Clifford still live in the mediæval Manor in which Fair Rosamund (*alias* Jane Clifford) was born. Like many houses of this part of the Vale, it is half-timbered, with a lower storey of fine stonework which dates from about 1500. If you go to Frampton in mid-August, you may see another survival from the Middle Ages in the form of Frampton Feast. Nowadays this is just a carnival, with round-abouts and dodge-'ems and cokernut-shies, for like all the other village revels and feasts, fairs and "mops" its original character and purpose have been mislaid. Traditionally, it took place on the Monday after the Assumption, and was the dedication festival of the church.

According to Fosbroke, Mr Edw. Gardner, the companion of Chatterton, lived at Frampton and celebrated it "in that sweet and plaintive poetry by which his amiable muse is distinguished". In a note to his poem *Barrow Hill* (a fine local viewpoint), Mr Edw. Gardner tells us that in the reign of Edward the Elder, on August 5th, 904, the Danes, loaded with plunder which they had gathered on the banks of Severn, were ambushed in Woodend field by an army of Mercians and West Angles, totally routed, and three of their "kings" slain.

Coming down to more recent times, there's the story of Cole, landlord of the *Horseshoes*, and his practical joke. This Cole was a vast, ponderous man with a liking for practical jokes. On this occasion he announced that he had in his possession a water otter, and challenged any dog to catch it. Along came the poachers and sporting farmers, not to mention the more disreputable gentry, so that Rosamund's Green was alive with dogs and spectators.

Out came Cole with a sack over his shoulder. Slowly he strode across the Green and waded into the pond. When the excitement and suspense was at its height, he emptied the contents of the sack into the pond and beat a hasty retreat. Instantly the dogs were loosed, but despite the noise and their fighting among themselves it soon became apparent that there was no wild animal, dead or alive, in that pond. Eventually the water otter was fished out, and found to be an old and rusty kettle. At first the crowd was angry. Then the absurdity of it came home to them. After all, what *is* a kettle but a water 'otter? Behind his bar, Cole—who had had visions of an angry crowd dumping him in the pond, with his kettle—was relieved to hear the sudden roar of laughter. And soon he was doing better business than he'd ever done in his life before. Frampton men still laugh about Cole and his joke over their mugs of cider.

Many retired seamen live hereabout. I cannot tell you why, except that Frampton has a whiff of salt-water about it and connections with Severn and the Berkeley-Gloucester canal. Mr J. H. Brinkworth told me he remembered when trows and sailing-barges were built at the neighbouring village of Saul. One of them, the *Arabella*, was wrecked, with loss of all hands, near Ilfracombe. He also remembers the schooner *Julia*, also lost, and the apple sloops (as they were called) which were built by Fred Evans of Saul. James Harper built a number of sailing-trows which carried coal from Bridgwater, and a Mr Rowles, who was also a barge-owner, had a repair-yard at Frampton until the end of the last century. Mr. R. Davis, whose father worked for Mr Rowles, is now owner of a repair-yard at Junction Dock, Saul, and an authority on shipbuilding hereabouts, as well as being chairman of the parish council.

Mr Brinkworth has lived at Frampton, on and off, since he was three months old. His father was a master-rigger on the wind-jammers that used, at that time, to trade to Sharpness, and until he was seventeen Mr Brinkworth helped him. Then he went "deep water", and soon saw the Cape Verde Islands, Carthagena, Philadelphia, Dunkirk and Baltimore. Fifteen years of voyages followed, after which he came back to Severn and the Bristol Channel on coasters. He has been a salmon fisherman too, so he knows Severn better than most.

Although Mr Brinkworth has been a mariner and fisherman all his life, he isn't afraid to try his hand at verse in order to express his affection for Frampton. This is how he ends a letter to me:

> *How sweet on the banks of the Severn to wander*
> *When daisies and buttercups spangle the mead,*
> *To hear at a distance the sound of the cuckoo,*
> *And gaze at the cows as they peacefully feed.*
>
> *I've sojourned a season in many a city,*
> *Each boasting some feature delightful to see,*
> *But when I compare all the walks I have taken*
> *This one by the Severn is dearest to me.*

There is a pleasant walk to the fifteenth-century church across the fields, between a fine avenue of elms. Its tower has a parapet of open tracery, crowned by pinnacles and battlements, which are given dramatic emphasis by the trees which grow near it. Inside the reredos is a colourful mosaic depicting the Last Supper, and the church possesses a Norman lead font, one of the nine in Gloucestershire already mentioned. There are three fourteenth-century effigies here, too. A tiny figure in a mantle, hands together in an attitude of prayer, lies under an arch almost hidden by pews, whilst William Clifford and his wife lie in two recesses in the north aisle. William is a knight in armour, his hand on his sword and his dog at his feet. His lady wears a wimple, and her hands also are pressed together in prayer.

Below Frampton church is Splatt Bridge, a swing-bridge over the Berkeley–Gloucester canal, and beside it is the usual Greek-style bridgeman's lodge. It was on this bridge that I met Sam Taylor, who was himself for many years bridgeman, but had to give up when the canal was nationalised, because "they said I were too old". The present bridgeman is his son-in-law. Sam told me that he worked barges up Severn and Wye when he was young, as well as up the Severn to "Ooster" (Worcester). In his day the motive power was sail, horse or human. Now all the craft are petrol-driven. "There ain't so much as a donkey on the whole canal now," says Sam. "'Tis all petrol ingines today." He told me it had been a bad year for the salmon fishing. "Haven't done too well wi' the long-nets, neither. An' dozens o' fine great fish coming down dead on top o' the water, they tell me."

"Pollution, I suppose?"

"Ah; that and the weather! This drouth have let the mud get foul. Not getting any fresh to carry off the foulness, it've soaked in, till the mud's stinkin'. *Stinkin!*" He repeated, profoundly, and spat emphatically into the waters of the canal.

All along the bank of the canal, at regular intervals, hopeful anglers were squatting, watching their floats. "Do you do any of that?" I asked. "What—fishing? No, couldn' never stick it! Not that sort. I've fished for salmon with a lave-net when I were younger, but this sort—why, 'tain't worth pullin' 'em out the water when they do bite. And half the time when they do catch a fish, they'll throw 'n back in. No doubt 'tis all right for city chaps as wants a bit o' fresh air, but there ain't nuthin in it when you've fished for salmon with a lave-net."

We stood aside to let an R.A.F. van cross the bridge. "Now, what's that doing here?" I must have asked, for Sam Taylor was astonished at my ignorance. "Haven't 'ee heard? I thought everybody knew." He pointed to a field between the canal and Severn. "See that thing stickin' up over there—well, that's an aeroplane!

She crashed down over there yesterday. All I can say, 'tis lucky for that pilot he's still alive. A bit farther on, and he'd a' been in the Severn. Not so fur, and he'd a' been in the canal. But there, it had to be! 'Tis all luck. When our turn do come, we got to go."

"Very true," I said in the lugubrious voice I keep especially for such occasions.

"Still," Sam brightened up, "I do keep up pretty well, considering."

"You look pretty fit."

"Oh, ah; I still do a bit (of work) now and then, even if I *be* 'too old'. The farmers is glad of a bit of help now and then, and last 'ear I done some apple-picking. That was in Arlin'ham. They grows a tidy few apples there. Don't make any cider now, though. They sends their apples down to Wickwar (the Gloucestershire Cider Co.)—down to the factory, to save 'em the bother."

In answer to my question, Sam told me he was "sebenty-seven". As we were talking it started to rain again, in earnest, and soon it was peppering the smooth wide waters of the canal. Sam Taylor smiled upon it. "Lovely drop o' rain," he said appreciatively. "Do more good than I shall today." He was thinking exclusively of farming, however; for it was an August Bank Holiday Monday, and I could hear, in my imagination, the thousands of curses which would greet this "lovely drop o' rain" at the seaside resorts. After that, the rain never stopped. It became a downpour, and when we drove away from Frampton we were surprised to see that the cricket match on the Green was still in progress, either because the players had not yet noticed it was raining, or because a critical stage had been reached and they were anxious to see it through.

A mile or so north of Frampton, another of these swing-bridges crosses the Stroudwater canal to Whitminster. I cannot separate the place from the day; for the only time I've seen Whitminster church was on a perfect day in May, when the lanes around it were fringed with the lace of wild carrot, the hedgerows sprouting herb-robert and the ditches holding pools of germander speedwell. Whitminster church lies back from the road, near Whitminster House. It is beautifully situated among the trees, with a charming fifteenth-century tower at the end of a path between yews.

One of the most repellent gargoyles on the tower has a man's head between its paws. Above the fourteenth-century entrance arch an old stone sundial tells the hours, but inside there are signs of nineteenth-century restoration. Apart from a fourteenth-century arcade, all I could find of interest was the unique and beautiful effigy of Rebecca Lloyd, who is depicted in gown, veil and ruff, leaning on a desk with a book.

Fretherne church, about a mile and a half westward of Frampton crossroads, is a weird pseudo-Gothic place, dating from 1851 when it was rebuilt by the Rev. Sir William Lionel Darell, Bart., whose seat was at Fretherne Court. Judging from his works, Sir William seems to have been a reader of *Vathek* and *Otranto*, for inside the church queer faces peer at you from odd corners in the most disconcerting way.

Sir Lionel Darell is grandson of the Rev. Sir William. One of the great sporting personalities of the Vale of recent times, Sir Lionel lives at Saul Lodge, near Frampton, and he has recently written and published his autobiography under the intriguing title of *Ratcatcher Baronet*.* Action predominates, of course, as it has done in Sir Lionel's life; his work as soldier and administrator sharing place with his hunting, fishing and shooting. At some time or other Sir Lionel seems to have pursued almost everything that runs and shot most things that can be shot. There are many thrilling accounts of hunts with the Berkeley and with his own Fretherne Beagles, as well as an expert's experience of rat-catching, for during the war Sir Lionel was chairman of the Gloucestershire C.C. Pests Committee, and during his term of office he made war on insurgent rodents with commendable zeal.

Ratcatcher Baronet is a spirited, frank, ingenuous account of Sir Lionel's life from prep-school to present. In his foreword the Bishop of Gloucester writes that "he reveals himself as a typical Englishman of the old school", and acclaims the book as a record of the life of the landed gentry before the social revolution of recent times. Sir Lionel was unhappy at his prep-school, though he seems to have enjoyed life as an Eton "fag". A fellow "fag" at Eton was Sir Desmond McCarthy, and the author tells how—

* *Ratcatcher Baronet*, by Sir Lionel Darell, printed for the author by Sir Joseph Causton & Sons Ltd., London and Eastleigh.

"One evening, when running up Keate's Lane to evening chapel, a jolly little boy stopped me with the remark: 'Have you a trouser button, Darell, to lend me for the offertory?' He was none other than Desmond McCarthy, a grand little fellow in those days, good in his work, good at football, and now one of our chief literary experts. Alas, I never meet him now, and our paths in life have, I think you will agree, gone in very different directions—do not smile, O Reader!!!"

From Eton to Oxford, where (Sir Lionel frankly admits) he acquired very little in the way of knowledge but had some glorious rags. The most spectacular of these was when the young Darell held a November 5th firework display *in his rooms*. Sir Lionel comments:

"The din of rockets, the smashing of glass, and the shouts of merry young gentlemen was a thing one's memory can never efface. I remember in the midst of this amazing scene a very foolish fellow lighted a squib and put it into my greatcoat pocket . . . he later finished his life in a lunatic asylum."

We are not surprised to learn, a little later on, that Sir Lionel's father soon decided that he'd had enough of Oxford, and that it was young Darell who gave Brandon Thomas some of his ideas for *Charley's Aunt*. There are stories of life in camp and at country-house parties; of the purchase and sale of horses; of dear old boys with nicknames like Jumbo and Wiggy, Algy and Floppy, who later became generals or bishops or died of obscure fevers in foreign parts. Of his operation for appendicitis, soon after he was commissioned in 1899, the author observes: "I was one of the first to undergo this operation, which has since become so popular." Ten years later he went to South Africa, where he hunted jackal, shot bush-buck, went whaling off Durban and big-game hunting near Simba. When the war came he saw service in "Alex" and Gallipoli before he was crocked in Egypt and had to come back to Blighty. In 1919 he succeeded his father and settled down to the life of a country squire, magistrate, county councillor, member of the Severn Fishery Board, etc. He tells an amusing story about one of his jobs, that of certifying lunatics. The call came on a Sunday for him to go over to Framilode to certify a mental case. Arrived there, he interviewed the lady in question, who, as it happened, had once worked for his family. She seemed to talk sensibly enough, so, turning to the doctor, Sir Lionel said: "I don't see much wrong with her", when, all of a sudden, she expressed a strong desire to kiss him. Sir Lionel certified her at once, whereupon the woman became very violent, tore up all the official papers and wrecked the room. Sir Lionel's mixture of manliness and naïveté is both charming and, at times, rather comic. Yet *Ratcatcher Baronet* describes a useful, active and happy life—and describes it with a good-humoured gusto that disarms criticism. It does more than that: it traces the development of a "character" who is also a sportsman.

Arlingham is near the end of a peninsula, surrounded on three sides by Severn. It possesses fertile farmland, apple and pear orchards, and a ferry to Newnham. There used to be a ford here too, the only place where a horse and carriage could ford the river between Gloucester and the sea, but it was destroyed in 1802 when the river altered its course and scoured out a deeper channel in the sand.

Both of the great houses of Arlingham are now farms. Slowwe House (the family motto was "Slowwe is Sure") is reputed to be haunted by the ghosts of two old ladies, whilst Wick Court once received a visit from Elizabeth and her favourite, Leicester. So pleased was Leicester with their reception that he presented the village with a charity. It seems that he was patron of a hospital at Warwick, and his charity meant that two aged people from the village could be accepted by the Warwick hospital and cared for in their declining years. All too often, it was said, the old people looked upon this "charity" as a penance, and it had been remarked that Warwick had a worse name at Arlingham than anywhere else in the kingdom.

Between Arlingham and Framilode, Unla Water is possibly the most dangerous reach of Severn. It is a maze of whirlpools and currents, even at low water, and was probably given its name after the tragedy described in Chapter II. Priding, a small hamlet, was named from the "pride" or "prid", which was the old name for the lamprey. Many centuries ago the lamprey was a fish much esteemed by gourmets. In the Middle Ages the city of Gloucester was under an obligation to supply the King with lampreys every year at Christmas, and King John once fined the city £12 13s. 4d. because it did not supply him with sufficient lampreys to please him. So great was the fame of Gloucester's lamprey pies that Catherine the Great ordered lampreys from Severn to be sent to Russia. Nowadays, as a result of a change in eating habits, the lamprey is neglected, and they no longer make cribs for the catching of them at Priding or Minsterworth.

"Framilode", Brian Waters tells us in *Severn Tide*, "would seem half asleep were it not for the watchful eye of old George. Leisure and a good pair of binoculars give an air of opulence to his workaday appearance, and . . . the small gold rings in his ears hint of the romance of distant places. The droop of his moustache betokens the inward arrogance of a man who has been accustomed to command. His deep, low voice has an almost Shakespearian familiarity with the English language, for he has a genius for adorning his conversation with the exact and unexpected adjective. . . . He sits all day long on top of Framilode's river bank, a solitary figure in the sun, or else like some phantom ship's figurehead looming out of the autumn mists when seen across the river. He surveys the moving water and no motion of fish or fowl escapes his eye, for the river runs as a continuous thread through his long life."

That is a fine bit of writing, and although I have not met George, I know him, having been introduced by Brian Waters. Why is it that you get so many "characters" beside the Severn? Is it the river that changes a man? Or do men of character tend to gravitate toward the river? Certainly the estuary of Severn is a force to be reckoned with—a psychical as well as a physical force. This was especially true in the old days when men deliberately pitted themselves against her, either by snatching salmon from the river-bed with a lave-net or by "riding" a Bore in a rowing-boat, as old George did. Men have even swum through a Bore, though I do not think many do that now. Perhaps we do not feel the necessity to combat the elements, as our grandfathers did. We have most of us found more sophisticated ways of expressing our exuberance.

As it takes 18 feet of water at Sharpness to show an inch of tide at Framilode, there are several days in the month, round about neap tide, when there is no tide at Framilode, where the Frome empties into the Severn and gives the village its name (Frome-lode). It is the only village of the Vale which stands on the brink of Severn. Brian Waters says it has a Venetian air, "not the Venice of the tourist, but the rural Venetia of the lagoons". This is because the original outlet of the Stroudwater canal has been sealed off, turning it into a charming backwater. The Severn has little power against Framilode, for the tide has weakened by the time it gets there, and it only recovers its virility a mile up-river when it enters a narrower channel. Framilode is an elver-village, and men who have known them to fetch as little as $1\frac{1}{2}d$. a pound have lived to sell them at $2s$. $6d$. a pound. Elvers are, of course, young eels, which arrive in great shoals in the early days of spring, three years old and about 3 inches long. They are fished for with an elver-net, about 3 feet long and 2 feet wide and 18 inches deep. The net is built on a cradle of willow and carried at the end of a 5-foot pole. Some fishermen favour a night tide, since elvers can be lured by the light of a lamp. They come at the turn of the tide, in their thousands and millions; but within an hour the catch falls back "from quarts to pints and from pints to teacupfulls". After each dip of the net, the elverer will tip his catch into a pail by his side, where the elvers "froth like newly-drawn beer", squirming up the sides of the pail in their efforts to escape. Although catches are not what they were, elverers may still make, on a couple of tides, as much money as they earn in a week at their regular jobs.

CHAPTER X

SOUTH OF GLOUCESTER

STONEBENCH is the favourite place to see the Severn Bore. For not only is it one of the few places where a road follows the river-bank and gives an uninterrupted view of the tideway, but it is here that the Bore is often most impressive. The submerged reef or ledge which gives Stonebench its name gives the Bore a crest, and it has been known to give sightseers wet feet. But it can be disappointing too. Early this year (1952) the newspapers announced that, with exceptionally high tides, there was a possibility of a record Bore which would equal, and maybe break, the 1918 record. Now there is nothing like the possibility of records being broken for collecting a crowd. Even so, the public response was staggering! Lanes around Elmore were in a state of confusion. The traffic was overwhelming. Half the cars in the West Midlands seemed to be bound for Stonebench, and there were hundreds of cyclists too. At Lower Rea, several fields had been adapted for use as car-parks, and soon hundreds of cars stood in rows, looking conspicuously out of place in that green countryside. It was a glorious morning, just the sort of morning on which records *ought* to be broken, and the press, expecting a Sensation, had sent along its photographers and reporters. The more enterprising of these had climbed into trees, possibly in the hope that this year the Bore would so exceed itself as to o'erwhelm its banks and maybe drown a few hundred of the spectators. And still the crowds poured into the normally peaceful hamlet of Stonebench—by charabanc and car, awheel and afoot —there were even a few people there on horseback. There was an atmosphere of cup-tie and holiday. And as the Great Event drew nearer, a wondering expectation possessed the sightseers, many of whom had never seen a Bore before. Tensely they waited, one eye on their watch and the other downstream.

At this point I should explain that a good Bore may be 9 feet in height when it reaches Stonebench. It sweeps along, smooth and sheer, with indescribable dignity, only the outer edges broken by obstructions on the bank which send up fountains of spray. Its speed is about sixteen miles an hour, and what at a distance seems to be a solid wall of water proves, on closer acquaintance, to be three or four separate undulations, each one as smooth as glass, behind which comes chaos; for no sooner have these three or four undulations passed than the river-bed is a riot of furious water, which in a matter of minutes rises level with the top of the deep bank, and sometimes tops it. When this happens, of course, those who are watching are likely to get wet feet. Yet out of all those thousands, I saw none with wellingtons. I smiled to myself at the thought of their neglect, for I *had* brought wellingtons. They had been a frightful nuisance to carry, but it would be worth the effort if, surrounded by several thousand wet feet, I alone could remain dry-shod, whilst the murmur went round, "Now, why didn't *we* think of that!"

. . . But now the Bore was due. People climbed railings, stood precariously on hedge-banks, tried to find a better viewpoint, panicked, and rushed back to the old one, only to find it taken. We looked at our watches, and held them against our ears to confirm that they hadn't stopped. Five minutes passed. The Bore was overdue! There were mutterings from the crowd, a vague feeling of discontent. A wag called out: "We've had it, chaps. They've called it off!" George (who was with me) looked bleak. And when I asked him how he accounted for the delay, he said he couldn't, didn't want to, wasn't going to. Why should *he* worry? He'd brought a terrific bore *with* him!

It is not, of course, unusual for the Severn Bore to defy time-tables. With a blustery sou'wester behind it, it has been known to arrive twenty minutes before it was due, so that many who had not made due allowance for this distressing eccentricity have missed seeing it. Similarly a north-east wind will delay it. The wind was north-east now. But it was not a gale. It was little more than a breeze.

We waited, and waited, and waited; and kept on waiting, until the Bore began to live up to its name. Sandwiches were taken from pockets, and flasks up-ended. Some of the spectators, with the edge of their curiosity blunted by delay, grew outright cynical.

George compared the behaviour of the Bore with that of certain local 'buses which, according to him ,arrived and departed in an equally unpredictable manner. Five, ten, fifteen minutes passed. Then someone downstream cheered. A fragment of spray caught the sunlight as it was tossed from the crest, and the Bore came into sight round the nearest bend, sweeping towards us.

Our first reaction was excitement, followed by puzzled incomprehension, then numbed stupefaction. We had expected great things, but this . . .

Ah, well—even a 4-foot bore is not unexciting; but it is very far from being a record, and when it had passed by there were grumbles. The grumbles were in a minority, however, for a very simple reason. Most of those present had not seen a Bore before, and had no means of drawing a comparison. Perhaps they still had an idea it really *was* a record-breaker, and wouldn't begin grumbling until the newspapers disabused them. Less disappointed than the sightseers were the nearby cottagers who, in expectation of an inundation, had moved all their furniture upstairs, leaving the ground floor empty for flood-water.

Most disappointed of all, perhaps, were the pressmen who had climbed trees. They duly reported that the Bore was a wash-out —it hadn't arrived on time, wasn't much to see, and hadn't wetted a single foot. One of them, in an excess of irritation (though when I taxed the editor about it, he blamed it on a bad telephone connection and/or printers' errors), reported that the Bore had been fifty minutes late, and only 3 feet high. Among those disappointed were George and I . . . I who had lugged a heavy pair of wellingtons all the way to Stonebench in the gleeful hope that everybody else would get wet feet, and now had to carry them back again, "like a damned fool", to quote George's vivid phraseology.

The annoying thing was that on the following day, when the so-called experts predicted nothing spectacular, the Bore was an 8-footer and arrived on time. Which, in George's view, all goes to prove that the directing-force behind the elements has a sense of humour. And a pretty malicious one, at that!

The first Bore I ever saw at Stonebench was unexpected, and, because of that, strangely impressive. I was sitting on the riverbank eating my sandwiches when I heard a curious rustling noise.

At first I thought it must be a motor-boat, and was really startled when, as it drew nearer, the noise grew louder and I could hear the uprush of water splashing trees and osiers on the bank. Surely a motor-boat wouldn't explain such a disturbance, I puzzled. And then I saw the Bore. It was nothing to speak of. A couple of feet high, perhaps. But because I was alone, and because it was about the last thing I expected, it made an impression upon me that repetition can never quite obliterate.

It is difficult to believe that Newnham and Arlingham are only a few miles downriver from Stonebench, for what is there a mile-wide estuary, open to the sky, is here a river confined between high banks. One day last autumn I followed the foot-path which takes you past people's backdoors and in between their outhouses before bringing you along the river-bank and into Weir Green. This is an entirely charming place, surrounded by orchards of apple and pear, and beside the Severn. It is, indeed, a country of orchards, for you may walk almost all the way from here to Framilode and have orchards all the way. One of the most conspicuous landmarks here-about (Stonebench and Elmore) is Robin's Wood Hill, which is as good a guide as Stinchcombe is down south. On a smaller scale is the local Hockley Hill, wooded and rather romantic-looking. No doubt all traces of romance would evaporate on closer examination, so it may be as well not to risk disillusionment. Why is it that hills, from afar, look so romantic, so interesting and unattainable, especially when seen through a faint-blue mist? Yet when you've struggled over the intervening obstacles, lost yourself a couple of times, torn your clothing on barbed-wire, fallen into ditches and scrambled through a horribly damp wood to reach the summit, what a dis-appointment it is! The magic has now moved down into the Vale. Your hill proves to be just another barren tump, whose only advantage is that it possesses a splendid view of the valley. Now it is the Vale which looks intriguing—winding lanes and orchards, cottage chimneys and clumps of elms which beckon irresistibly through the same faint-blue mist. "Distance lends enchantment", as one poet remarks. Unfortunately it is the distance which is en-chanted. Knowing this, I was not seduced from my intended walk by Hockley Hill, but was quite content to admire it from a distance.

Frampton Pond on Rosamund's Green, Frampton-on-Severn

Facing the river at Weir Green is a black-and-white, half-timbered cottage with a thatched roof. There are many such cottages between Elmore, Epney and Hardwicke. And what a pleasure it is to find them! At Barhouse and Kenton Green I found some lovely examples of this style of building, once characteristic of the Vale, but now surviving only in these more remote places which have not yet attracted the attention of planners and development boards. Another structure which is peculiar to this part of the country is the wooden, thatched barn, though most of those I came across were unfortunately in disrepair, sagging at the corners and sprouting ivy at the seams. All this points to a shortage of local stone. Even the recently-built houses are of brick, usually bare of plaster, and seen at their best in autumn when their reds and yellows match the tints of the dying foliage. In spring, I imagine, these brick-built houses are out of place. In contrast to the delicate fresh green of the budding trees, they probably look like raddled old tarts.

Elmore Court, home of the Guise family, is a fine Elizabethan manor, seen through iron gates beautifully wrought with flowers. Oddly, the church is over a mile distant at Farley's End, presumably because Elmore is such a scattered parish that, standing where it does, it is equally far from Elmore (proper) and Elmore Back, and is fairly central for the hamlets of Bridgemacot, Kenton, Barhouse, Weir Green, Wicksgreen and Waterend. Much of the church is thirteenth-century, and the old benches have linenfold ends. It contains a tomb with an engraved portrait of a fifteenth-century de Guise, in armour, with a dog at his feet, whilst outside in the churchyard are four great pillars which formed part of the Guise family mausoleum.

I had intended to take a short-cut from Kenton Green to Farley's End, but I must have chosen the wrong path, for after walking nearly a mile my lane deposited me in the cowyard of Velthouse Farm. There I stood trying to puzzle out my whereabouts, whilst the farm dog announced the arrival of a stranger by barking furiously. Out came the farmer, surprised to see me. "Hullo," he said, "where did you spring from?" I told him I was walking to Longney and had contrived to lose myself. Like most farmers I've come across when walking in the Vale, he was friendly and helpful, taking me through his orchard to point out

The Severn Bore, as seen from Minsterworth

the way. "Just keep down along this hedge, with that three-cornered wood on your left and the cottage ahead of you. When you get to the cottage, bear across a rough piece, and take the cart-track that'll bring you out at Madam's End." But when he heard that I was hoping to walk on to Longney, Epney and across the canal to Parkend, he looked doubtful. "I don't reckon you'll do it in the time. It'll be dark before you've got round that way. Better turn left at Madam's End and go back through Hardwicke."

Thanking him, I followed down the hedge, stopping to pick and eat some blackberries, for the day was warm and sultry, before I came to the cottage beside the "rough piece". Having arrived there, however, I didn't quite see what he meant by his instruction to bear across it. Anyway, I crossed it and began to follow a cart-track through a clover field and into a wood. This obviously wasn't the way. I must have crossed the rough ground at the wrong angle. So I took what I thought was a short-cut back to the cottage, and was very soon lost again. The field in which I found myself seemed to be bewitched. For, having got into it, I couldn't find a way out, nor even the gap by which I entered. This happens sometimes when you are walking alone in country strange to you, and are anxious not to be caught afield by the darkness. You lose your path, and instantly the country appears to close-in around you. Trees loom ominously; wood-pigeons suddenly clap out from the branches over your head; blackbirds shriek as they fly low in front of you; the sun, which until now has beamed on you like a benevolent uncle, suddenly slips behind a dark black cloud. When you stop to listen for some sound of humanity, there is a complete and utter silence. And then you discover that the cows are really young steers, and are disposed to be playful.

Suddenly the tousled head of a small boy appeared above the hedge, his brown eyes questioning, and, crossing the field to where he stood, I found that he was actually standing in the garden of the cottage, which had been obscured from my view by a couple of trees. Near him was a gap in the hedge which brought me, once again, into the "rough piece", and I pushed through it before asking him if he could tell me how to get to Madam's End. The grave brown eyes opened wider as he said: "This *is* Madam's End."

"Can I help you, sir?" his father asked, coming out of the cottage.

"I'm trying to find the road to Longney and Hardwicke," I said.

"It's about a quarter of a mile from here. Down that cart-track." He pointed, indicating the track which I should have seen and taken first time.

We stood chatting there a few minutes, and I asked him if he didn't sometimes get to feeling lonely. Like Mr Palmer, the light-keeper at Sheperdine, he laughed at the idea. But I persisted. "Surely in the winter-time——" I began. "It's nice and quiet and peaceful," he said. "It depends what you're used to, I s'pose. Now, I can't stand towns. All that noise—that hurry and bustle, traffic and crowds, smokes and smells—it gives me a headache; and whenever I go into town I wonder to myself how folks can stand it."

That gave me something to think about, for the quiet common-sense of his manner and his healthy, sunburned face added point to the argument, and when I compared his attitude to that of the ordinary town-dweller, who requires frequent doses of excite-ment in the form of football, pictures and newspapers to make life bearable, I couldn't help thinking that this cottager had got something. Not that he's a typical countryman, or that country folk don't like a little excitement. A few miles away, up at Elmore Back, there is a strong tradition of country roguery which suggests that here, at any rate, there was no lack of excite-ment in the old days. One rank of cottages used to be called Rogues' Row, because they were inhabited by men who made a living carrying contraband up to London. Their local head-quarters and rendezvous was a cider-house called The Shark, which went out of business towards the end of the last century. Contraband liquor was brought to The Shark by bargees, and conveyed to the cities in barrels, quite openly, except that the barrels were marked "CIDER".

I did not go to Longney or Epney that day. That was a pity, for I'd like to have seen Longney church with its curious gar-goyles, Tudor porch and memorial to Richard Littleton, a parson with curly hair who was rector here for fifty-eight years and died in 1713. I might even have tasted a Longney russet, an apple which, though it has lost its popularity elsewhere, is still to be found in the place which fostered it and gave it its name. Epney is best known as an elver depot, since elvers caught in the Severn are sent out from here to stock rivers at home and abroad.

Instead, I turned left, along the quiet country road to Hardwicke. From this rising ground were fine views across the Vale to the Cotswold slopes, misted now by the blue haze of distance. And presently I saw, below me to the south-east, the tower of Hardwicke church, rising above the trees. Dignified and creeper-clad, Hardwicke Farm stands back from the road among its apple orchards; and then, turning a bend in the road, I came to the Berkeley–Gloucester canal. Here, again, was the white-painted swing-bridge with its Arcadian lodge. And in this lodge lives Mrs Prosser, the bridge-keeper's wife, who once broadcast in "Country Magazine". According to Mrs Prosser, bridge-keepers work seven days a week, from six in the morning till ten at night, though it isn't all work, of course, for even the Berkeley-Gloucester canal isn't a perpetual stream of craft. Nevertheless, it's not quite so easy as it looks to be a bridge-keeper. Every time anything wants to come through, there's a matter of seven tons to push each side of the bridge. Seven tons of water takes some pushing. Even so, bridge-keeping is reckoned to be one of the best jobs on the canal. Many of the bridgemen only got their jobs after they'd been working for the canal company for many years. For instance, Mr Prosser had been working for the company thirty-four years before he landed his job as bridge-keeper at Hardwicke. He is a countryman, and usually finds time to take part in local sheep-shearing. Once he was shearing sheep at Colethrop Farm when a tramp came along. Seeing that the tramp's hair was long and neglected, Mr Prosser said: "Looks as if you'm about ready for shearing yourself, guv'nor." The tramp agreed, and invited him to give him a haircut. Knowing nothing about haircutting, Mr Prosser sheared him as he would a sheep, which was apparently what the tramp wanted. "There," said Mr P. when he'd finished, "now that'll last thee a twelvemonth."

On the other side of the canal is the Pilot Inn, a large modern public-house. I imagine it used to be smaller when it was the resort of bargees, but it is now frequented largely by the anglers who come from near and far to fish the waters of the canal, and by the owners of canal-side chalets. These chalets are a recent innovation. They are presumably week-end "escapes" from town. Some of them have small boats moored to the tow-path, and from more than one, on the day I was there, came the sounds of radios in full blast. A motor-tanker, carrying oil to Worcester, chugged upstream; the radios blared out jazz and running commentaries; a jet aeroplane streaked across the sky; and a man in one of the chalets was busily sawing wood; whilst a little way up the canal bank sat a line of silent anglers, contemplatively watching their floats. Beside them, in the grass, were little discs of metal numbered in black paint.

Following down the tow-path as far as the next bridge, I crossed it and came to the village of Hardwicke. In spite of the proximity of the factories and installations of Quedgeley, Hardwicke village retains its charm. It really is a charming place, with a large Georgian mansion, a lovely old church, and a stone seat for travellers on its village green. Charlie Smith, whose father was sexton here, told me that the most interesting house in Hardwicke is the Old Hall, half-timbered and with a stone-tiled roof, reputed to have been occupied by Cromwell's troopers during the Civil War. It was Charlie Smith who told me about a Hardwicke worthy called Thomas Dainty, who lived in a cottage near Stank Bridge, and worked for the Sharpness Dock Co. This old man walked from Hardwicke to Sharpness, a distance of about twelve miles, every day, *arriving at 6 o'clock a.m. in time to start work*. Fortunately, Thomas didn't have to walk home at the end of his day's work as well, for there was a passenger boat (commanded by Captain Pegler) coming up the canal, which gave him a lift. But when, as sometimes happened, he missed the boat or worked overtime, Thomas Dainty would have to walk home. The Morning Star at Hardwicke is very old, but has not always been an inn. When Charlie Smith's grandfather was a young man, it was a private dwelling. Surgery was crude in those days, before anæsthetics were used, and when the man who lived in this house had to have his leg amputated, the vicar sent over a bottle of brandy. When the recipient had drunk it, neat, and was well and truly intoxicated, the surgeon took his leg off.

Inside Hardwicke church is an intriguing tomb with the carved figures of John Trye and his son, the father in armour of the

Tudor period and the son in court dress. A great bell (pre-Reformation, with the words *Santa Maria, Ora Pro Nobis* upon it) stands on the floor of the nave, and the massive font, 700 years old, contains a Woolaston Basin.

I have already mentioned travelling up to Hardwicke on a day of winter sunshine (p. 209). In point of fact I was on my way to Hardwicke Court, where I was to meet Miss Olive Lloyd Baker, the present "Lord of the Manor". I still remember every detail of that journey: the cold clarity of the air, the incisive brightness of sunshine, revealing detail with almost microscopic clearness, spotlighting some things, shadowing others. In the Park, grey squirrels were active, and I left the drive to look at a great old poplar which was festooned with mistletoe, growing all over it in bunches, like queer savage heads of fuzzy hair. Rooks got up, cawing, at my approach, and rabbits scuttled. It was amazing how the birds and animals had responded to this burst of sunshine early in the year.

Although I would have liked to see the Italian garden, laid down a little over a century ago by Mrs Barwick Lloyd Baker, I did not like to do so before I had introduced myself, so I pulled the bell and waited. Presently I was shown into the smaller library, which I imagine Miss Lloyd Baker uses as a study, and was made comfortable beside a blazing log-fire. Soon afterwards I was joined by Miss Lloyd Baker, who had very kindly got together some old manuscripts and books which she thought might interest me. But before she left me to study these books and manuscripts alone, we talked about Hardwicke village, past, present and future, with special reference to ways and means of making village life more satisfying and complete. The problem of Hardwicke is, of course, the problem of all villages near large cities: how to maintain the essential and characteristic internal life of the place in face of the attractions of the city? I said that too often a good bus service meant a poor social life, the town sapping its vitality until the village became no more than a dormitory. Miss Lloyd Baker smilingly reassured me that Hardwicke wasn't yet as bad as that. There were still many social activities, and I gathered that Miss Lloyd Baker herself took part in some of them.

She told me how she came into the estate, which is still quite a considerable one. Her father, Michael Lloyd Baker, was killed in Katia in 1916. Knowing that Miss Olive would inherit, her grandfather gave her several lectures to prepare her, and although she was a young girl at the time, with other things to preoccupy her, Miss Lloyd Baker still remembers much of what he said. One thing he told her was: "In the course of a year a lot of money will be paid into your bank account. Don't lose your head and imagine it all belongs to you, because most of it, you'll find, will have to be paid out again."

When, in 1924, Miss Lloyd Baker opened the telegram which told her that her grandfather had passed away, her feelings were mixed. She felt sorrow at his death, and apprehension at the prospect of her responsibilities. Until then, she was gay and fond of pleasure, chiefly interested in driving her car faster and leaping her horse higher than her friends and rivals. Now she would be burdened with all the cares of running an estate, at a time when such estates were threatened with extinction, beset with difficulties on every side. Anyway, she shouldered the difficulties and, with the help of her tenants, who were "unobtrusively helpful and very patient", she kept the estate together during those troublesome years between the wars. Quite soon she found herself taking up social and local-government work, and so Miss Lloyd Baker reached maturity, and, as it were, put away childish things.

Unfortunately I am not a note-taker. So that, when Miss Lloyd Baker left me alone, with a parting injunction to close the window if I felt a draught and put on more logs if the fire went down, I didn't start copying down everything in sight. Instead I lit my pipe and looked round the room. It was a pleasant, comfortable room, well supplied with bookcases, easy-chairs and a writing-desk, and with a large open fireplace beside which hung fox-brush hearth-brushes. Over the fireplace was a picture, reputedly a Gainsborough, though there is no real evidence for that claim. It is a curious thing but a large number of Gloucestershire country houses contain pictures which may be Gainsboroughs.

I picked up a manuscript book, to discover that it was the Memoirs, hand-written, of Barwick Lloyd Baker. Now, Barwick Lloyd Baker was a famous man in his day: a prison reformer, model squire, and pioneer of the reformatory system. But he was no author, and long before he had completed his Memoirs, he grew tired of them and abandoned the work. Oddly enough, one of the best accounts of Barwick Lloyd Baker, his work and life, was written by a German professor who met him by chance and stayed a few days at Hardwicke Court as his guest.

They met in Dublin, at the Social Science Congress of 1861, a German professor and a Gloucestershire squire. Von Holtzendorff was (of all things) Professor of Criminal Jurisprudence, and Barwick Lloyd Baker told him he was a typical English squire. If he was, the squirearchy have been grossly and unfairly maligned. But I do not think he was typical. For one thing, he (like von Holtzendorff) was interested in the treatment and rehabilitation of young criminals. At Hardwicke he had started a reformatory which was a great success. Holtzendorff, who was interested in this idea, also expressed curiosity in the English squirearchy. It was a class they didn't possess in Germany, and he wondered about their mode of life, customs and habits, social conventions and political power. He wondered to such effect that Barwick Lloyd Baker suggested he came for a week to Hardwicke Court, for

"the entrance into Bristol harbour is worth the voyage, and Gloucestershire itself is well worth visiting. If you're anything of an antiquary, you'll find antiquities in abundance, for our county was the centre of Roman power and the first territory which Christianity conquered in Britain. The first Christian king, Lucius, was buried at Gloucester. . . . The first known translator of the bible, John Trevisa, was vicar of Berkeley. If you are a lover of nature, the valley of the Severn will charm you. If you care for hunting and fishing, you'll like to make the acquaintance of the Severn salmon, which in the London market realizes a penny a pound more than any other; and our lampreys were, until 1830, sent to the kings of England as a Christmas gift, and were decorated with gold. . . . I can also promise to show you a few choice specimens of sharpers and thieves."

Jocularly the professor said that he would gladly come, but not to inspect all the excellences of which Barwick Lloyd Baker had spoken, since to do so would in all likelihood keep him at Hardwicke so long that his wife, in Germany, would divorce him "for cruelty and desertion". He would be quite satisfied if he could be introduced to two aspects of life at Hardwicke: the treatment of criminals and the habits of the landed gentry. This was agreed upon, and the two of them set sail for Bristol.

After a somewhat rough passage, they proceeded by coach to Hardwicke, which they reached just as (to quote the professor) "twilight was casting its shadows over the landscape". Next morning, however, "as soon as the early sun shone through my bedroom window, I was able to admire the beauty of this part of Gloucestershire. Over the nearby parkland and fields, bright with flowers, dotted with ancient beeches and elms now illumin-ated by the clear autumnal sun, I could see, stretching out in the distance, the blue range of the Cotswold hills."

It was a Sunday, so Barwick Lloyd Baker took his German friend straight to the smoking-room, since, he observed humor-ously, he was aware that Germans possessed three national characteristics—smoking, singing and Sabbath-breaking. Later in the morning the professor talked to the lady of the house, Mrs Barwick Lloyd Baker, who gave him the domestic, everyday details of life in a country manor. These details were subsequently published in Germany in a book called *An English Country Squire*.* If all our squires had been so conscientious as Barwick Lloyd Baker, however, the domestic history of England would have been very different. He was the model squire, taking part in the administration of affairs, interested in his property, and seriously concerned with reforming young criminals.

Barwick Lloyd Baker's reformatory was not the first, nor even the first of its kind, but it *was* the first to be successful. He himself gave much of the credit to his young friend George Bengough, of The Ridge, who (with an income of £10,000 a year) devoted the whole of his time to mending broken lives; first at Hardwicke, later at Kingswood, near Bristol. When they began the Hardwicke Reformatory it was in a house not much bigger than a labourer's cottage. A bailiff was employed to look

* *An English Country Squire, as Sketched at Hardwicke Court in Gloucestershire by Professor von Holtzendorff.* Translated into English by Rosa Gebhard and privately printed by John Bellows Ltd., of Gloucester.

after the boys' work out-of-doors, because it was felt he'd be more likely to treat them as employees than as prisoners—an essential part of the scheme. By 1854 they were able to take twelve boys at a time, and it was a success. A leading article about it appeared in *The Times*, and meetings were held to petition Parliament for similar institutions.

The main principle was to set the boys to work—hard manual work, in the open air. To this was added an education in essentials, and religious instruction intended to encourage the growth of a moral sense. Barwick Lloyd Baker had no illusions about the boys, and he certainly did not pamper them. Actually he was motivated by a conviction that to lock up young offenders with "old lags" was to sentence them to a lifetime of petty knavery. That was wasteful and absurd, so something must be devised to attempt reformation. There are, of course, obvious parallels between Hardwicke and Leyhill insofar as one led, by stages, to the other. But listen to Barwick Lloyd Baker, speaking, it must be remembered, at a time when crime was inevitably followed by punishment, and was looked upon by respectable people as an unpardonable sin:

"A boy comes to us, usually, quick and energetic by nature, and with *a restless craving for excitement and change*. If we set him to tailoring, or any other sedentary occupation, he would still remember his old ways, companions, haunts. But give him hard work in the open air to do and his energy expends itself, not only harmlessly but profitably, on our stiff clay soil. The very feel of the fresh air and the appearance of liberty tend to tranquillize . . . and when the labour of the day is over, the boy is disposed to enjoy his rest."

When they came there first, the boys sometimes wanted to run away. But the fact that there were neither walls nor locks had, if anything, a restraining effect. It made them suspicious, and their suspicions gave the system a chance to work. The bailiffs were "kind, but firm". And when the boys discovered that the managers were not only doing their work without pay but sacrificing pleasure to do so, it had "a softening effect, and brought them into a state to profit by instruction". In fine weather the boys at Hardwicke worked on the land. When it was wet they made their own clothes and mended their boots. Results speak for themselves. Of the ninety boys whose sentences had expired by 1884, eighty-five were doing well, three were doubtful, and two were failures, having been again convicted.

Barwick Lloyd Baker was not, however, a sentimentalist. He did not say, with some reformers, that, since the boys could not differentiate between right and wrong, they should not be punished. Disgrace, he thought, ought never to be separated from crime, since it was one of the most powerful deterrents. It was really remarkable how many of his Old Boys rose in the world. His explanation was that most of the boys who came there were naturally quick-witted and eager, and, unable to find a normal outlet for their high spirits and intelligence, had turned to crime. When, however, their exuberance was diverted into the right channels and their wits put to work, they frequently outdid the more staid and sober boys who had never gone wrong.

Barwick's father, T. J. Lloyd Baker, came to Hardwicke Court in 1815 with his wife and children. The house to which they came was Elizabethan, but, discovering dry-rot in the beams, T. J. had the whole place pulled down and the present house built. Judging from his manuscript notebook T. J. Lloyd Baker was chiefly interested in farming and the management of his estate. The brute facts of stockbreeding are faithfully recorded: "APR 15. The sow was driven to Field Court and took the boar." "DEC. (1815): The Stouts Hill Cow was bulled by Mr Watt's bull about the 17th of the month."

Among the pile of books which Miss Lloyd Baker had left for me to read in the library was another notebook, kept by her grandfather, Barwick's son. Granville Lloyd Baker was interested in anything curious and bizarre which had to do with Hardwicke or his own family. He writes of Nanny Cross, who lived to the ripe old age of 102:

"When she was young she suffered from chilblains. Told to break ice and dip her foot in leech-pool, did so, and the leeches clung fast (to it as she drew it out). Her foot was so swollen that she couldn't get up next day. But she lost her chilblains."

When this old lady had achieved her century, he sent her a special dinner of roast chicken, plum-pudding and a large mince-pie to celebrate. It was in this notebook of Granville Lloyd Baker that I found a brief anecdote which might well be called

CHARLOTTE,

or *The Advantages of Thrift*

"Charlotte Davis (now Mrs Sterry) was the daughter of a poor widow. She told me she went to service at 11 years old for £1 a year, and had to pay for her first pair of shoes. At the age of 13, she came to the Old Hall, at Hardwicke, where she stayed till she was 30, when her wages were £10 a year. By that time she had saved £100.

"Then she bought a small piece of ground near the Old Hall from my father and built Apricot Cottage for £86. . . . It is covered with apricot trees of her own budding. She was a capital gardener and always begged her husband not to do anything to the garden as it was sure to be wrong. She had in one year 210 apricots."

Other anecdotes have nothing to do with either family or locality. One of them is worth quoting, however, for its own sake:

"My grandfather told my father that he remembered the Splashing-House, somewhere near the corner of Park Lane and Piccadilly. You could go in, dressed in riding clothes with a whip, and be splashed with the mud of the Oxford road or the Kent road, or whatever place you wished to be supposed to have been riding. This impressed people in the street and perhaps your acquaintances with the idea that you possessed a horse."

. . . That was all the notes I took at Hardwicke Court, for at this point Miss Lloyd Baker's housekeeper brought in tea for me, and soon after Miss Lloyd Baker came back to show me the house. In the larger library, a very fine one, I noticed Gould's *Ornithology*, the *Flora Londiniensis* and a Second Folio Shakespeare; and the same room had a family boating-party by Zoffany over the fireplace. The drawing-room was remarkable for its Chinese hand-painted wallpaper, and in the corridor was a clock encased in a representation, in carved oak, of Siena Cathedral. Round the walls, in all the rooms, in the hall and in the corridors are the family portraits. Gentlemen in armour and in ruffs, ladies in silks and muslin, hoops and bustles, gowns and bodices; grave and gay, young and old, beautiful, plain and peculiar. Their eyes look down on you, as though summing you up. For my part, I don't think I could stand being permanently quizzed by so many censors.

When I left the Court, it was dark and rather cold. Gusts of icy wind blew across the open spaces between the trees. Overhead an owl glided on noiseless wings. You could hear the sounds of cattle breathing and see the white steam of their breath when you passed close by them. In spirit, however, I was still in the smaller library of Hardwicke Court, a friendly room, in which I had felt completely at ease. Going to someone-else's house, seeing the things they use and admire, you share with them a strange and partial intimacy, the extent of which depends on your sensitivity to atmosphere and your powers of observation. For a while you live, as it were, within the same envelope, and feel the impress not only of your host's personality, but, to a lesser extent, that of his (or her) ancestors who lived there before him. To that extent all houses are haunted by echoes, vibrations, emotions; and you have only to sit and wait in silence to experience them. That is expressing it clumsily, of course. But it cannot be expressed directly or easily, since the experience is more essentially spiritual than physical and therefore incomprehensible to materialists.

Here I must leave you—here at Hardwicke, on a cold evening early in the new year. I am standing on the kerb, beside A.38, waiting for the bus which will take me back to Bristol; and I am being alternately dazzled and plunged into darkness by the headlights of traffic. In places I have said hard things about this road, and it cannot truthfully be described as a thing of beauty at any time; but its utility has never been in question. It is a straight road, and a wide one, and will take me home.

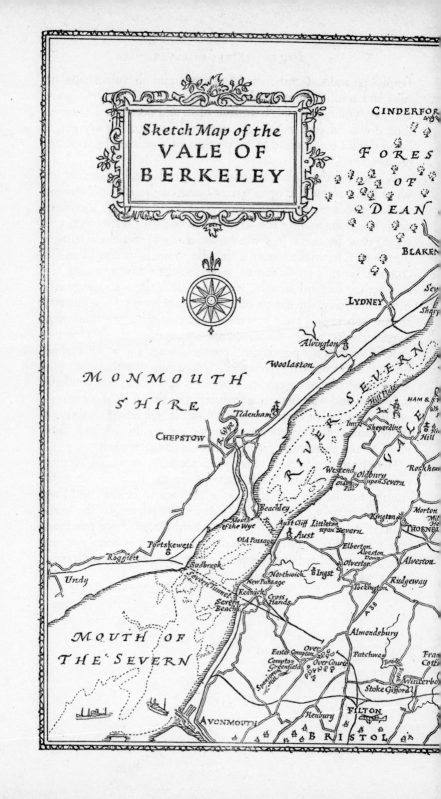

Sketch Map of the VALE OF BERKELEY

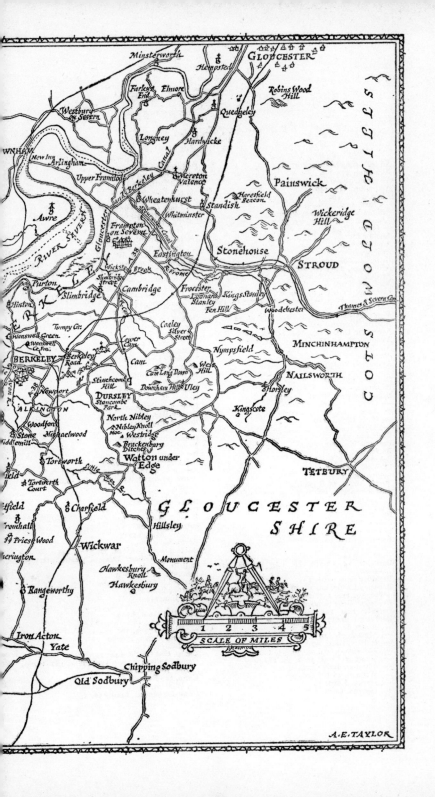

INDEX

INDEX

INDEX